Images and Identities in Public Administration

*To the over six hundred scholars and practitioners
who have made the Public Administration Theory Network possible
since 1979.*

EDITED BY
Henry D. Kass • Bayard L. Catron

Images and Identities in Public Administration

FOREWORD BY
Gareth Morgan

Published in coooperation with the
Public Administration Theory Network
of the American Society for Public Administration

SAGE PUBLICATIONS
The International Professional Publishers
Newbury Park   London   New Delhi

For information address:

SAGE Publications, Inc.
2111 West Hillcrest Drive
Newbury Park, California 91320

SAGE Publications Ltd.
28 Banner Street
London EC1Y 8QE
England

SAGE Publications India Pvt. Ltd.
M-32 Market
Greater Kailash I
New Delhi 110 048 India

Printed in the United States of America

Library of Congress Cataloging-in-Publication Data

Main entry under title:

Images and identities in public administration / edited by Henry D.
  Kass, Bayard Catron.
       p.   cm.
    "Published in cooperation with the Public Administration Theory
  Network of the American Society for Public Administration."
    Includes bibliographical references.
    ISBN 0-8039-3787-3. — ISBN 0-8039-3788-1 (pbk.)
    1. Public administration.   2. Public administration—United
  States.   I. Kass, Henry D.   II. Catron, Bayard L.
  JF 1321.I43   1990
  350—dc20   90-5730
                                                            CIP

FIRST PRINTING, 1990

Sage Production Editor: Diane S. Foster

Contents

Foreword

Language is a wonderful tool for expressing ourselves and our relationships with the world. But it can also create blind spots and traps, binding us into unthinking, knee-jerk and large unreflective ways of seeing.

In my book *Images of Organization* (1986) I addressed this problem in relation to the study of organizations. Organization. An indispensable word in the modern age, conjuring up an image of neat, tidy, efficient disciplined activity. But what is organization? What does it mean to say "let's organize"? What image guides us when we set about our organizing activity?

In *Images* I showed that much of our thinking about organization is metaphorical. When we organize we often have an image of organization at the back of our mind—usually a mechanical one! When we organize we mechanize—splitting and shaping complex activities into neat and tidy parts, exactly as if we were designing a machine or some mechanical process.

But organizing and organization can take other forms as well. For example, we can organize by creating an adaptive process, by creating shared understanding among people—"getting them on the same wave length," through political wheeling and dealing, or through exercise of brute force. Organization can take many forms, and be understood in many ways.

But when we talk about organization, it's usually the mechanical version, typified in the process of bureaucracy, that usually comes to mind.

To break free of this conception I ended *Images* with the suggestion that there may be merit in replacing the concept of organization with that of *imagination*. The purpose—to recognize that organization is a creative activity that can be developed and understood in many creative ways.

Why should we be constrained and limited by our shared history of mechanistic thinking about organization? Why not break free and imaginize? Why not recognize that organization embodies images in action, and that we can organize in many different ways?

The concept has enormous implications for modern management because in turbulent times mechanistic concepts of organization do not serve us very well. New images and ideas are needed to hold people and their actions together in "organized" fashion. To organize, we need to imaginize the organizing process to create flexible free flowing forms that have more in common with balloons, bubbles, and umbilical cords than inanimate parts of a machine.

This book takes a first stab at applying the concept of imaginization to public administration. Before you read, why not think about what public administration means to you now. What images does it conjure in your mind? What are its main metaphors? *Then*, devote some time to thinking about what it could be. Strip away the constraints of language and conventional definition. Imaginize and see the possible.

The ideas in this book will help you continue the journey.

Gareth Morgan

Prologue: Emerging Images and Themes in the Reexamination of American Public Administration

HENRY D. KASS

INTRODUCTION

This volume represents an attempt by a variety of observers to explore alternative bases upon which to legitimate public administration in the American system of government. The role, and thus legitimacy, of public administration in the American republic has always been problematical. While we have recognized the need for an administrative establishment since revolutionary times, we have feared the potential power of an administrative elite to undermine cherished individual freedoms.

Accordingly, we have moved from one legitimating myth for public administration to another in a vain effort to assuage our discomfort with an administrative establishment we need, but seem bound to fear and even revile. At one time or another, we have tried to base the legitimacy of public administration on one or more of the following: the superior virtue and character of an administrative elite; direct partisan appointment and control of all administrative officers; the competency of a politically neutral, technically rational public service; and the belief that administrators were loyal, self-effacing, but politically astute, "Bill Bureaucrats" capable of guiding the country through war and depression.

However, collective experience with two decades of the New Public Administration, neoliberalism, and Reaganite conservatism seems to suggest that we are rarely happy with any of these formulations for long. Thus, the fragile legitimacy of the administrative establishment lies less in the organic and constitutional character of our political system, than in the vicissitudes of the popular mind and the national fortunes. The purpose of this volume, then, is taken from this text, namely the need to develop legitimating concepts for American public administration that can send their roots deep into the soil of American political culture.

THE APPROACH TO WRITING THIS VOLUME

Any attempt to undertake a project of this sort on this scale poses two challenges: first, the challenge to go beyond the traditional legitimating myths that have been used in the past to justify the role played by public administration in the political system; and, second, the task of dealing critically with the complexities, ambiguities, paradoxes, and oxymorons inherent in terms like *democratic administration, separation of powers,* or *the politics/administration dichotomy.*

Those planning the conference[1] that initially prompted this volume attempted to address these issues by asking the individuals writing chapters to employ a technique called *imaginization* (discussed in the preface). As a technique, imaginization was originally developed by Gareth Morgan (1986) as a means to conceptualize another complex, ambiguous, and paradoxical phenomenon—organizations.

Imagination involves thinking and rethinking the implications of a variety of possible images (metaphors) for a phenomenon under discussion. These images can then be used to develop full blown conceptualizations of the phenomenon incorporating different themes, possible linkages, and contrasts that can be employed as a new way of framing action.

In the present context, this approach has a number of advantages. Since it starts with the conceptualization of a variety of images, it is possible to use these images creatively and even playfully, to think about administrative legitimacy. For example, Harmon's image of a "tortured soul" is one rarely associated with bureaucrats, yet it succeeds in linking administrative life with the anguish of taking ethical action.

Using imagination, complex concepts and events can be succinctly, and cogently related to one another (e.g., White and McSwain's "Phoenix project," Hummel's "circle" and "pyramid"). Images can help clarify ambiguous situations by allowing seemingly conflictive and paradoxical notions to be compared. For example, Fox and Cochran attempt to conceptualize the role of public administrators in a republic that continues to link liberalism with democracy and bureaucratic accountability with separation of powers. To do so they use an image that is a seeming oxymoron, "mass elite." By reducing concepts to a metaphoric kernel, imaginization can reveal underlying value systems that are normally taken for granted (e.g., agency norms [Kass] or technicist assumptions underlying the information-processing image [Zinke]). As in this volume itself, a set of images can also reveal the genuine complexies, contrasts, and relationships that comprise a single phenomenon—in this case, the identity of the public administrator in our political system.

Finally, images can be used not only in a descriptive, but prescriptive manner. We can employ diverse images to express the alternative futures we desire to enact. It is important to note that this is precisely what the contributors to this volume were asked to do. The result is a complex, often paradoxical and conflictive picture of what these observers would like to see as the legitimate role of the public administrator in our political system. Nonetheless, it can be argued these chapters have a master image, White and McSwain's "Phoenix project"—the literal rebirth of the field.

BASIC TYPES OF METAPHORIC IMAGES DEVELOPED

The resulting chapters generated at least two sorts of metaphors. A number of chapters focused on metaphoric images meant to express the roles public administrators ought to play in the political system if they expect to obtain legitimacy. These role images included conceptualizing the public administrator as "phronemos" (practical reasoner) (Douglas Morgan), as member of a "democratic elite" (Fox and Cochran), as "steward" (Kass), and as "responsible actor" (Harmon).

Other contributors selected images that symbolize and capture the tasks they believe face the whole enterprise of public administration before it can claim legitimacy in the political system. As already noted, Orion White and Cynthia McSwain use the powerful image of rebirth from the ashes—the Phoenix project—to picture the challenges they are convinced lie before public administration. They then couple it with the image of the public agency as an "enclave" in which this rebirth will be

nurtured, and from which the Phoenix of postmodern public administration can arise. The Evergreen Group (Adams, Bowerman, Dolbeare,
and Stivers) adopt the image of an unfinished democracy revolution,
which they insist public administrators must help citizens complete if
they are to win legitimacy for themselves or the republic they serve. Jay
White employs the metaphor of "political discourse" to argue that
public administrators can only enhance their legitimacy if they become
capable of exercising "interpretivist" and "critical," as well as technical, rationality. Lastly, Ralph Hummel projects the "icons" of the
"pyramid" and the "circle" to argue that the task of public administration is to transition society from the modern era of hierarchical
(pyramidal) power, instrumentalism, and technical rationality to the
postmodern era dominated by shared power, wholistic thinking, and
cooperative action (the circle).

THESIS AND THEMES

Apart from these two broad approaches to utilizing the metaphors
generated in these chapters, the images themselves at first seem quite
diverse and even contradictory (e.g., Platonic guardians and democratic
revolutionaries). Yet it is argued here that a close reading of these
chapters reveals these themes that emerge and reemerge in various
guises throughout this volume. One theme—legitimacy—arises naturally from the charge given the authors; the other two themes—the
restoration of a sense of community in the U.S. political system and the
use of practical wisdom to accomplish this end—are the result of the
authors' attempts to grapple with the issue of administration legitimacy.

Consequently, these themes do not merely coexist with each other;
they can be linked to form a thesis concerning the legitimation of public
administration in the American political system. This thesis can be
expressed as follows: The legitimacy of American public administration
rests on the legitimacy of the political community itself and the administrators' ability to serve and represent that community. In the
United States this sense of political community has been severely
eroded by the extreme pluralism that characterizes contemporary American politics. Therefore, public administrators can play a significant
role in rebuilding their own legitimacy to the degree they can help
restore a shared sense of political community at all levels of our
political system.

However, this project requires that the administrators take a leading role in resolving those ethical issues of justice and welfare that are always present in the process of constructing a community. In turn, such involvement will require that public administrators escape the narrow technical-instrumental role in which they have often been cast by American political orthodoxy. They must then go on to find a place in the American political system as persons capable of engaging in the full range of practical (applied-ethical) reasoning and discourse.

Now let us turn to examining each of the major elements that make up this thesis and their relationship with one another. A good place to begin is the linkage between a sense of community in the United States and the political legitimacy of American public administration.

Given the hierarchical and unitary assumptions that underlie the modern administrative state, the connection between administrative legitimacy and community should come as no surprise. As Kass observes in his chapter, the notion of agency underlies much modern administration. This concept of agency requires some form of coherent, unitary principal for the agent to serve. Starting with Wilson's (1987) classic formulation, administrative legitimacy in the United States has been heavily dependent upon the assumption that the administrators act as agents implementing the collective public interest of a political community (Ostrom, 1974). Moreover, as White and McSwain point out in this volume, the Depression and World War II years saw the development of a generally well-regarded and prestigious public service whose legitimacy was clearly drawn from their success in guiding the United States successfully through a series of community-threatening crises.

In retrospect, from Wilson to Roosevelt, those who have sought a strong and legitimate public administration in the United States have rooted their arguments in what Bellah, Madsen, Sullivan, Swidler, and Tipton (1985) called the "second language" of American politics—communitarianism. In doing this, the apologists for public administration desired to avoid the problems posed by a national constitution whose preoccupation with preventing concentrations of power provides a far better justification for interest group politics than it does for traditional hierarchical bureaucracy. Yet those who seek to develop a sense of community consciousness in our political and social system must always face the power of the "first language" of American life—individualism. Balancing these two languages without losing the value inherent in either is clearly a major problem faced by the authors in this collection.

This volume starts with the work of several authors who feel that any sense of community and common public interest we formerly enjoyed is in a period of decline. With that decline, there has come a predictable loss in the legitimacy of American public administration. White and McSwain are most pessimistic in this regard. They depict a hyperpluralist American society with thoroughly narcissistic and decultured underpinnings. Here the public administrator lives a dicey existence, attempting to placate the demands of transitory and opportunistic political elites with his or her technical know-how as a "management scientist." For his part, Douglas Morgan explains part of this development by noting the erosion of those institutions (families, schools, churches, and voluntary associations) that once mediated between the demands of individual interests and the obligations imposed on individuals by the larger political society.

Consequently, by undermining the sense of community and common purpose that does exist in the United States, extreme pluralism does two highly undesirable things from the standpoint of public administration. First, it undermines the communitarian basis upon which public administration is traditionally and most easily legitimized. Second, pluralist politics casts public administrators in roles that make it difficult for them to be seen as representatives of the entire political community (e.g., technician, interest group representative, mediator, etc.).

Despite the decline of communitarian sentiment in American society, most of the contributors feel that community, and with it administrative legitimacy, can be restored in the nation. Once more, these same authors are convinced that public administrators will play a significant role in this process.

The less optimistic chapters in this collection hold that the social and political forces that underwrite pluralism are so strong that they can only be resisted at present in communitarian "enclaves" (White and McSwain) or by guardian elites within the larger society (Fox and Cochran). For example, White and McSwain believe that public agencies can form the basis for one such enclave, while Fox and Cochran argue that a "mass elite" composed of openly recruited, demographically representative, mid-level civil servants can play much the same role. By contrast, other chapters (Morgan, Kass, Hummel, and the Evergreen Group) argue that the potential sense of community is still strong enough in this country that it can be revived on a nationwide basis without the necessity of incubation in an enclave or containment within a mass elite of activists. In a sense, these authors argue that under the right conditions communitarian and public interest arguments can still have a mass appeal in the United States.

The chapters that call for some sort of restoration of community as a basis for administrative legitimacy in the United Stated also differ in the way they view what constitutes the foundation for such a community. As a result, they vary in the tasks they assign to public administration in the project of rebuilding those foundations.

Some chapters see the nation's new sense of community based on a continuous process of dialogue that builds and rebuilds a shared sense of meaning and value (White and McSwain, Fox and Cochran, Morgan, and Hummel). In this scenario the public administrator plays an active role in generating and maintaining this dialogue and the political and administrative processes that support it.

Other chapters supplement, or go beyond, such linguistic (inter- pretivist) strategies to suggest institutional approaches to the project of community building. For instance, Morgan argues that the unique in- stitutional position of public administrators in our system allows them to take a longer range view of issues than the legislative branch or the political executive. Providing public administrators are capable of sound, ethical judgment and action, this institutional position enables them to facilitate the "covenanting process" upon which we are able to build a strong, constitutional republic.

Kass holds we can restore our sense of community by realizing that modern, technological society creates as many indissoluble interdepen- dencies as irreconcilable diversities. He argues that once we grasp this, we can base a new American community in the institutional arrange- ments of the repubic which we have founded to mediate and manage these interdependencies. Public administrators can facilitate this pro- cess if they are willing to go beyond their traditional roles as apolitical technicians or interest group mediators and become "stewards" of this republic and the mutual reliance on which it stands.

The Evergreen Group holds that the resurgence of communitarianism in the United States depends upon completion of our democratic revo- lution, both politically and economically. This event would allow us to build political institutions that are based not only on liberty, but on fraternity and equality as well. These authors cast public administrators in the role of helping citizens to foment this revolution.

Robert Zinke brings yet another perspective to the problem of community building in the political system. He argues that public administration must avoid a technocratic solution to the problem posed by the loss of community consciousness in the United States, no matter how beguiling this solution appears. To underscore his point, he paints a bleak future in which administrators have imposed an autocratic and dehumanized order on American life that is rooted in the metaphor of electronic information processing and technicist ideology.

Despite their diversity, all the community-building roles suggested for public administrators share one view in common: The public administrator becomes capable and worthy of rebuilding an American political community because he or she has the ability and virtue to exercise some form of "practical" (ethical) wisdom that transcends the technical rationality traditionally required of public administrators.

This observation then suggests a linkage between the two themes just discussed, legitimacy and community, and the theme we have yet to analyze, practical wisdom. It is the practical wisdom (phronesis) necessary to carry on ethical discourse, make ethical judgments, or take ethical actions that gives the administrator the capacity to help sort out the issues of justice and public welfare that lie at the heart of building any republican community. While David Morgan is most explicit about the public administrator's unique role in exercising phronesis, most of the other administrative roles discussed in this volume require the same capacity. It is hard to think of someone building the humane and democratic world of Hummel's "circle," exercising Kass's "stewardship," or acting in a guardian capacity as a member of a "mass elite" (Fox and Cochran) without the ability to act ethically. The same is, of course, true of helping citizens build a political and economic democracy (the Evergreen Group) or developing communitarian "enclaves" within public agencies (White and McSwain).

Given this linkage, predictively a number of chapters devote some attention to examining practical wisdom and discourse. In various ways Morgan, Jay White, and White and McSwain suggest that phronesis requires a process similar to legal reasoning in which experience is used to apply general principles to the particular circumstances of a given situation.

Jay White holds that practical wisdom necessitates the ability to employ practical discourse as a basis of decision making and action. In such discourse "interpretivist" and "critical" rationality is used along with technical rationality to make choices among means and ends that are both ethical and efficient.

Michael Harmon treats the challenge and personal turmoil facing a public administrator who seeks to exercise practical wisdom and act responsibly. He argues that practical wisdom in such cases necessitates that the administrator balance three distinct concepts of responsibility—personal, governmental, and professional. Finally, Robert Zinke paints a pessimistic picture of the future of public administration if it refuses to require of practitioners the ability to exercise phronesis.

ORGANIZATION OF THE VOLUME

The reminder of this volume is devoted to exploring the thesis and related themes just outlined. This exploration is divided into three parts and an epilogue. Each part has a brief introductory essay providing an overview of the works included.

In Part I, Orion White and Cynthia McSwain review the factors that they feel have led to the declining legitimacy of public administration since World War II. As indicated, they describe what they call a Phoenix project to affect the rebirth of the field.

Part II consists of five chapters that explore the major themes outlined in this prologue—legitimacy, community, and practical wisdom. As already stated, chapters by Douglas Morgan, Charles Fox and Clarke Cochran, and Henry Kass use the images of the "phronemos," the "mass elite," and the "steward," respectively, to stake out a legitimate role for public administrators in our political system. In doing this, each of these authors forges one or more of the connections among administrative legitimacy, political community building, and the application of practical wisdom by administrators examined earlier. The section closes with the two chapters that deal exclusively with the exercise of practical wisdom. These are Jay White's discussion of practical discourse and Michael Harmon's treatment of responsible, ethical action in public administration.

Part III provides three projected possible futures for public administration. Robert Zinke uses the image of a robotic "Administron" to sketch out the implications of a future public administration that tries to use the metaphor of electronic data processing to create a technocratically based political community. Ralph Hummel argues that the future is already here as administrators help society's transition from a hierarchical, technically rational world to a human-centered, democratic one. Lastly, the Evergreen Group sees the future of public administration and the nation itself as dependent upon completing the democratic revolution by extending it to the economic as well as the political sphere.

In the epilogue to this volume Bayard Catron and Barry Hammond reflect on these chapters and the numerous images that have been generated. They suggest some pattern in the images and argue that they can be seen in a developmental frame of reference. In this manner they address the implications of the images for the identity of public administration. Distancing themselves from these chapters and the conference that stimulated them, they close by offering comments on the current state of practical discourse in public administration theory and by implication on the field itself.

This collection represents the work of many people. In particular the editors would like to thank the following colleagues for their advice in preparing this volume: Robert Denhardt, John Rohr, and Curtis Ventris. We would also like to take this opportunity to express our thanks to Blaise Donnelly and Diane Foster of Sage Publications for their unfailing support and understanding during this project. In addition, we express our appreciation to Sharon Barnes, Claire Farmer, Aileen Fisher, and Rosetta C. Kass for their continuing assistance in the preparation of the manuscript. Needless to say, any errors or omissions found in this volume are the responsibility of the editors and authors.

Finally, this book would have been impossible without the existence of the Public Administration Theory Network of the American Society for Public Administration. The editors feel special indebtedness to Guy Adams, who spearheaded the foundation and early efforts of the Network, and Barry Hammond, whose tireless work is a major factor in its present success.

NOTE

1. This volume was the product of the first national meeting of the American Society for Public Administration's Theory Network, which was held in conjunction with the 1988 Conference of ASPA in Portland, Oregon.

REFERENCES

Bellah, R., Madsen, R., Sullivan, W., Swidler, A., & Tipton, S.M. (1985), *Habits of the heart: Individualism and commitment in American life*. Berkeley: University of California Press.

Morgan, G. (1986). *Images of organization*. Beverly Hills, CA: Sage.

Ostrom, V. (1974). *The intellectual crisis in American public administration* (rev. ed.). Tuscaloosa: University of Alabama Press.

Wilson, W. (1987). The study of public administration. In J.M. Shafritz & A.C. Hyde, *Classics in public administration* (2nd ed.). Chicago: Dorsey Press.

PART I:

Reconceptualizing American Public Administration: The Phoenix Project

In this section, Orion White and Cynthia McSwain outline what they call a "Phoenix project" for public administration. This project essentially calls for a reconceptualization of the technical/rational image of public administration that has dominated the field since Simon's work in the late forties (Simon, 1976).

White and McSwain see the necessity of the Phoenix project arising from a narcissistic and hyperpluralist society that is thoroughly "deconstructed" and at odds with itself. This society constitutes a world in which the only basis for cooperative action is the transitory, disjointed, and opportunistic coupling of individual interest and passion.

The social and human costs of this situation are great. First, it is a society dominated by a highly instrumental worldview the authors designate as the "technicist episteme." Paradoxically, given its liberal foundation, this worldview condones using technically rational administration to instrumentalize the very individuals whose interests and "self-realization" it seeks to achieve. Second, equally important, it is a worldview incapable of sustaining culture as a unifying and contextualizing force. This not only makes the construction of community on any scale extremely difficult, it prevents any authentic self-determination by individuals. As White and McSwain put it, ". . . in our belief system human discretion can be worked and exercised through culture and the social process that expresses culture where people are related to themselves and others authentically and validly. . . ." Therefore, in a hyperpluralist society with a technicist worldview, the inability to sustain culture, and with it community, implies nothing less than the ". . . loss of human control over human destiny."

White and McSwain argue that while hyperpluralism, and with it the technicist episteme, will remain dominant in the immediate future, the possibility of restoring the social capacity to maintain culture and community will remain alive and can be nurtured in a variety of "enclaves." It is from these enclaves that a new world-view replacing the technicist episteme will issue forth.

The authors argue that one of the enclaves capable of nurturing a new episteme is modern public administration. However, to realize this potential, public administration must undertake the Phoenix project of its own rebirth. This will entail casting off its postwar image as an apolitical and instrumentalizing "administrative science" and embracing the values of the "traditionalist" public administration of the 1930s and 1940s.

Before it was replaced by the modern administrative science movement in the 1950s, traditionalist thought and practice was based on a series of "axioms," the fundamental values of which can provide the foundation for the rebirth of contemporary public administration. Traditionalists viewed the public administrator as a politically, socially, and ethically responsible actor whose major role was to build and maintain a strong, national community in a pluralist society. Once more, they saw the key to performing this task as the application of a form of practical wisdom and discourse that bears a strong resemblance to contemporary notions of interpretivist and critical rationality (see Jay White, this volume).

White and McSwain recognize the impossibility of recreating the social and political conditions that gave rise to traditionalism. However, they do feel modern public administrators can use the axiomatic basis of traditionalism to good advantage. Administrators can create communities of common political and ethical meaning within their own agencies. Using contemporary interpretivist and critical theory, they can defend the form of practical wisdom and discourse advocated by the traditionalist. Finally, they can even restore the traditionalist's cherished concept of public interest to some of its former luster. To the degree public administrators are successful in these ventures, the authors argue, they will have made a significant contribution not only to the renaissance of their own field, but to the larger "Phoenix project" of restoring human control over human destiny.

REFERENCE

Simon, H.A. (1976). *Administrative Behavior* (3rd ed.). New York: Free Press.

1

The Phoenix Project: Raising a New Image of Public Administration from the Ashes of the Past

ORION F. WHITE, JR.
CYNTHIA J. MCSWAIN

INTRODUCTION

This essay begins from the premise that a pervasive shift in world societies is occurring, a shift toward what we shall call the *technicist episteme*, the axiological foundation of advanced societies. Indeed, we would hold that what appears to many as the almost bizarre relativism of the present social scene could only occur, in the sense that it could only be considered sensible, under the social conditions that are produced by fundamental historical disconnects of the sort we are currently experiencing (Foucault, 1970). Our prognosis for this development is rather grim: we see societies of the future afflicted with an extreme hyperpluralism—a hyperpluralism so deep and widely spread as to deny the possibility for culture in the traditional sense of the term. In place of culture—which we define as the indigenous, spontaneously arising symbols and rituals by which people are related to each other through their collective unconscious—technology has installed a set of control routines and the amelioratives and palliatives necessary to make the whole situation at least tolerable. The salient of this major trend has appeared already, and the main body of the change it portends is close behind.

In sum, we see a future where the foundations of meaning in life are idiosyncratically, rather than socially, based, and where in place of a regulating consensus there is outright behavior control of many varieties. Because, at least in our belief system, human discretion can only be evoked and exercised through culture and the social process that expresses culture, where people are related to themselves and to others authentically and validly, this development means, simply, the loss of human control over human destiny.

We see the march toward this condition of technicism as, at this point, inevitable. The United States and other advanced technological nations, and then the rest of the world, are going to become technicist societies. Changes are never monolithic, however, and every new condition also carries into being its opposite. Our hope is that this contradiction of the technicist worldview can be identified and carried in an enclave within the broader technicist reality. If such an enclave is large and influential enough, it can deny the full effects of technicism and hence afford an essential element of human control over human affairs.

We believe that public administration can serve as such an enclave. Our belief is based on an interpretation of the history of the field, an interpretation that focuses specifically on the transition from what we shall call the *traditionalist* era in the development of the field to the current *modernist* era. Our interpretation holds that the conditions under which the traditionalist viewpoint developed—the Great Depression and World War II—were, like today, conditions of great social upheaval. In societies with a weaker sense of constitutional community than the United States such conditions can lead to replacement of traditional value systems and/or to the relativism that seems characteristic of the current day. The approach to administration developed by the traditionalists both avoided relativism and upheld existing principles. As we see it, this traditionalist approach was overwhelmed by the theories and methodologies—sociological functionalism, behavioralism, and positive science research techniques—that arose as component aspects of the general trend toward the technicist episteme that began to take hold in the 1950s. What we wish to do is to resurrect the traditionalist image of the public administrator as an answer to the issue of technicism that we have just described. The technicist episteme overturned the traditionalist viewpoint in the name of greater scientific precision and certainty. It seems, though, that the end result of the change is to plunge the human race into an abyss of relativism. By raising the traditionalist image of the public administrator into a contemporary form, like the mythical Phoenix from the ashes of its own destruction, we hope to avoid this abyss.

THE TRADITIONALIST APPROACH

The traditionalist approach, as used in this chapter refers to the group of men who founded the Inter-University Case Program (ICP) in the late 1940s (Stein, 1952). Some key names (just to evoke an image of them) are:

Paul Appleby
Wallace Sayre
Roscoe Martin
York Wilburn
Emmett Redford
Phillip Selznick
Don Price
Emery Olson
Phillip Moneypenny
Arthur McMahon
Merle Fainsod
George Graham
Norton Long
Ed Bock
Dwight Waldo

While of course, any attempt to group a collection of academics into a school or an approach is fraught with difficulties and danger—the main one of which is torturing their individual viewpoints onto a procrustean bed—it is notable that they did fashion a rather comprehensive and shared philosophy of administration as a foundation for the ICP program. Hence, there is some justification for characterizing them as generally sharing an approach.

The traditionalist approach arose as a reaction to the classical era in public administration, with its pretensions to becoming a general science of rational administrative action. In fact, it was the classical era attachment to the symbols of rationalism and science, the explicit denigration of politics, and the implicitly antidemocratic overtones of the public administration movement that led to a reaction against and critique of it. This critique is epitomized in Dwight Waldo's classic analysis, *The Administrative State* (Waldo, 1984). Waldo exposed the seeming contradictions in the new form of government represented in public administration—its naive assertion of a value-neutral technical methodology, its overweening faith in and commitment to rationalism and instrumental action, and the inconsistency of this commitment with the field's equally ardently expressed commitment to the values and processes of democratic government.

Waldo's critique, along with the experience of the nation and its officials in the war effort of 1940-1945, produced a context that led to a revision of the identity of the field in the post-World War II period. A number of key figures in the field were drawn into federal government service during wartime, gaining in the process a firsthand sense of the complexity and gravity of the process of governing a nation. They brought to the field in their postwar writings a new, more mature sense of what were the possibilities for rational action in a government like that of the United States. In addition, they gained from their war experience, as did the whole world, an acute sense of the role that collective, irrational, unconscious factors can play in human affairs, even at the broad level of society. The world had witnessed directly the dark insanity of Nazism and Fascism.

The academics who had served in the government during the war then returned to their respective universities to begin teaching about public administration. The framework through which they began to write a research and teaching literature and within which they delivered their courses reflected strongly their experiences in government service. This was a most important phase in the development of the field. This phase we are calling the *traditional* era in American public administration.

We choose this term for the way it seems to reflect the heavy reliance that this group or school placed on the Constitution as an engine of *governance*, that is, the idea that the Constitution both generates (makes possible) and limits (defines) lines of government policy and action. This is, in our view, precisely how traditions function to maintain a community in a viable form: they provide a stable, structured, yet open context (because of their general and symbolic nature) within which the "dialogue of governance" can generate *new* and *legitimate* responses to the ever evolving issues of social life. The unifying orientation of the traditionalists can be described in terms of a set of four axiomatic assumptions with a corollary group of six methodological or working principles. Axiom 1: The broad social system can serve as a real and workable point of reference for administrative action. Axiom 2: National integration must be achieved through the linking of sub-communities of interest, of which administrative agencies are the center. Axiom 3: Leaders of institutions, through their personal capacities, give expression to institutional imperatives. Axiom 4: Administrative events can best be understood structurally.

Axiom 1

First, we must recall that the Roosevelt administration marked a major stage of constitutional development in the United States. The great tension that is built into our Constitution, a tension that derives from its roots in the English emphasis on political liberty, on the one hand, and in the French emphasis on communitarian equality, on the other, sought resolution at this historical moment. Specifically, the free-market tradition of libertianism seemed to have brought the country to a crisis point. One interpretation of the Rooseveltian project was that it was a balancing of this apparent overemphasis on liberalism by embarking on the building of a *national community*, a nationally shared perspective on what was at least a minimally just and humane way of life that should be made available to all Americans (Schambra, 1982).

Hence, the period carried an ethos, an ethic, of agreement, if not consensus. The vehicle for the carrying forward of this project was to be a newly expanded and vigorous public administration, and the workers who were to do the required construction were the public administrators. Each administrator was to refer administrative action and choice to the broad context of society and social well-being generally. This perspective went beyond the demands of any group or set of group interests. It included these and contained in addition a concern for the stake that specific interest holders shared in the well-being of the overall social system. This ethos was quite palpable and was vitally energized by both the experience of the Depression and World War II. It seemed eminently sensible at the conceptual level and directly practical at the level of action to shape one's decisions and actions to accord with the requirements of the well-being of the national system when one had just been living through the consequences of the economic failure of that system, and even more immediately, through the threat of that system's being overwhelmed and dominated by a foreign enemy.

Hence, it was axiomatic that an orientation to the broad social system could serve as a real and workable point of reference for administrative action.

Axiom 2

Second, following from this orientation toward the national system is a derivative emphasis on subunits or subcommunities. While the broad national interests seemed clear enough, there remained the fact that not even the catastrophes of economic depression and war could permanently unite the disparate geographic, economic, and ideological subgroups that make up a large heterogeneous nation like the United States into a national consensus. *Hence it was taken as axiomatic that national integration could only be achieved through the linking of subcommunities of interest. The administrative agency was seen as the center of most of these subcommunities.* The agency, then, was postulated to be a storehold of meanings, the kind of meanings that can only be developed through an ongoing process of working out day-to-day issues of business and social life in the context of contending interests.

Grant McConnell (1966) and Theodore Lowi (1969) have both argued that the decentralization of the center of policy-making to interests, agencies, and congressional committees was a result of the Progressive revolution with which the rise of public administration was concomitant. This seems an accurate analysis. This phenomenon probably was seen at the time as the natural and positive development of a vehicle for policy-making that was appropriate to the newly emerging American community. Each subcommunity centered in an agency was to have discretion over a wide range of policy issues that were important to it, but aspects of policy that represented the newly emerging national norms and values—the values that defined the American way of life that was to be made available to all—were to be powerfully represented to the agencies through the political controls available to the president. The general image was one of a nation of linked policy communities, communities that expressed some values idiosyncratic to them and some values that reflected the minimal standards defining a humane and just life in America. The centers of the subcommunities, the public administrative agencies forming the arena where policy was initiated and implemented, were to be the stable repositories of these two sets of meanings and the enactors who brought them both to life.

Axiom 3

Third, the context of the Roosevelt administration was one of turbulence and rapid growth. The social problems extant in the 1930s were real and immediate. There seemed to be no easily available explanations as to what had gone wrong, no certain theories as to why the system had failed. Further, as noted earlier, the events unfolding in Europe appeared even more darkly mysterious. No one really knew what was going on and solutions were not apparent. Social events appeared to be overdetermined, the result of an enormously complex set of causal forces some of which were irrational. The dynamics behind events indeed seemed so complicated as to not be amenable to any complete, rational comprehension. The scale and pace of events induced what might be called a social ontology of institutionalism. The affairs of human beings seemed to follow from the dynamics of institutions rather than from the choices and actions of individual people. *Hence, the idea of leadership was in vogue, when those at the top of institutions were seen as powerful historical forces because they possessed the personal capacities required to give expression to the imperatives of the institutions they headed.* This, of course, was particularly evident in the understanding of the critical role of the president. The active leadership of the president was crucial to the correct functioning of public administration. The subcommunities of policy formation, centered in administrative agencies, were to be linked together and given coherence through the macrolevel leadership of the president. Thus leadership was a key element in shaping the human project through the institutional process.

Axiom 4

Fourth, this context induced a specific axiomatic belief about the possibilities for understanding human affairs. *The broad patterns that characterized events seemed clear and stable enough to be rendered conceptually comprehensive and hence were the basis for a kind of structural understanding that seemed appropriate and possible.* Another way of putting this is to say that this view held that any given event was the expression of an *archetype*, a fundamental pattern that recurs repeatedly, even though at the surface level there might be innumerable variations in the themes signified and hence many apparently different manifestations of any given single archetype. While it was not seen as possible to comprehend rationally all of the complex events that constitute administrative life, it was postulated that administrators could discern (or be schooled to discern) their basic shape and direction, that is, the tendencies of the specific situations in which they found themselves (Stein, 1952).

At the level of methodology or working principle these axioms were matched by six applied concepts. Working Principle 1: The idea of the public interest can guide administrative action. Working Principle 2: The public weal and the well-being of public agencies are synonymous. Working Principle 3: The Congress and the political executive can effectively control agencies. Working Principle 4: The case study method is the most effective way to learn the correct sensibility of a public administrator. Working Principle 5: Effective administration is achieved through a pragmatic, experimental approach to action. Working Principle 6: Collaboration achieved through dialogue is essential to effective administrative action and policy-making.

Working Principle 1

Foremost among the working principles was the concept of the public interest. The public interest was seen as the practical embodiment of the well-being of the American nation, broadly considered. It was taken as a direct, even palpable point of reference for action in day-to-day administration and policy-making. The public interest referred to the stake shared by all members of the social system in the continued well-being and viability of the society itself. It served as the operational definition of the societal or national interest (Redford, 1958).

Working Principle 2

Because in the emerging administrative state policy-making and political action are the multiple arenas of decision and action that form around the agencies, the theorists of this time, as was mentioned earlier, saw the agency as an important repository of social meanings or consensus. *This view produced a faith that those in agencies could regard the well-being, even the growth, of their agency as equivalent to the public weal.* That is, in order to produce the kind of process of choice and action that this way of government depended upon for effective operation, the agency had to participate actively as a member with full status in the policy-making system. The agency had an important role in what has come to be called the iron triangle of policy formation in American politics. It had, in short, to push its programs and seek to extend its domain (Schattschneider, 1960; Truman, 1962; Heclo, 1978; Wamsley, 1985).

Working Principle 3

The compensatory idea was that agency ambitions would be held in check to a proper extent by the controls imposed through the Congress and the political executive. Such controls, though, were not to be carried to a degree that would undercut the integrity of the agency as a partner in the process, just as the rules of the adversarial process in a court proceeding are structured so as to keep the contending attorneys on an even footing as regards the court. Analogous to the adversarial process producing justice in the courts is the institutional process of struggle in policy administrative subcommittees, producing right policy and administrative action. The people, the actors, were seen as participating in the affairs of the institutions they peopled.

Working Principle 4

The perspective and the sensibilities needed by administrators in a world conceived this way were to be gained through the case study method. Indeed, the core of the literature of public administration at this time was constituted of a philosophical or normative literature focusing on the idea of the public interest and, beyond that, a series of purely descriptive case studies depicting the usual situations and events that one encounters in the world of administration (Stein, 1952). Most of these case studies were published under the auspices of the Inter-University Case Program, and hence were based on an explicit philosophy and methodology that were set out by the governing board of this program.

According to this philosophy, students of public administration, as prospective administrators, could best be prepared for the real world of administration by reading comprehensively factual accounts of actual administrative events in the presence of and with the help of mentors. The case was regarded as what would be called in contemporary jargon a *text*, which, in a sense, spoke to the reader. What the text revealed, through study and analysis, was the underlying structural pattern, the universal elements, that characterized situations of the sort of which it was an example. The student was schooled to perceive the archetypal forms of administrative events. The discernment of these forms, in turn, would provide an indication of what the fundamental tendencies of events in such situations were, including how actors involved in such situations would be disposed to behave. Thus, although the world of administration was enormously complex and a specific situation might take any one of an almost infinite variety of appearances at the surface, it was nevertheless possible for the trained administrator to identify the basic nature of the situation; that is, to understand the situation's essential and underlying form or structure. It was as if administrators were trained to be able to tell when they were in the presence of a horse rather than a cow, no matter what color, size, or breed the horse might be and no matter what behavior it might exhibit. While this may appear to contemporary minds to have been a mundane level of knowledge, it was at the time seen as a significant conceptual handle on a reality that the administrators/scholars who formulated this perspective had directly experienced as almost overwhelmingly complex and dynamic.

Working Principle 5

The concept of action consistent with this perspective on administrative reality might also appear to be mundane or simplistic to the contemporary mind. *Effective administration was to be based on a pragmatic attitude and the experimental method, whereby new lines of action were tried out so as to see what effects they would produce.* The history of Roosevelt's programmatic responses to the economic crises of the 1930s is a history of social experimentation much more than it is a history of the implementation of an ideological or rational plan. A process-oriented model of iterative action comes much closer to describing the theory of action that guided this era of public administration than does the modern idea of "decision." This point is epitomized by the famous Rooseveltian style of fomenting conflict among the members of the cabinet and other subordinates, sometimes pitting one against the other, so as to see if the struggle would generate new and better ideas and proposals.

The traditionalist school of administration did not put much faith in the possibility for definitive rational apprehension of correct lines of action in administrative situations. The best that could be done was to follow and situationally apply general rules of thumb that could be derived from a generic structural understanding of administrative affairs. The famous span-of-control guideline was one such rule of thumb. In essence it amounted to the ambiguous prescription "not to put too many subordinates under one supervisor." Unity of command was another, the idea being that people will have difficulty working for and responding to more than one boss. Such prescriptions, however, were to be applied situationally, in response to the immediate realities of the actual situations that an administrator faced. There were no pat answers or easy solutions in the world of administration as seen by the traditionalists. A struggle with ambiguity was simply what one must face.

The key to effective action lay in how one engaged the struggle. As with the cases one read in school, the actual situations one faced as an administrator were to be regarded as like a case text that could be understood as a set of tendencies that themselves might indicate appropriate lines of response. Nothing was ever certain, however, and all action was necessarily tentative. The understanding and clarity that could be gained came through subordinating oneself to the text of the situation, and this meant, necessarily, to the institutional position one occupied in the situation. The idea was that through the process of reading the text of a situation the right answer, or correct line of action would emerge—that is, would be indicated implicitly—and should be expressed by the administrator. The will of the administrator and his or her individual opinions, values, preferences, or concept of rationality were not to be brought into play explicitly, as they would in a process of rational decision. A metaphor for what was to happen is, again, the adversarial process in a court proceeding or, perhaps more on the point, what a Supreme Court judge is to do in interpreting the Constitution. We in a democracy accept the judgment of the Court because we regard the opinions of the justices on it as being inspired directly by the Constitution itself, as a text. We believe that the Constitution speaks to the judges independently of their own individual viewpoints (Corwin, 1928). We must stress that this way of shaping action is not an easy process or a manner of proceeding that comes naturally to people. Rather, it is acquired through experience and training in how to "read" the text of a situation while holding one's belief in the reality of the public interest as a superordinate symbol to which all must subordinate themselves.

Working Principle 6

Collaboration through dialogue, in the sense of listening attentively and sincerely to all those concerned with and involved in a situation, played a large role in this model of administrative action and policy-making. The willingness to consult, to listen to, and to consider thoroughly and genuinely all the technical information, political advice, and personal feelings, from helpless complaints to aggressive anger, was a primary indicator that the administrator was holding the appropriately subordinate posture toward a situation. When the administrator placed himself or herself in the role of student, and allowed the people involved in a situation to act as teachers to him or her, the danger that the administrator would impose a personal viewpoint onto the situation was minimized. In the traditionalist world, this role posture of allowing oneself to be taught was the key trigger to the administrator's gaining creative insight into the structure of the situation and being able to form an appropriate and original line of action toward it. This occurred in much the way that students in any learning situation are able to understand and then surpass their teachers. It is the learner, whether in the classroom, the specific laboratory, or the simple listening situation, who is most apt to gain the powerful and instructive new insight. While this was not a participative model of administration, it definitely was a collaborative one that stressed openness and insight as opposed to unilateral rational analysis. It bears noting here that many of the participatory group devices that are currently in use by group dynamics specialists were invented and used in the field programs of the U.S. Department of Agriculture.

We hope it is evident from this picture of the traditionalist model of public administration that the public service could be regarded by those who chose it as a vocation. First, there was (in the idea of the public interest) a transcendent vocational symbol, ineffable, according ultimate seriousness, and taken as a guide to practical action or at least as having real and direct implications for practical action. Then there was the embodiment of the vocation in the institution itself, most immediately one's agency and then more generally the government, and it was identified with the protection and furtherance of the general weal (to further one was to further the other). Last, but of great importance, was the training, done either formally or through the institutional ethos of the time, that schooled one to the subordinate, open, contemplative posture of the learner who was to create lines of policy and administrative action from insights gained into specific situations. All the major aspects of this model of the administrator's role deemphasized the individual—as ego or career oriented, as objective rational decision maker, or as independent willful political actor. Rather primary stress was on the context, and the individual administrator's connection to it at every point—to the others in the situation as listener, at the agency and the government as protectors of general well-being, and, ultimately, to the public interest as symbol and guide.

The aspect of this model that is most difficult to communicate is the feeling of commitment and connection that it gave to those who were involved with it. To those who experienced it at the time, as one of the authors did during his own MPA training, the sense of connection between the public service commitment and the well-being of American society was palpable. It was made real primarily because the public interest was felt to be a living and powerful symbol, one that was active in the public administrator's mind and heart.

THE ECLIPSE OF THE TRADITIONALISTS

Introduction

The traditionalist model of public administration did not prevail for long. In fact, almost as soon as it reached a point of having a fully developed identity as an approach to education and practice for the public service, it began to wane in influence. While ICP case studies continued to be used in public administration classrooms, more and more they were regarded as illustrative material for teaching the mushrooming literature of what came to be known as modern organization theory. What caused this rapid cycle of waxing and waning? How it is that the laudable, appealing, even inspiring model of the public service created by the traditionalists was pushed prematurely into the background? The answer lies, again, in the ethos created in America by the experience of World War II. Just as it was the war that created the sense of national identity that played so strong a role in consolidating and giving final form to the traditionalist model, it was also the war experience that inspired its antithesis.

Before describing specifically how this change took place, the nature of the change should be outlined. For this purpose we borrow a concept from the French epistemologist Michel Foucault. Foucault's theory of the history of consciousness rests on the idea that the movement of human consciousness through time proceeds discontinuously (Foucault, 1987; Merquior, 1985; Rabinow, 1984). These discontinuities are marked by shifts in the *episteme* that frames consciousness at a given historical moment. Epistemes are frames of mind that are much more deeply rooted in unconscious processes than, for example, Thomas Kuhn's paradigms (Kuhn, 1970). They are completely incommensurable. Foucault identified four epistemes: a preclassical, a classical, a modern, and a last contemporary one that he believes began to shift in the 1950s. Foucault said little about the nature of this episteme, and he avoided discussion of the question of what causes an epistemic shift.

Our view is that perhaps what happened after World War II, and probably as a result of it, is that human consciousness began to shift to a technicist frame—or at least a quantum level movement in this direction occurred as a result of some sort of critical mass effect of technical developments brought on by the war. We wish the story or analysis we present below to be seen in this context. The change that eclipsed the traditionalist perspective was a most profound shift in the very sense of life that prevailed in the United States. To our view it is important to realize this fact: There is no accepting or turning back technicist consciousness.

Therefore, we want to stipulate that we do not see the shift to technicism as an entirely aberrational development. We may deplore it, as we made clear earlier, but because it is an inevitability, it is best seen as a new condition. A condition that human beings now face in the perpetual struggle, generic to the human condition, to maintain and further the human principle by becoming conscious of the self-alienation that stands as the archetypal obstacle to their own humanity. Hence, we are not romantics who find the modern world abhorrent. Technicist consciousness simply *is* our current condition. It may be likened to a problematic life stage such as adolescence, a stage that one may regret being in at the time, but that itself contains the potential for its own resolution. The main figures in the following story, then, (behavioralism and sociological functionalism) are not *betes noires*. Rather, they are simply the vehicles of a change of consciousness. Further, we shall argue in the conclusion to this chapter that they both can be valuable in creating an image of the public administrator that can countervail technicism and thereby establish the dialectical tension that is essential for carrying the human project forward.

The Rise of Technical Consciousness

World War II created a new interest in and emphasis on understanding social process in a rational, objective manner, a manner that could yield applicable information and practical lessons. Money supporting this type of research began to flow into universities during the 1950s and 1960s in unprecedented amounts. A new consciousness about knowledge was forming, a consciousness that regarded research as a process for improving technique. The priorities for what techniques needed to be improved or invented were set through the device of government and foundation research grants. Emphasis began to shift away from social philosophy to social theory and from wisdom and experience to empirical data. Clearly this new consciousness was at odds with the traditionalist model because at every point, from the belief in the public interest to the structural awareness training of the case method, the traditionalist model was founded on a metaphysical grounding. The new approach stressed *rational technicism*, based on empirical data, the furthest thing from metaphysics.

It seems incontrovertible that the person most responsible for bringing the new technical consciousness to the field of public administration is Herbert Simon, specifically, in the initial stage, with his book *Administrative Behavior* (Simon, 1976). Space is not available here to do justice to such a seminal work. Rather, the few key points that indicate how the position that Simon took contrasted with the newly predominant traditionalist model will be outlined briefly. First, and of major importance, is the fact that Simon adopted an explicitly logical positivist epistemological stance. He is distinctive among social science theorists in doing this, in that usually theorists leave their epistemological beliefs unstated and implicit in their work. (Perhaps to avoid evoking the critical reaction that making such basic assumptions explicit frequently brings about.)

This epistemological commitment carried with it a highly important implication. Positivists of the sort with whom Simon allied himself hold that facts and values are necessarily and incontrovertibly separate. Facts are ascertainable through the direct information of sensory data and can be delineated more or less certainly. Values, on the other hand, can only reflect visceral, emotional reactions and the preferences based on such (Ayer, 1936). They cannot be subjected to scientific study.

Simon drew a direct analog between this epistemological axiom and the nature of the relationship between policy (and by implication, politics) and administration. That is, policy, as he stated it, is the proper province of politics, where emotionally based preferences can be given expression as policy. Administration, on the other hand, is the arena where policy can be translated into the factual question of how efficiently to produce most of the preference that the policy defines and demands—for example, reduction of crime. The result is a specific question and an essentially technical issue: What line of administrative action will consume the least amount of resources per unit of policy outcome produced? This was Simon's standard of efficiency and the core of his idea of what administration is or ought to be. Hence, Simon rejected the idea, newly espoused by the traditionalists, that policy formation is an inextricable part of administration. Rather he stood (curiously, since his work marks a major innovation in the field) with the classical, beginning stage of the field, whose proponents also argued that administration is a realm separate and apart from policy-making and politics.

Where Simon parted from the orthodoxy of the founding stage of the field was on the point of the classical school's commitment to a general science approach to the study and practice of administration. Simon saw this as an overreaching attempt to construct scientific generalizations that could never be specific or definite enough to be applied usefully in the actual organizational world. As evidence to support this point, he parodied what he called the ambiguous, self-contradictory proverbs that the general science approach had yielded. An example, to his view, was the span-of-control principle, which to him gave two conflicting messages: do not put too many subordinates under one supervisor, and, on the other hand, do not put too few subordinates under one supervisor. This to Simon sounded like the twin proverbs "Look before you leap," but, on the other hand, "He who hesitates is lost." What he asserted as a replacement for this grand science approach was what might be characterized as an engineering level of science, where specific technical knowledge about definable issues in the administrative process could be developed and made available to those who operate organizations. Simon saw the emerging emphasis on behavioralism as the way in which such knowledge could be developed (Stein, 1952).

This acceptance of the behavioralism perspective was the major point of contention between the two schools or approaches to administration. The difference lay in the level of understanding sought in each approach and, as a consequence, in the way in which the administrator regarded and intervened in the situations that arose in administrative life. This can be illustrated from the case study literature of the traditionalists. The "National Labor Relations Examiner" case involves an issue of a rather psychologically volatile supervisor and a zealous subordinate (Stein, 1952). An administrator working from the behavioral approach would seek enlightenment as to how to cope with such instances by consulting studies explaining the correlates of employee identification with program objectives or organizational goals as opposed to professional standards or corollary political goals. Armed with such understanding, the administrator might be able to manipulate or explicitly alter the key independent variables involved in the situation so as to produce the balance or pattern of commitment that is desired for a specific organization.

Another famous case study provides a similar illustration, namely the "Indonesian Assignment" case. In this case the central issue involves the question of a subordinate's possible disobedience and a rather direct affront to his immediate supervisor. In this case, the administrator would consult studies indicating the correlates of obedience to authority and, given the special circumstances of the case (in this case a foreign field office), structure or control the appropriate variables so as to produce the desired degree of certainty of compliance. The book *Organizations*, on which Simon collaborated with James March, is a compendium of such information—in essence, it constitutes for the state of the research findings of that time a reference book of information as to what variables directly affect a wide variety of key organizational behaviors (March & Simon, 1958).

By contrast, the traditionalists viewed such cases in much broader but deeper terms. That is, they felt that such cases represented to the reader circumstances and situations that inevitably arise in administrative life—in a myriad variety of permutations, perhaps, but all with basically the same underlying form. Just as, for example, a tension between generations is inevitable at some stage (usually during the chronological adolescence of children) in family life, so are episodes involving employees who are zealots. The question for action, in this light, was not how to *predict* and *control* the situation through the manipulation of key independent variables. Rather it was how to *respond appropriately* to the situation as it presented itself. The question of right action, then, involved, together and at once, a moral dimension and a correctness dimension. A right action would resolve or settle the circumstances of the situation (i.e., be correct) and would also further the larger processes of individual and organizational development and thus serve the public interest (i.e., be moral). This required an ability to understand the structural, underlying dynamics of the situation at hand so that the response that most optimally fitted might be chosen. Right action was seen as *synergistic*, as resolving at the same time the situation itself, the organization's stake or interest, the individual's stake or interest, and the overreaching public interest. Mary Parker Follett's "law of the situation" is an appropriate image for the process of right action (Follett, 1924, 1926).

The idea of technically and value-neutrally controlling organizational situations was to the traditionalists both ethically repugnant (for denying the inevitable moral component of all action) and invalid (for assuming the power through the operation of intellect alone to control and determine the course of events in something as complex as an administrative organization peopled by human beings). In the eyes of the traditionalists, the new image of the administrator that was indicated by Simon's behavioral approach amounted to a significant denigration to the status of a functionary technician. Simon was even quite happy to predict and call for the elimination of middle-management bureaucrats in organizations when computer technology had developed to a level where it could take over what he saw to be their essentially routine roles (Simon, 1960). All important discretion, namely the discretion to set policy and make reasoned judgments on issues of fairness, justice, equity, etc., was removed from this new role definition and given to the political sector of government. Not only was the degree of subordinancy implied by this role definition unrealistic and inappropriate in the traditionalists' view, but the substantive dimension of the role was reduced to the mechanical application of expertise. This was a direct threat to the traditionalists, in that the expertise they had to offer was not mechanically applicable—indeed, it was an expertise not even specified in any great detail. The change Simon represented amounted to a true paradigmatic shift whereby the old perspective and the knowledge produced under it was rendered obsolete.

As was mentioned earlier, there is a curious paradox in this story. While it was the experience of the Great Depression and World War II that largely produced the traditionalist approach, it was the pattern of sociocultural changes that these events and the attempts to cope with them set in motion that also produced the new view, as embodied in Simon's work. It was the very events that created it that ultimately overwhelmed the traditionalist perspective. This paradox probably derives from the predominantly dual nature of the war effort. That is, the war effort was both a communitarian struggle and a vast technological enterprise, as symbolized by its culmination in the dropping of newly invented nuclear weapons. It is further significant that Truman's decision to use the bomb was apparently based largely on the fact that it had been invented, that it would work, and that the nation had incurred an enormous cost in developing it—a veritable paradigmatic schema of a technicist choice (Neustadt, 1961). The symbol of science, especially engineering science, took on a virtual omnipotence. There was little or no room in the ethos created in the postwar period for the sense of metaphysics; the ambiguous, bewildering complexity; and the profound mystery of the human world that characterized the traditionalist approach. People believed answers to any question were now, in principle and in fact, possible, and they wanted answers. The idea of the public interest, it seemed, was necessarily general and vague—it could better be reduced to specifically resolvable technical questions. This technical ethos set off broader changes in all the institutions of society, but among the most heavily struck was the university, which now was drawn under the influence of government through the vehicle of sponsored research.

If the demystification and technologicalization of society were to proceed, however, it was necessary to develop a new understanding of social process, an understanding that rendered social institutions in specific, and then in technical, terms, free of such ideas as the "emotional substructure" and the irrational (Waldo, 1984). The task of constructing this image sat naturally in the province of the social sciences, and it is no surprise that it was here that one can see the vanguard of the movement creating this effort mounted specifically in the field of sociology. The demise of the traditionalist perspective must be seen in this larger context of a transformation of the social sciences and indeed of the popular view of society. This change went in a direction that was antithetical to the fundamental axiological assumptions of the traditionalist approach. As the paradigm shift occurred, the traditional approach simply lost its plausibility.

Functionalism in Sociology, Political Science, and Society Generally

Unlike the present day, when the field of public administration, along with policy studies, has established and continues to define ever more clearly an identity independent of the field of political science, during the period when the traditionalist viewpoint predominated, public administration and political science were closely allied. Indeed, one could even say that the study of administration, especially the emphasis on the development of administrative law and the executive function of the president, constituted key elements in the core of political science. This difference with the present-day situation is reflected in the fact that the term *political science* was less in use than the more generic term *government* (i.e., the study of government) to refer to the field. The literature of the field was composed largely of historical-legal studies of the institutions of government, along with classical political philosophy. This pattern began to change dramatically during the late 1950s and early 1960s, however, largely as a result of the influence of the field of sociology and especially the work of the functionalist school of thought led by the famous Harvard sociologist, Talcott Parsons (Black, 1961; Collins, 1988; Parsons, 1949, & Wilson, 1983).

For our purposes here, we need only mention the few key aspects of Parson's functionalism that had the greatest impact in creating the new ethos that emerged in political science after the Second World War. Primary among such influences was Parson's conceptualization of society as a *system* that manifests adaptive, survival-oriented activities. This notion of system, because it depicted society as almost a self-conscious, purposive (in the sense of seeking to survive) entity, amounted to a powerful reification, lending to it a virtual physicality. This effect, when coupled with Parson's idea of *functional requisites*, was especially compelling. The functional requisites identified in Parson's theory defined the presumed activities of any social system, the activities that the system had to accomplish if it were to survive. At the most general level these were identified as *goal attainment, integration, adaptation,* and *latency*. The functional requisites completed the process of reifying the idea of social system (i.e., of coming to regard it as an integral, real entity that is concretely distinct from its surroundings) and provided a source point for the notion that definite, convincing judgments could be made as to which behaviors, events, and so forth helped the survival of society, and which hindered it. The "helps" were referred to in the theory as *functional*, while the "hinders" were labeled *dysfunctional*. Hence, we can see in these core ideas that while Parson's functionalism definitely rejected positivism, it nonetheless adopted an implicitly objectivist mood and epistemological stance (Black, 1961).

This posture is in evidence also in another key aspect of Parsonian theory—the emphasis placed on the idea that social order is normatively grounded, meaning that people's behavior in society is regulated through processes of socialization that teach people values or normative rules that they subsequently follow as a guide to appropriate behavior in social settings. To Parsons, deviant behavior is produced by the dysfunctional configuration of structural vectors (e.g., conflicting role expectations), perhaps the main one of which is the socialization process. In one sense, his entire theory hinges critically on the belief that people can be taught, effectively and unambiguously, how to achieve correct role performances. This belief itself is founded on an undisclosed assumption: namely, that language, as the key vehicle of socialization, can carry definite, positive meanings that will be received in a standard manner by the objects of socialization processes. In short, Parsons believed that social*izees* could at least in principle hear precisely what social*izers* intended to communicate to them, and, of course, that the socializers themselves knew clearly and shared a common understanding of what they wanted to communicate to socializees. This theory of language is sometimes referred to as *legal positivism*. It means simply that words have definite, standard meanings that, to some extent at least, are independent of context. This is a highly important aspect of Parson's theory for what we wish to explain here. Not only does it reinforce tremendously the positive epistemological stance of the theory, it establishes by implication that rational agreement is the basis of human communication and that collective relationships can and should be based on such agreement. The consequence is that if a term is brought into discourse (e.g., *the public interest*), it carries an implicit demand that others agree to it as meaningful, and this, in turn, means that the term must be specified or defined in a positive, definite way.

As Parson's hegemony in sociology was climbing to its zenith in the 1960s and emanating strong influences into the field of political science, a corollary development was occurring from within the field. This change was the shift from institutions to behavior as the focus of study. One of the founding events of the movement toward behaviorism was the publication of David Truman's *The Process of Government*, which advocated a shift from the study of patterns of institutional development to the study of the human dynamics that occur within institutions (Truman, 1962). Truman's book had the effect of strengthening the move toward the behavioral approach, but this influence was no doubt helped by (or perhaps grounded in) the more general ethos that was being fostered by the spreading acceptance of functionalism. One bit of evidence to support this point is the interpretation that was put on Truman's work regarding the mandate it seemed to imply for political science research. Truman's book leaned heavily on a source work:

Bentley's *The Process of Government* (1908). Bentley, in turn, was influenced by Dewey's philosophy of pragmatism and the social philosophy of George Herbert Mead. It is difficult to see how these roots in process philosophy could have nurtured what turned out ultimately via Truman's work to be the behaviorist's central project: the construction of rather broad-scale, empirically grounded generalizations that comprehended the human events of politics and government. This seems plausible only if one forgets the process philosophy grounding of Truman's work and refers instead to the context of Truman's times, that context being set by functionalism. By so doing one can take Truman's call to study the surface dynamics of institutions as it was predominately taken—as a challenge that the field shift its emphasis to the task of constructing a theory of political behavior. It is further consistent that the research methodology for pursuing this product was borrowed largely from sociology, at least in the initial stages of the change.

The theoretical literature of political science during the 1960s includes many instances of direct incorporation of one version or another of functional analysis; numerous examples of a shift to new sociological, logico-deductive modes of theorizing; and an emphasis on empirical research focused on the behavioral dynamics of political institutionalism. Further, the research is primarily quantitative rather than qualitative. This rapid shift toward behavioral, quantitative, empirical research occurred within a new kind of reality-oriented scientific attitude. The attitude was based on a belief that the social world in general and the political world in particular could be rendered understandable in explicit, rationally conceived, causal terms. This attitude seemed to portend that, eventually, all or almost all ambiguities about how things worked in the world of politics would be resolved and clarified. The move toward an orthodoxy of scientific rationalism gained the momentum, virtually, of a juggernaut. Indeed, the entire range of intellectual diversity, as retrospective accounts indicate, was contained within the paradigmatic assumptions of functionalism (Burrell & Morgan, 1979). Symbolic interactionism, based on the social psychology of Gorge Herbert Mead, constituted the far left wing of social theorizing. Nonetheless, even as close as symbolic interactionism is to mainstream functionalist modes of thought, had it had more of an audience, and greater influence, the positive attitude of mind and the rampant scientific rationalism of the new trend would have been substantially qualified, at least in its pretensions to a comprehensive logico-deductive understanding of the social world.

The traditionalists did react vigorously, at least initially, to this major new development, particularly to the denigration of the administrator's role that seemed clearly to be entailed by Simon's reassertion of a separation between politics (i.e., policy-making) and administration. They were hampered by two dominant facts, however. First, they lacked the conceptual tools they needed, in the form of both philosophically based social theories and psychologically based social theories of the sort that are currently labeled humanist theories. With these two theoretical tools, which are available today, the traditionalists would have perhaps been able to marshal a convincing defense of their essentially process approach to administrative action and their essentially idealist approach to the public interest as the main ethical guide for the administrator. Second, the ethos from which public administration had arisen, the ethos of twentieth century America, was itself more consistent with the new trend toward scientism than the position from which the traditionalists worked. Therefore, not only were the short-term contextual forces of the postwar scientific mood working against the traditionalists but the longer run historical and structural trends toward a technicist society supported their adversaries. The result was that the traditionalists rather quietly adapted themselves to the new trend by taking on at least the appearances of following it and by deferring to the new hegemony that began to appear in the field's professional associations.

It was in this circumstance that the tremendous influence of Herbert Simon's writing was felt. From a position of being far ahead of his time (the text he co-authored with Smithburg and Thompson [1950] sold only a few hundred copies in its first year), Simon's work quickly gained prominence as the exemplar of the trend toward behavioralist social science in the field. It was through his influence that a broad-scale, pan-social science approach to the study of administration and organizations became legitimate. Further, because Simon (remarkably) made explicit his definite commitment to positivism as his epistemological standing point, the "wisdom of experience," "reason," and "mature good judgment" approach to knowledge that was the core of the traditionalist school seemed limited and intellectually parochial by comparison. With Simon, discourse was narrowed to a degree that left the supremely important idea of the traditionalists, the public interest, out in the cold, without support. Hence, it was rather easy for Glendon Schubert to, in effect, destroy the term, or remove if from dialogue in the field, with the publication of his book *The Public Interest* (Schubert,

1961). The argument Schubert made was that the term *public interest*, because it cannot be referred to the realities of the social and political world in a way that fits the positivist criterion of meaningfulness, is useless as a term of social science. Schubert's was an easy argument to make in the context of the times, much easier than it would be to make today. In the current situation, the orthodoxy of the behavioralist era has broken up, though behavioralism remains perhaps the largest of the resulting pieces. The work of Thomas Kuhn, from a history and philosophy of science perspective, and Peter Berger, from a social theory perspective, gained widespread readership and did much to crack open the functionalist orthodoxy in the 1960s and 1970s (Berger & Luckman, 1967; Kuhn, 1970). As the '60s and then '70s progressed, a variety of critiques emerged, ranging from critiques of the Enlightenment, to methodological critiques of the claim of value-neutrality that underpinned behavioralism, to critiques of the pluralist version of democratic process that was espoused by the leaders of the behavioralist revolution in political science, to social theory critiques of the adequacy of behavioralism for understanding social interaction (usually these were based on the phenomenology of Wilfred Schutz), to attempts to define and assert a new, normatively based, and subjectively sensitive postpositivist epistemology. The simple, positivist-inspired line of thought that Schubert (1961) used would meet with a myriad and vigorous counterattack today. Nonetheless, the behavioralists were successful in giving a definite and new shape to the intellectual profile of public administration, of political science, and, indeed, to the generations of students who studied under its aegis. In fact, it bears mention here that the typical reader of these pages will be reading them from a mindset that was shaped by the functionalist ethos. As a result, what is being said here about the traditionalist viewpoint may seem strange and to some extent incomprehensible. The positive science mood that was released and diffused by functionalism remains the dominant mood of the day.

This wide-ranging influence should not obscure the reality of the transition that this chapter has been reviewing, however. What the positive view of society propagated by the rise of functionalist thought did was substitute a new metaphysics for the metaphysics of the traditionalists. The metaphysics of the traditionalists was the metaphysics of community. It grounded all social institutions in a social process that was in turn grounded in relationships between people. These relationships, taken collectively, form a context that has a life of its own and a spiritual voice that can guide the practical affairs of the collective toward the common weal. This metaphysics was grounded directly in the higher law tradition of the American Constitution, the tradition on which judicial review is founded (Corwin, 1928). What the traditionalists sought was to establish a relationship among the actors in the administrative arena and between the administrator and the text of an administrative situation that was analogous to the relationships among Supreme Court judges and between them and the text of the Constitution. By so doing they hoped to have the administrator guided toward the public interest in the way that judges are guided toward the will of the Constitution. The ultimate reality to which the traditionalists' metaphysics referred was the reality of what exists between and among people. To the traditionalists the sense of community was the reality of community and thus of society and all its constituent processes, like politics and economics.

The functionalists seemed to destroy this metaphysics by emphasizing the positive, tangible aspects of social process and institutional events and by asserting a set of essential, universal requisites that are so clear and standard that they can serve as workable guides to arranging the affairs of the system. Functionalism accomplished this through the conceptual device of reification, however, and as a consequence, it was not truly grounded. Rather the functionalists simply treated individuals as if they processed a reality independent of social context. It was as if individuals had a set of self-contained motivations that they sought to express in their social lives. Similarly the overall social system was also reified by treating it as if it possessed a discrete boundary and independent reality.

These reifications amount to a massive discounting of the human principle, the human spirit. While the ideas underlying them are true, they are great half-truths. The other side of the story is that individuals have no human shape outside the moral context of human community, and society's requisites for survival can only afford guidance in social affairs when they are refined and defined through the operation of individual moral sentiment. Society and the individual are inextricably connected through community. The one makes the other in a reciprocal, seamless relationship. They cannot justifiably be considered as discrete and independently separate real things.

Worst of all, though, the functionalist ethos reified language. Whereas the truth about language appears to be that it, too, is a fragile creation of the relation of human beings to each other in community, the functionalists gave it an independent reality and asserted that it carries definite meanings. The special, ineffable, indefinable connection between people that is the essence of community was thereby reduced, in this view, to a social contract and an explicit agreement. Their idea was that there can be no other real or true connection between people. People in a situation governed by such an ethos begin to seek explicit and positive guidance for their behaviors. They frequently look first to law and to traditional and explicit role definitions, taken literally and explicitly. Alternatively, they look to market processes for guidance.

We are currently living in the midst of the problematic circumstances that such a theory of language can engender. On the one hand, there is widespread confusion about what are the standards and norms that govern various institutional roles. It seems that standards are simply changing when in fact standards are actually disintegrating. Such confusion is evident in instances ranging from the issues of how we as a people should appropriately assess presidential candidates to figuring out what are the appropriate responsibilities of a surrogate mother. The ambivalent attitude of the public toward the press and the press toward its own real role is a particularly illustrative case. Traditionally, the press has constrained its investigatory activities through the guidelines set by a sense of national community. There is a famous story about Babe Ruth's being chased, naked, through the dining car of a train on which his team was traveling to play a baseball game in another city. The person chasing him, with raised knife in hand, was his current lady friend, who, according to the report, had just discovered him in bed with yet another woman. In the dining car was a table of sportswriters traveling to cover the game Ruth was about to play, and they all witnessed the spectacle of Ruth's flight firsthand. One turned to the others and said, "There is no need to report this, is there?" and that was the end of the matter as far as public reports went. This would scarcely happen today. The press has expanded its coverage of news to virtually all the details of the private lives of major and sometimes minor public figures. The "Geraldo Rivera syndrome" and the case of Gary Hart's presidential candidacy have led leaders among journalists to wonder and debate publicly what is their appropriate role. They seem caught between market forces, the whims of the public, and various attempts to assert guiding principles.

What the transition from the traditionalist to functionalist ethos in public administration marked is a broader transition in American society generally. At the surface, this transition appears to be a perhaps simple, certainly predictable, development into a new stage of scientific and technological sophistication as a society and the positive science consciousness that goes with it. At a deeper level, though, it is a deterioration of our national constitutional community and the ineffable sense of higher law, moral relationship, and unconscious connection that unite people who share a viable national identity. The standard of *agreement*, to which we increasingly hold ourselves, we increasingly fail to meet.

THE PHOENIX ARISING—A SKETCH OF THE NEW IMAGE OF THE PUBLIC ADMINISTRATOR

Because we deplore the monolithic rise of technicism in the modern world and because we believe that the traditionalists held a position that worked directly counter to technicism, we see it as regrettable that they held center stage in the field for as short a time as they did. Nonetheless, their rapid fall from influence was no doubt inevitable, in light of the broad-scale epistemic shift toward technicism after World War II. Given this general condition as well as the structural conditions that were increasingly uncongenial to their views, they had little ground for appeal. Where the traditionalists offered belief in a vague normative standard, the modernists proposed accepting the hard, clear guidance that they saw as emanating from the political arena. Where the traditionalists saw the world as overdetermined and hence impossibly complex, the modernists offered a view that held it could be reduced through the sure methods of science to sensible lawlike patterns. Where the traditionalists proposed a tentative, process-based approach to action, the modernists promised specific techniques informed by scientific understanding.

Even more telling than those matters, though, was the fact that the traditionalists lacked the philosophical, theoretical, or even conceptual devices necessary to the defense of their position. Indeed, lacking this ideational grounding, they were unable to formulate their position in such a way as to make it seem like a position, that is, a conceptual system with integrity and grounding. In the Introduction to Harold Stein's *Public Administration and Policy Development* (1952), where the traditionalist viewpoint is given a rather comprehensive statement, one can find homage paid to much of the belief system that underpins the modernist position. The traditionalists' own approach is stated there as a pattern of emphasis within a thoroughly catholic framework for understanding public administration. Hence, it is plausible that many of the traditionalists felt that they could, as the Hindus did with Mohammed, simply incorporate the new views into their own framework. While there was resentment at the rise of the modernist view, and conflict with it, the fight soon was abandoned.

A different approach is possible now. Within the past 20 years the social sciences have become sufficiently heterodox and this heterodoxy has generated sufficient alternative conceptualization to support a reconstitution and reassertion of the traditionalist approach. This section of this chapter will take each of the axiomatic assumptions and the working principles of the traditionalists and reexamine them in light of these contemporary theories. When these new conceptual tools are used, the traditionalist image of the public administrator can be renewed in terms that are both eminently plausible and at the same time preserve the essence of their approach.

The romantic images of the traditionalists' first two axiomatic assumptions, which concerned society as a reference point and the linkage of subcommittees, must now be drastically revised. The contemporary and future public administrator must see the development of technology and technologically oriented forms of social organization as the fundamental conditioning fact of society. As we noted in the chapter's introductory remarks, our view is that the only realistic image of the future is one that depicts technicism as having a pervasive impact on social life. There will, therefore, be no possibility of community in the sense that the traditionalists envisioned it. There will not even be, in our opinion, a possibility for a consensus-producing political process. That is, as politics and political decision processes become more and more reliant on technical devices such as television, polls, electronic voting, and—who knows what the future will produce—they will be reduced ultimately to market processes themselves. David Stockman's insider's account of the Reagan administration shows that this pattern is already present in more than outline form (Stockman, 1986).

What this means for the public administrator is that he or she must accept these highly problematic conditions as normal. Not only will it be impossible to refer to a general social construction such as American society or any standard like that—that is, any commonly shared value base—but in addition the political system will for all intents and purposes continue to act as a source of random value inputs. The values institutionalized by the political process will become as capricious as the marketplace itself. Now values, in the form of new programs and new interferences in the administrative process, will begin to appear with the rapidity of new products in the economy.

A third axiomatic assumption the traditionalists held was the importance of leadership (especially presidential leadership) and institutionalism. This concept, too, must be made contemporary by reflecting it against the reality of advanced technicism and the degradation of culture that it entails. Institutions cannot embody normative principles when no shared normative principles are held in the society of which they are a part. The public administrator, then, must see the agency not as an institution so much as an enclave or redoubt against technicism and the social incoherence it tends to generate. Within the enclave or redoubt, rather than leading in the historical sense, the public administrator must act as a mediator of meaning. This means that the administrative agencies must be the loci for the creation of a shared social reality. Preceding this is the more fundamental task of creating a *lingua franca* by which value issues can be discussed. (A lingua franca is a common way of talking that is shared by people from different linguistic communities.) The great increase in social incoherence that we have experienced since the 1960s and the emerging literature of interpretivist sociology have taught us that, indeed, *all language is a lingua franca* in that participants in a linguistic community must constantly do interpretive work in order to construct meaning and coherence from each other's communication acts.

Congress and the political process generally can only respond to complaints and raise issues. Answers must be worked out as a process of living through the issues of real life. Only here can the parties find a way of talking—again a lingua franca—about the shared body of knowledge and the shared values that solutions require. This is the role of the agency as enclave. Where the traditionalists could assume a value base and proceed from there, the modern public administrator faces the task of creating the very basis for communication itself, and must work from the modern realization that this lingua franca itself constitutes the shared body of knowledge and consensus on which policy and administrative action must be based (Douglas, 1986). What we are saying comes down to this: The agency is the place within the hubbub where reason can be spoken. The voice of the surgeon general, as leader of the Public Health Service, speaking about the threat of AIDS in the name of public health is an appropriate image from which to draw an illustration.

A fourth axiom of the traditionalist approach was that the immense complexity of the real world of administration could only be understood *structurally*, that is, in terms of basic, archetypal mechanisms and patterns. We take it as the task of the academic wing of public administration to provide the public administrator with a solid grounding in modern structural analysis and in general to reorient the field away from complete reliance on the behavioralist model of organization theory and behavior. Drawing from structural anthropology, structural linguistics, depth psychology, and a broad concern with myth and symbolism, a new way of understanding administrative life—as the traditionalists did but more grounded and more intellectually sophisticated—must be developed. Charles Goodsell's study of the architectural symbolism of city council chambers (1983) marks precisely the direction in which the field ought to go in accomplishing this task.

Similar revisions must be made in each of what we designated above as the working principles that derived from the traditionalists' axiomatic assumptions. The first of these mentioned was the idea of the public interest as a normative standard for guiding administrative action and policy. Presently, however, and again with the aid of conceptual tools made available by the perspective of interpretivism, the concept of the public interest can be placed on much firmer ground. One way of doing this, for example, is by using the analog of Berger and Kellner's concept of sociological consciousness (1981). Berger and Kellner have argued persuasively that human beings have the capacity to choose consciously the set of typifications that they employ in constructing an interpretation of any event. Such a choice both distances one from the event and, at the same time, creates a special type of involvement with it. This distinctive relationship, they say, is what constitutes sociological objectivity. In Berger and Kellner's view, sociological analysis conducted in this manner should not be made to serve as the basis for policy formation and action because it is an artificial or exogenous manner of interpreting human situations. Hence to act within actual situations on the basis of sociological typifications can only serve to degrade the shared reality that has been constructed through the interpretive work of the participants in the situation.

This caveat seems hinged, though, on the assumption that there is a stable and shared reality existing that would be degraded. While, of course, this must be true at the micro level of the community if there is to be any coherence at all in social life, it is less and less true (and possible) at the level of society itself, or even for the supracommunal sectors of society with which public agencies typically deal. In such contexts as these, the task faced is one of constructing social reality itself out of the specific life worlds represented in the agency's arena of action. Metaphorically speaking, the public interest would serve as the grammar, or methodological rules, for a common language. The work that needs to be done in order to construct such a grammar is to compile the typifications that constitute the public interest consciousness, or the frame of mind that one employs when constructing interpretations of events from the perspective of the public interest.

When then is the rule of decision or choice? This is a key point in that it was here that most damage was done to the traditionalists' idea of the public interest. While indeed they did stress individual decision as a focus for understanding administration, they viewed the individual as acting in an institutional context. This meant that policy and action emerged from the ethos of an institutional process. Individuals expressed this ethos. It was context that informed policy and action. This is the critical point: By viewing the public interest as an ideal type that constitutes a mode of consciousness, we can return to the idea that human action derives from a sense of meaning rather than from decision.

A second traditionalist working principle is derived from the axiom of institutionalism mentioned earlier. It was assumed that public agencies were appropriately an active part of the process of governance and that, indeed, for the administrator to work to further the program and well-being of the agency was in a sense to work for the public interest. The public administrator was seen as a *doer*, as one who could have a direct hand in accomplishing great tasks. It seems evident that this image of the public administrator is now anachronistic. First, there is the fact that a great bulk of government activities is carried out by contractors, and no end to this trend is in view. The public administrator is becoming a contracting manager. Some decry this development as marking a diminishment of the public service role in social life and wonder how far it can go without compromising the very function of government itself. This complaint must assume, however, that going back to the programmatic model is a possibility. We believe that even if such a possibility exists now, it will not be real for much longer.

The reasons for this, again, are the conditions of complexity, change, and social hyperpluralism that characterize advanced technological society. Program implementation assumes a clear sense of what needs to be done, that is, that there are answers to problems and that conditions are not so complex as to deny implementing these answers instrumentally. The conditions faced by government presently and in the future are not like that. They are so diffuse and complex as to make it impossible to find points of leverage from which to mount programs against them. The illegal drug trade in the United States is one obvious example; AIDS is another. The issue, then, becomes one of constructing a basis for mounting broadly based, diverse, multiple initiatives in both the private and the public sectors. In this the agency must act as an enclave within which relevant parties can begin a reality-constructing conversation, that is, begin forming an institutional ethos out of which multiple lines of action can emerge. The public administrator must play the role of mediator and negotiator, sometimes of meaning, sometimes of policy and action alternatives, as when contractor relations are involved. We see this mediator-negotiator role as even more important, and indeed more dramatic and exciting, than the program implementation role idea of the past. Rather than improving society through programs, the public administrator will be central to the process of reconstructing society.

A corollary to the idea of agency activism in the traditionalist approach was the notion that agencies are an integral part of the policy partnership, the system of checks and balances, by which governance in the United States is achieved. This meant that while they were to be responsive to political controls from the Congress, they were not to be dominated by these. The traditionalists did see agencies as subordinate to the president, however, in that the president was viewed as the chief public administrator.

A revision of this notion, more appropriate to the conditions of the present, is to see the agency as a full partner in the process of government. This means at bottom that no political element is seen as legitimately being able to compromise the integrity of agencies. A rationale for this position that is grounded in the traditions of the Constitution itself has recently been provided by John Rohr (1986). Another reason for this revision rests on the emerging realities of politics under conditions of technicism. As has been suggested several times already in this essay, political processes, including those that energize the presidency, are becoming so fractionated and responsive to market controls that they lack the coherence necessary for providing publicly interested control of agencies.

Our view is most certainly not that administrators ignore or rebuke mandates, pressures, and controls from political actors. Indeed, the balancing of interests as reflected through politics is a tradition of the very definition of the idea of the public interest. Public administrators must be responsive to political controls, and such controls must be seen as properly resulting in real changes in the behavior of agencies. Those controls that go so far as to impair the capacity of the agency itself, as an element of governance, though, can and must be legitimately resisted. This, we believe, is the implication of John Rohr's analysis of the Constitutional grounding of the agency's position in our system of government.

The fourth working principle of the traditionalists had to do with the training of public administrators and, more generally, with the way in which they understood the world of administration. The structural understanding that was axiomatic to the traditionalist position was to be created through training based on the case study method, as described earlier in this chapter. Rather than revising it, we would extend the principle of education that underpinned this approach. At bottom, the case approach deemphasized the educational material and instead placed most importance on the development of the future public administrator as a person. The point of education was not so much to install technical information in students (though there was some of this in the form of skills training) but rather to help students acquire a kind of vicarious wisdom, a premonition of experience, that would give them the confidence and the fortitude—and some situationally applicable insights and practical tips—to face the problematic reality of the public administrative world. The idea was something like what parents attempt to do with their children or mentors with proteges: Build the person, the rest takes care of itself.

Certainly the emphasis on behavioral social scientific knowledge has diminished the extent to which this philosophy is employed in public administration programs today. Our view is, though, that not only must this approach be resurrected, it must be extended to include all aspects of the prospective public administrator's educational experience. All aspects of testing and evaluation of the student, particularly, should be revised so as to reflect a concern with the development of the student—that is, with evoking his or her best performance—rather than with producing a judgment as to the fitness of the student to pass through the educational gate into the world as an authorized person.

This does not mean that modern social science and the knowledge about behavior that it has produced should be ignored or eschewed. Rather, these approaches and their research products would be regarded in a different way. Instead of holding out the vain hope of producing cumulative, empirically verified generalizations that are (and this is the most clearly impossible part) specific enough to be applied in real-life settings, these literatures would be mined for patterns that suggest the underlying archetypes of administrative life. These archetypes can be discerned through research as well as through experience.

The last two working principles of the traditionalists that are relevant to a reconstituted image of the public administrator are their idea of action as process—that is, as an iterative, experimental approach to dealing with a complex, shifting reality—and their commitment to collaboration. The central image here is that the administrator, through achieving a proper relationship to the various elements in a situation, could respond to it in an emergent fashion. The idea was that reasoning together would provide guidance in the correct and right direction.

Current perspectives on process, especially interpersonal relations and group processes, have much to offer in the way of material for making the traditionalists' commitment to process a practical working principle. The research literatures of group dynamics, organization development, humanistic psychology, principled negotiation, and, more generally, the theory of learning systems, indicate rather clearly how to establish a working process approach to action, one where lines of action can emerge because the relationships among the parties involved are not distorted, or suffer minimal distortion, from issues of power, manipulation, and so forth.

CONCLUSION

Earlier in this chapter we discussed Michel Foucault's concept of the episteme, the dominating mode of consciousness that he claimed characterizes moments in history and that conditions all perception and action at those moments. Foucault recognized, though, along with some of his critics, that the evidence that a given episteme completely dominates thought and action at any point is anomalous. It seems that even during the reign of a given episteme, there are pockets or centers of consciousness and institutional action that reflect alternative epistemes.

Foucault drew hope from this, seeing it as a possible source of escape from domination.

This is consistent with our belief that even though we seem, certainly in the United States and probably in the world generally, to be well into an era that is dominated by technicist consciousness, there is hope for maintaining a foothold against it. The bottom line issue is one of how human beings can reestablish and maintain a common language, and with it the base of mutual values and shared knowledge that a language entails, for discussing the nature and direction of their societal fate and the destiny of humankind. Such questions are not open within technicist consciousness because, in effect, it imposes a kind of artificial language, one that does not carry true meaning because it does not carry human sentiment. Language, as the primary organizing agency of sentiment, acquires this quality when it arises spontaneously from indigenous patterns of living together. As we increasingly substitute calculated technical routines for folkways, we begin to speak technically, communicate technically, and the direction of our lives comes to be set by technical necessity and opportunity, that is, by the requirements of the system rather than the people within it. We begin indeed to equate, as Manfred Stanley points out (1972, pp. 273-322) the humanly possible with the technically available.

We are by no means saying that this situation is or should be reversible. There is no going back to the tribe, the village, the town, or the ghetto. Probably human beings of the future will never know meaningfulness in these traditional senses. The human project has moved into a new phase, onto a different plane, and we are hence facing a whole new set of problems and potentials. What we are saying is that perhaps the task we face is one of building a new, and truly different, form of human community, a form consistent with the level of consciousness and individualism that has come to characterize the human race. It seems that given the way in which political processes and the market have come to work, and given the degree of secularism that has developed in modern societies, public administration is one of the better possibilities for countervailing technicism. Of course, it too could be taken over by the technicist mode of consciousness. It already has been to a substantial extent. Further, there are many deficiencies and dangers in looking to public administration to serve as a redoubt from which the human principle can countervail technicism. Nonetheless, its traditions are the high ones of modern society.

REFERENCES

Ayer, A.J. (1936). *Language, truth and logic* (2nd ed.). New York: Dover.

Bentley, A.F. (1908). *The process of government*. Chicago: University of Chicago Press.

Berger, P., & Kellner, H. (1981). *Sociology reinterpreted*. Garden City, NY: Anchor Books.

Berger, P., & Luckman, T. (1967). *The social construction of reality: A treatise in the sociology of knowledge*. Garden City, NY: Anchor Books.

Black, M. (Ed.). (1961). *The social theories of Talcott Parsons: A critical examination*. Englewood Cliffs, NJ: Prentice-Hall.

Burrell, G., & Morgan, G. (1979). *Sociological paradigms and organizational analysis*. London: Heinemann.

Collins, R. (1988). *Theoretical sociology*. New York: Harcourt Brace Jovanovich.

Corwin, E.F. (1928). *The "higher law" of American constitutional law*. Ithaca, NY: Great Seal Books.

Douglas, M. (1986). *How institutions think*. Syracuse, NY: Syracuse University Press.

Follett, M.P. (1924). *Creative experiences*. New York: Longmans, Green.

Follett, M.P. (1926). *The new state*. New York: Longmans, Green.

Foucault, M. (1970). *The order of things: An archeology of the human sciences*. New York: Pantheon Books.

Foucault, M. (1987). *Mental illness and psychology*. Berkeley: University of California Press.

Goodsell, C. (1983). *The case for bureaucracy: A public administration polemic*. Chatham, NJ: Chatham House.

Kuhn, T.S. (1970). *The structure of scientific revolution* (2nd ed.). Chicago: University of Chicago Press.

Lowi, T. (1969). *The end of liberalism*. New York: W.W. Norton.

March, J.G., & Simon, H. (1958). *Organizations*. New York: Wiley.

McConnell, G. (1966). *Private power and American democracy*. New York: Knopf.

Merquion, J.G. (1985). *Foucault*. London: Fontana Press/Collins.

Neustadt, R. (1961). *Presidential power: The Politics of leadership*. New York: Wiley.

Parsons, T. (1949). *The structure of social actions*. New York: McGraw Hill.

Rabinow, P. (Ed.). (1984). *The Foucault reader* (1st ed.). New York: Pantheon Books.

Redford, E.S. (1958). *Ideal and practice in public administration*. Tuscaloosa: University of Alabama Press.

Rohr, J. (1986). *To run a constitution: The legitimacy of the administrative state*. Lawrence: University Press of Kansas.

Schambra, W.A. (1982, Spring). The roots of the American public philosophy. *Public Interest, 67*, 36-48.

Schattschneider, E.E. (1960). *The semisovereign people: A realist's view of democracy in America*. New York: Holt, Rinehart, & Winston.

Schubert, G. (1961). *The public interest: A critique of the theory of a political concept*. Glencoe, IL: Free Press.

Schutz, A. (1967). *The phenomenology of the social world*. Evanston, IL: Northwestern University Press.

Simon, H., Smithberg, D., & Thompson, V. (1950). *Public administration*. New York: Knopf.

Simon, H. (1960). The new science of management decision. New York: Harper & Row.

Simon, H.A. (1976). *Administrative behavior* (3rd ed.). New York: Free Press.

Stanley, M. (1972). Technicism, liberalism, and development: A study in irony as social theory. In M. Stanley (Ed.), *Social development*. New York: Basic Books.

Stein, H. (1952). *Public administration and policy development, a case book*. New York: Harcourt, Brace.

Stockman, D.B. (1986). *The triumph of politics: How the Reagan revolution failed*. New York: Harper & Row.

Truman, D.B. (1962). *The governmental process*. New York: Knopf.

Waldo, D. (1984). *The administrative state* (2nd ed.). New York: Holmes & Meier.

Wamsley, G. (1985). Policy subsystems as a unit of analysis in implementation studies: A struggle for theoretical synthesis. In T.H.A. Toonen & K. Hanf (Eds.), *Policy implementation* (pp. 71-96). Hingham, MA: Martinus Nijhoff.

Wilson, J. (1983). Social theory. Englewood Cliffs, NJ: Prentice Hall.

PART II:

Toward a New Image of American Public Administration: Themes of Community and Practical Wisdom

The chapters in this section represent diverse attempts to work out the reconstruction of public administration advocated in White and McSwain's "Phoenix project." Collectively they cover and develop the major themes of this volume: public administration's search for political legitimacy, the role of the administrator in rebuilding a sense of community in the nation, and the role that practical wisdom and discourse must play in this difficult task.

Douglas Morgan's chapter introduces these themes. He argues that in attempting to legitimatize the role of public administration in the American political system, we have become preoccupied with preventing illegal action. Thus we have failed to legitimize a positive role for the administrator in furthering those substantive and procedural democratic values that ultimately support the constitutional covenanting process upon which our national community rests.

Morgan points out that this positive role in administration is all the more important to make legitimate, given the rise of hyperpluralism and a corresponding decline in the sense of national community. This decline has left the other elements of the governmental system, tied to the electorate—the legislature and the political executive—increasingly unable to come to coherent, long-range community regarding solutions to national problems. As a result, the administrative establishment, and to a lesser extent the judiciary, is left with a greatly increased responsibility to represent a communitarian view of our national interest.

While both judges and public administrators have been under attack for their activist role in the policy-making process, the judiciary has on the whole fared better, according to Morgan.

Here Morgan argues that the judiciary's success in maintaining its legitimacy in the face of strong criticism lies in the widely recognized competency of the justices to come to fair and equitable decisions, based on their special experience and institutional position in the American constitutional system, is widely recognized.

He holds that public administration can win its own legitimacy if it too grasps that it provides its practitioners with unique training and a particular institutional position that makes them especially well suited to represent the interests of the political community. In this regard, Morgan makes the case that the special competency of the public administrator to govern lies in his or her position in the institutions and processes of constitutional government. These allow the career official to see the varied ramifications of issues, take the long view of policy, consider diverse and competing demands for action, and at the same time fully appreciate the value and importance of knowledge in solving problems.

However, in order to fully realize this role, public administrators must rise above the instrumental, technically rational role they have been assigned in the political system since the Progressive era. They must see the unique competence they bring to government as the ability to exercise judgement that is at once ethical and politically astute. He calls this capacity *phronesis* after Aristotle's concept of practical wisdom.

Morgan believes that armed with the capacity to exercise practical wisdom, reinforced by training, and advantaged by their position in the political system, administrators can win legitimacy. They can do this first by mediating between individual interests and the welfare of the political community, and, second, by providing a government that is both politically vigorous and regarding of individual liberty.

Thus Morgan makes an explicit linkage between the themes of this volume. He argues that the administrator's legitimacy will ultimately rest on his or her ability to exercise administrative phronesis in ways that will rebuild the fragmented national community and reinforce the constitutional covenanting process upon which it rests.

The chapter by Charles Fox and Clarke Cochran also deals with the themes of legitimacy, community, and the exercise of practical wisdom. However, it shifts from the unique contributions administrators make as they employ political discretion to the task of legitimizing that discretion.

The authors begin by noting an increase in literature advocating a "discretionist" point of view in public administration. While they find some "proximate" causes for this (i.e., the current venality and weakness of elected public officials, etc.) they ultimately discover the argument for increased discretion rests in the greater burden American administrators must bear for maintaining community and community-regarding policy in a highly pluralist society.

Against this background, Fox and Cochran first examine the concept of administrative discretion itself. Using Plato's exposition of the guardian class in the *Republic* as a benchmark, they compare the viewpoints of a number of contemporary "discretionists" (e.g., Friedrichs, Rohr, Hart, Kass, & Wamsley).

Based on their analysis of Plato, the authors assert that those who seek to give an administrative class a major role in setting the course of a political system must be able to contend that members of the class can educate themselves to know the communal good, act effectively to achieve that good, and help the citizenry do so as well. Thus, the claim of any group of administrative "guardians" ultimately rests on their proven ability to exercise the kind of virtuous judgment associated with practical wisdom. Given these criteria, Fox and Cochran conclude that, taken as a body of literature, the discretionists have made "a good and sophisticated. . ." case for their viewpoint.

This chapter closes with the authors' attempt to develop a theory of administrative discretion compatible with political democracy. Here they argue for a guardian administrative class composed of mid-level, career civil servants. This class would be an "elite" in the sense that it is specially educated in the knowledge and practiced in the virtues necessary to ascertain and effectuate the communal good. It would be a "mass" in that it would recruit openly and representatively from all strata of society. The authors contend such a class would be legitimated both in terms of its elitist training and its democratic (representative) composition.

Fox and Cochran point out that the mass elite they depict constitutes ". . . a relevant political and democratic community

divorced not by intent, but intentionality from apathetic others. . ."
It would appear, then, the authors have sought to construct what
White and McSwain would call an "enclave" within a pluralist and
often self-seeking society—an enclave that would accept anyone
willing to engage in the search for a communal good through a
rigorous and virtuous political and administrative practice.

Like Fox and Cochran, Henry Kass is interested in enhancing the
legitimacy and credibility of the public administrator in the political
system. He too recognizes the legitimacy of administrative discretion. However, unlike Fox and Cochran, he sees the problem involved in achieving legitimacy not so much overcoming the apathy and selfishness of the pluralist political system, as reducing the
vulnerability and fear felt by alienated, isolated individuals in such
an atomistic society when they are confronted with potentially
powerful, integrated bureaucracies.

Kass argues that the concept of agency, if adopted to the notion
of governance, can serve to reduce this sense of vulnerability. This
is because agency as a normative social system is designed to
allow the specialized, socially fragmented individuals who populate a modern, pluralist society to act on each other's behalf
without sharing the classic ties of family, community, and culture.

Agency, as a social institution, reduces the vulnerability of putting one's trust in a stranger by pledging the agent to a set of norms
that not only ensures his or her faithful service to the principal, but
the principal's fair treatment of the agent. Finally, agency protects
third parties from the combined action of agents and principals
since agency norms are always subject to the more fundamental
ethical principles of justice and beneficence.

Despite his advocacy of agency as a normative model for public
administrators, Kass is aware the concept will have to be revised
considerably from its current social usage (notably in commercial
law) to be of value in governance. In particular, he is sensitive to
the problem posed by the fact agency is normally thought of as a
relationship between a single principal and an agent or agents. In
his view, considering the "public" a unitary principal in a pluralist
society is unrealistic in the extreme.

However, relying on Tussman's (1960) theory of the associational
state, he holds that even a pluralist political entity is a *res publica*,
a "business of the people," founded to manage the very real,
common interdependencies of its members. Therefore, he argues

that public administrators as agents do have a unitary principal to serve—the *res publica* and the community of interdependence upon which it is based.

Thus, to Kass, the basis for the legitimacy of public administration in a pluralist political system lies in two sources: first, its ability to make citizens aware of the community formed by their interdependence upon one another, and, second, its capacity to decrease their sense of potential vulnerability in joining that community by enhancing the credibility and trust they can place in the agents of the republic. Kass calls a public agent who attains excellence in practicing so as to achieve this task a *steward*. Accordingly, he argues stewardship must be at the heart of any concept of administrative legitimacy in our political system.

The last two chapters in this section focus on what Morgan referred to earlier as *phronesis* or practical wisdom. The reason this concept plays a significant role in this volume has been addressed in the prologue: The exercise of some form of practical wisdom by American public administrators is seen as key to the restoration of a sense of community in our hyperpluralist society. In turn, successful restoration of community is viewed as the basis upon which American public administration can claim legitimacy in our political system.

In the first two chapters, Jay White joins a number of others in this collection in arguing that technical rationality is inadequate for administrative practice. His point of view is based on the observation that a technical/rational decision-making process can neither help the reasoner make value choices among ends and means nor can it account for noninstrumental action and behavior. To White, technical/rational thinking has dominated not only public administration, but much social and political thinking. This has limited the possibility of "practical discourse," that is, a dialogue among those in a situation over the value choices (especially ethical choices) involved in setting ends and selecting means to achieve them.

White argues that the arena for practical discourse can be widened to the degree public administrators are willing to practice not only technical but "interpretive" and "critical" forms of rationality as well. Interpretive, like legal rationality, requires a situational application of decision and action principals in which "part" and "whole," "fact" and "value," and "situation" and "principle" reciprocally define and redefine one another through the power of language. Critical rationality allows individuals in the situation to evaluate their own interpretive position and that of others in terms of the values and interests the position serves. White holds that while technical rationality is necessary to make sure things are done, interpretive and critical rationality are required to make sure they are done right and well.

Michael Harmon's work serves to show the ethical challenge to public administration posed by White's prescription that interpretive and critical rationality become a basic part of administrative practice. Using C.S. Forester's gallant and troubled hero Horatio Hornblower as his example, Harmon contends that practical wisdom and discourse ultimately serve responsible administrative action. However, he points out that the term *responsible action* has had at least three meanings in public administration: political responsibility, professional responsibility, and personal responsibility. Pursued singly and single-mindedly, each of these concepts of administrative responsibility can result in more vice than virtue. For example, political responsibility taken to its extreme can result in opportunism or reification of political authority as absolute.

After a careful analysis, he argues that the demands imposed by any one of these concepts of responsible administrative action limit the excesses inherent in the others (though he argues that personal responsibility takes ultimate precedence over professional and political responsibility). Accordingly, he holds that public administrators who seek to act ethically must face the agonizing task of balancing the excesses of each form of responsibility with the imperatives of the others. It would appear, from Harmon's viewpoint, that the essence of exercising practical wisdom as an architectonic ethical virtue lies in accomplishing this challenge successfully.

REFERENCE

Tussman, J. (1960). *Obligation and a body politic.* New York: Oxford University Press.

2

Administrative Phronesis:
Discretion and the Problem of Administrative
Legitimacy in Our Constitutional System

DOUGLAS F. MORGAN

The Senate trial of Evan Mecham does not concern merely this one officeholder but instead addresses the very essence of democracy in our State Constitution.
—Alan Stephens, Democratic Minority leader, Arizona State Senate

This man hasn't dipped his hands into public funds. He hasn't ripped off the treasury. He hasn't committed high crimes in office. . . .
—Jerris Leonard, attorney for Evan Mecham

Even if it turned out that Mecham hadn't violated state laws, his conduct would be grossly offensive to the people of this state.
—Paul Eckstein, prosecutor of Evan Mecham

The impeachment trial of Governor Evan Mecham by the Arizona State Senate raised a perplexing and constantly recurring question for citizens of our constitutional democracy. What is the appropriate framework for judging the relationship between public officials and the citizens in whose name they serve? As is illustrated by the more recent cases of John Power and Jim Wright, we tend to vacillate between two standards of judgment.

On the one hand, many citizens want to raise broad and far-reaching questions about the person's ability to carry out the duties of the office in a manner that will be respectful of the procedural and substantive values of the larger structure of public authority within which the person will serve. Can a potential officeholder be trusted to exercise power with restraint? Does the person respect competing democratic values, such as liberty and equality? Can the person carry out his/her duties in a manner that preserves the integrity of institutional processes and structures created by our constitutional order—a system that separates, divides, and checks and balances powers?

Despite our tendency at times to rely on such sweeping questions in determining fitness to serve, we just as frequently invoke much narrower standards of judgment—what may be termed the "smoking gun" approach to wrongdoing. Such an approach identifies wrongdoing with a violation of the specific rule, law, or regulation.

While some of this ambivalence can be explained by the narrow legal standards that apply to formal removal from office, at a deeper level we are in doubt about the criteria that should be used in judging the overall fitness of our public officials to serve. Should we confine our judgments to evidence of actual illegal acts of corruption, or is it sufficient simply to show that a person has abused or is likely to abuse the office in a manner that offends "the very essence of democracy"? These questions are not limited to judging the fitness of elected and appointed public officials. They strike at the very heart of the current debate over the role and function of nonelected career administrators within our democratic process.

In the past we have been preoccupied with controlling, structuring, and limiting administrative discretion with an eye to eliminating corruption. Little attention has been paid to the larger role of public administrators as democratic standard-bearers with responsibility for protecting and promoting both procedural and substantive values of our democratic polity (Morgan & Rohr, 1986; Morgan, 1987). The prevailing paradigm at the political and administrative levels of government still remains little changed from the terms set by the early debates in the 1940s between Herman Finer (1941) and Carl Friedrich (1940). According to this paradigm, administrators are to be governed either by neutral technical competence or simple notions of rule-oriented accountability to policy choices made by elected public officials.

This rule-oriented paradigm is supported by two deeply rooted influences in American administrative life. One influence derives from our constitutional system of government that seemingly places the administrative function in a clearly subordinate role to the elected and/or appointed executive. The other major influence derives from our view of organizations that (regardless of how open or participatory they may be) places subordinates in a hierarchical relationship to someone higher on the rung of the bureaucratic ladder. Both influences have helped to sustain the view that administrative discretion is illegitimate until a policy directive can be found to justify its exercise and/or the discretion can be carried out in a so-called "neutral" manner.

At a political and academic level, this view has had two consequences in shaping responses to abuses of administrative discretion. When faced with such abuses, we either attempt to tighten political control or impose new legal constraints on the exercise of administrative discretion. Both of these responses deny administrators the governing role they play as democratic standard-bearers.

There is increasing recognition, however, of the inadequacy of the traditional rational/legal paradigm for judging the relationship between administrators and those they serve. This paradigm has almost always been rejected by the average citizen who tends to see all public officials as undifferentiated agents of the public trust. This responsibility for the public trust usually includes two expectations: that officials practice the negative merit of refraining from wrongdoing as well as the positive merit of making wise and fair democratic decisions that are similarly implemented. For the average citizen, there is little or no distinction between good government and good administration. Despite our best academic efforts to separate politics from administration the average citizen refuses to make judgments according to a paradigm that pits neutral competence against democratic responsibility.

The citizen's view has gained increased respectability as members of the academic community have begun to develop alternative models or metaphors for guiding thinking about the proper relationship between professional career administrators and the citizens they serve in a democratic polity. These efforts tend to fall into two broad categories. One category emphasizes the unique role administrators play in the democratic process, while the other places more emphasis on the role of administrators in shaping the substantive values of our collective lives.

Whether one seeks to ground an alternative to the Finer/Friedrich paradigm in the unique contributions administrators can make to the process or substance of American political life, one is faced with the same two fundamental questions. First, by what right can a public administrator exercise independent discretionary authority over others within a constitutional democracy? Second, what particular competence do and/or should public administrators possess in their exercise of such authority? It is these two questions that will be addressed in the sections that follow.

TWO APPROACHES TO LEGITIMACY

During the late 1950s and 1960s when the U.S. Supreme Court was single-handedly reweaving the political and legal fabric of the land, the question was frequently asked: By what right do nine appointed judges who hold their positions for life play so large a role in a country that calls itself a democracy? Is it appropriate for members of the Supreme Court, rather than elected legislators, to reform the country's criminal procedures, its race relations, and its electoral processes? In the last decade, particularly during the Reagan administration, similar questions have been asked of the administrative branch of government. By what right do tens of thousands of career administrators play such a large and seemingly independent role in our democratic society? Is it appropriate that they should reform land and water practices, reverse environmental policies of yesteryear and oppose many of the forces set in motion by the Warren Court? Of course, it is only when such changes have been made in the absence of clear political directives from above, or have been made in response to the directives of one branch against the other, that any question is raised about the proper exercise of discretionary authority. To insist that career administrators should be frozen from action until they receive clear marching orders from their elected and/or appointed political superiors is both dangerous and unworkable.

It is dangerous because it ignores the dual responsibilities career administrators have to the policy directives of both the legislative and executive branches of government. When political control of the two is divided, tightening the reigns over administrative bodies by one branch can precipitate an escalating tug of war in which administrators become political footballs (Aberbach & Rockman, 1988). This can quickly result in institutional gridlock, a situation in which public officials point to each other and their respective agencies as an excuse to do nothing.

Holding administrators to the strict control of the policy directives of elected officials is also unworkable. There are too many instances in which such officials cannot or refuse to provide the clarity necessary for clear administrative action (Morgan, 1987). To refuse to act until sufficient clarity can be provided would simply further weaken the institutional capacity for collective action. Consider what would have happened, for example, to many of the Great Society programs of the 1960s, the environmental protection programs of the 1970s or the current planning requirements placed on natural resource agencies if we adopted the strict administrative rule "Don't act until clear policy directives have been provided by the elected officials you serve."

When career administrators are forced to take action without clear policy directives from elected officials, they may claim, like judges, to confine their actions to "the black letter of the law." But this notion of neutrality has as little credibility for administrators as it has for judges who make the same kind of defense of the exercise of their discretion from the bench. Just as we needed a better justification for judicial discretion than that provided by the mechanical jurisprudence model, so too we need a better justification for administrative discretion than that provided by our rational/legal tradition.

In seeking to construct an acceptable alternative to this tradition, we can find some useful guidance in the debates over the proper exercise of judicial discretion. These debates provide two different schools of thought for legitimating the exercise of discretionary authority by judges. One has come to be called a *result-oriented* approach to legitimacy, and the other has been characterized as a *process-oriented* approach. Corresponding analogues can be found for each of these approaches in the debates over the proper limits of administrative discretion.

Result-Oriented Approaches to Administrative Discretion

There are those who defend the supreme power exercised by non-elected judges on the Supreme Court in terms of the substantive advantages it brings. For example, some argue that the main task of the Court is to defend the First Amendment rights of the minority against a tyrannical and oppressive majority. A somewhat broader set of purposes is to be found among those who argue that courts, particularly the

Supreme Court, can often provide a forum for the despised and rejected who have no effective voice in the legislative chamber. Finally, at the broadest substantive level, appellate courts can also be seen as a "safety value, relieving intolerable social pressures that build up when legislatures are unresponsive to urgent needs" (Lewis, 1966, p. 211).[1]

Much of the literature spawned by the New Public Administration movement falls into this substantive due process tradition. For those who take the position that administrators, like judges, should use their discretion to promote substantive values, there immediately arises the question, which values? Some respond by pointing to universal human values like benevolence (Frederickson & Hart, 1985); humanism (Thayer, 1978; Dvorin & Simmons, 1972); and equity (Hart, 1974; Marini, 1971). Others single out those values to which a constitutional system of government is especially partial, such as liberty, property, equality, and so forth (Rohr, 1978, 1986; Nigro & Richardson, 1987; Sedgwick, 1987).

The most dominant strain within these result-oriented approaches sees the bureaucracy as a facilitator of humane values, a counterpoise to the findings of those studying large complex organizations through the lens of organizational theorists, on the one hand, and of sociologists/political scientists on the other. Organizational theorists became increasingly concerned in the 1960s about the way in which the informal and dysfunctional dimensions of organizational life create severe and inevitable tensions between the needs of an organization and its participants. In the 1970s political scientists and sociologists added their concerns about the growing problems arising from agency/bureau co-optation as well as the inherent tension between the needs of large complex organizations and the underlying values of our democratic society (Lowi, 1979; Scott & Hart, 1979).

As a result of these studies, many organizational theorists, sociologists, and political scientists concluded that individuals in large complex organizations could not achieve self-actualization within organizations without some massive restructuring of authority relationships. Many believed that through such restructuring it was possible to reconcile the tension between individual self-interest and the larger public good (Likert, 1961; McGregor, 1967). Many came to view public administrators as facilitators of the substantive humane values that would be necessary to initiate a restructuring of these authority relationships.

Process-Oriented Approaches to Administrative Discretion

The result-oriented arguments in defense of administrative discretion that are outlined above are at best negative justifications for the exercise of power by career administrators. They are grounded in the failings of processes and practices elsewhere in the political system.

Following the example of students of the judicial process, there are those who would look beyond the substantive contributions of career administrators to the unique characteristics of the administrative process itself that enable career administrators to make a distinctive contribution to the governing process. In the case of our judiciary, it is easy to identify a variety of unique characteristics of the process that set our courts and judges apart from other institutions of governance: a focus on concrete controversies between individuals, a partial responsibility of each judge to respond to the claim that is raised, a search for principle, a need to give reasons for one's judgments, and, finally, the need to make these reasons available in a published opinion. Taken as a whole these characteristics enable our courts and judges to make distinctive contributions to democratic governance. Can the same kind of argument be made for the bureaucracy and career administrators?

Traditional answers, of course, have focused on the rational/legal characteristics of bureaucratic forms that enable administrators to be the guardians of efficiency and procedural equity. These include guaranteeing consistency of treatment for the clients being served (Davis, 1971); helping to determine the correct fit between organizational means and ends (Pressman & Wildavsky, 1973; Wildavsky, 1979); and helping the citizenry understand the complexity and urgency of problems that need to be given immediate attention in order to forestall even more serious difficulties in the future (Friedrich, 1940; McGregor, 1984).

But there is a growing recognition that the special role that career administrators can play in our governance process consists less in what McSwain and White in this volume characterize as "technicism" and more in their understanding of what is likely to work. Three things are meant here by "what will work." First, it means that there is a good fit between means and ends. Administrators are expected to put the pieces of a policy puzzle together so that a course of action will accomplish its intended policy objectives. At the same time, administrators are expected to be sensitive to the limits of popular acceptability. In a system ultimately governed by the consent of the governed rationally, crafted policy implementation is a starting point not an ending point. In the first instance, then, the moral challenge of administrative discretion is to facilitate policies that "hit their mark"—policies that simultaneously are workable and acceptable.

But there is a third kind of knowledge that is important if policies are to "hit their mark." It is not only important that policies be both workable and acceptable. In our rule-of-law system, it is also important that the exercise of administrative discretion be "fitting." By that is meant the ability to justify a course of action that is consistent with the larger backdrop of constitutional principles and values that inform and guide the ongoing communal covenanting process (Cooper, 1987, p. 144).

Career administrators are uniquely situated to make a distinctive contribution to this ongoing covenanting process. In fact, it will be argued here that they possess, through the mediating role they play between citizens and elected officials, a special kind of prudence, or what Aristotle called *phronesis*, that enables them to coalesce considerations of workability, acceptability, and fit.

In the *Nichomachean Ethics*, Aristotle (McKeon, 1947) characterized phronesis as the capacity to conjoin knowledge of the principles of right action with considerations of what is suitable—the ability to relate principles to practice. It is the practical wisdom that ensures that one will pursue a proper course of action in the service of the proper ends desired by moral virtue. It is the capacity that enables one to recognize the right thing to do both in a world of particulars and variability. Within the framework of our constitutional polity, it is the deliberative capacity to know how to make the right thing work.

For judges this quality is captured by the term *jurisprudence*—a person who possesses a knowledge of legal principles and the ability suitably to apply them to the circumstances of the moment. At the administrative level of government, there is an analogous kind of prudence that performs the same functions for administrators that American jurisprudence performs for our judges (Nigro & Richardson, 1987, n. 6, p. 218; Hart, 1984). Such prudence is to be found in two sources—first, the unique role that career administrators play in our constitutional system of separation of powers and, second, the distinctive role they play in our system of checks and balances.

ADMINISTRATIVE PHRONESIS I: SEPARATION OF POWERS AND ADMINISTRATIVE COMPETENCE

Career administrators have long been viewed as the guardians of efficient government. While such a view tends to be associated with Woodrow Wilson and the Progressive Era advocates of social engineering, American concern for efficiency at the administrative level antedates Wilson by more than a century.

In fact, a desire to secure a more efficient administrative arrangement was one of the major factors that contributed to disenchantment with the Articles of Confederation and brought forth increased pressures for a new constitutional system. When it became evident that war supplies and materiel could not be delivered to the troops on time, disenchantment mounted with the system of government established under the Articles. As a result, many of the delegates went to the Constitutional Convention in 1787 with the specific goal of correcting the inefficiencies and ineffectiveness that had resulted from dispersed and fragmented administrative authority in the early days of the Articles, which had been designed almost exclusively to prevent executive tyranny (Thach, 1969, chap. III).

The various waves of reform that have swept through the administrative branch of government in the last century can be seen as variations on this original theme of designing a system that could work administratively. As McSwain and White argue in this volume, success in making things work depends upon our ability to build on that part of our tradition that defines competence more broadly than does the technicist part of our tradition. Certainly those who became increasingly disenchanted with the administrative effectiveness of the Articles of Confederation did not equate competent administration with efficient administration. By narrowing our universe of administrative discourse away from questions of competent administration to issues of efficiency, we have cut ourselves off from a consideration of the distinctive competence that the administrative process contributes to the governance process.

Administrative competence, like judicial competence, is very much shaped by the way in which the formal structure of administrative authority interacts with other governmental functions. Taken together such structures shape the way questions are posed and answers are framed. This can be illustrated by summarizing the distinctive differences in process, structure, and personnel that set the work done by administrative agencies apart from the work done by courts and legislative bodies (see Robson, 1951 for a useful comparison of administrative and judicial functions).

The characteristics of the administrative process as a whole create a decisional forum that is more forward-looking and more attentive to the long-term social complexities and interplay of public problems than is likely to be the case with either a legislature or a court. This is true for at least two reasons. First, the administrative process has due process requirements, or "rules of evidence," to govern its decisions that place a heavier burden on standards of rationality than are placed on legislative bodies. The so-called rational person test, or mere reasonableness, is sufficient to produce a legislative conclusion in contrast to the far more demanding tests used by the courts. The somewhat intermediate due process requirements of administrative bodies are not so narrowly protective of the claims of the individual that they restrict an agency's capacity to see larger social patterns and interconnections, what Donald Horowitz has called "social facts" as opposed to "historical facts" (Horowitz, 1977 pp. 47-49). For this reason, administrative bodies are much better suited than courts to making projections about how the interplay of complex social variables is likely to affect the future than they are in reconstructing the "who done it" kind of historical facts faced by courts.

A second reason why administrative agencies have a greater potential to be more forward-looking and more attentive to the long-term social complexities and interplay of public problems than either courts or legislatures results from the decisional rules that govern how evidence gets transformed into conclusions. This transformational process within administrative arenas is governed both by standard operating procedures and by expediency. Like lower courts, which tend to follow the dictates of *stare decisis*, and unlike legislative bodies that follow the short-term dictates of the electorate, administrative agencies roam the middle ground between low expediency and high principle. In roaming this middle ground, public agencies perform roles that are probably closer to state and federal supreme courts than lower courts, largely because they are less constrained by the past and by the principle of *stare decisis*.

These characteristics of the administrative process mean that the bureaucracy has a greater capacity to plan for the future, especially for a future where the problems are essentially *polycentric* in nature. This is a term used by the late Lon Fuller to describe those problems that resemble a seamless spiderweb (Fuller, 1978, pp. 51-52). Such problems, like a spiderweb, have many interlocking strands. No one strand can be singled out and dealt with individually without disturbing the rest. The administrative branch is well suited to take the lead in helping to define such problems, not only because of the process characteristics mentioned above, but also because of the characteristics of the administrative structure and personnel.

As is suggested in Table 2.1, the administrative structure fosters the development of a repository of experts who are supervised by generalists. In turn, these generalists must be sensitive to the political climate of opinion in order to shape and implement public policy effectively. Sensitivity to political cues is thus important not only to keep administrators on tap to their political superiors but also to keep them on top of their responsibility for effective policy implementation (Long, 1962, pp. 86-93).

In short, as the table illustrates, career administrators are better situated than elected officials to see the multiple ramifications of an issue, take the longer view, consider more encompassing competing demands, and value the importance of knowledge and information in solving public problems. In addition, they are better able to understand the problematic character of the public interest and to exercise a kind of constitutional prudence (Long, 1962, pp. 73-77).

ADMINISTRATIVE PHRONESIS II: CHECKS AND BALANCES AND ADMINISTRATIVE COMPETENCE

Public administrators in the United States not only operate within a scheme of government that *separates* functions, they also operate within a scheme that *mixes, checks, and balances powers*. However obvious this may be, its implications for administrative competence and responsibility are often overlooked. First, it places an obligation on administrators to understand the problematic character of democratic government. Second, it obligates administrators to instruct those they serve in the nature of these problems and, when possible, to use their discretionary authority to ameliorate them (or at least not make them worse).

TABLE 2.1: Comparative Characteristics of Judicial, Administrative, and Legislative Decisional Forums

Characteristics	Courts	Administrative Agencies	Legislatures
Process			
Orientation	Retrospective	Prospective	Transitory
Types of facts	Historical	Social	Temporal
Rules of evidence	"beyond reasonable doubt" "preponderance of evidence"	"reliable, substantive and probitive evidence" based "on consideration of the whole record"	Mere reasonableness Expediency Prudential
Decision rules	*stare decisis*	*partly stare decisis,* partly polycentric	Electoral survival
Decision mode	Reason	Fiat	Vote
Structural			
Organization	Professional with political independence	Hierarchical with political dependence the exception	Personalized with little or no political independence
Mode of conducting business	Collegial—a relationship of autonomous equals	Bureaucratic—a relationship of unequals held together by rules that define role and function	Political—a relationship of equals (except where seniority is heavily relied on) held together by quid-pro-quo agreements
Personnel related			
Orientation	Referees in a remedial proceeding	Advocates in a prophylactic proceeding	Agents in a bartering proceeding
Training	Generalists	Specialists supervised by generalists	Generalists
Tenure	Generally based on good behavior	Political loyalty and technical competence	Outside: none; Inside: combination of seniority and election

Understanding the Problematic Character of Democratic Government

Those who framed our constitutional polity agreed on at least two things: first, democratic rule was the only acceptable form of government and, second, such government was problematic. It was regarded as problematic by the framers not so much because the ends of government were contested but because they were uncertain about what practical courses of action would best achieve a regime of ordered liberty.[3] This uncertainty grew out of disagreement about the major sources of danger to liberty and, consequently, what kind of protections needed to be established to preserve a democratic polity in perpetuity.

There were three major sources of danger to liberty, each having its own distinctive set of advocates. Some, like Alexander Hamilton and James Wilson, emphasized the need for energy at the center to maintain domestic tranquility, foster nation building, and protect against foreign intrusions. Others, like James Madison, emphasized the danger of a tyranny of the majority operating to the detriment of the interests and rights of the minority. Finally, there were those who were concerned that the decisions made by government be well and wisely informed and competently implemented.

How can the need for safe, competent, and energetic government be brought into harmonious tension? There were two kinds of answers given to such questions by those participating in the debates on the framing of the American Constitution. These answers parallel the distinction that was drawn previously between a process-oriented and a result-oriented approach to the exercise of administrative discretion. Following the result-oriented approach (with its emphasis on substantive outcomes as opposed to the procedures by which the outcomes are reached), there were those who believed that a healthy polity could not long survive without having a substantial and distinctive level of virtue among rulers and followers alike (Morgan & Rohr, 1982; Storing, 1981). Men like Alexander Hamilton and Benjamin Franklin emphasized the virtues of the best and the brightest. The antifederalists, on the other hand, emphasized the virtues of the numerous yeomanry of the country who were thought "to be more temperate, of better morals, and less ambition, than the great" (Storing, 1981, p. 158).

The views of both groups were defeated by those who argued that it was possible to construct a well-ordered regime of liberty without paying too much attention to the virtues of human excellence, whether they be the high-brow virtues of the best and the brightest or the low-brow virtues of the hardworking yeomanry. The passions and interests of individuals could be used by a rightly structured constitutional order in such a way that officeholders could be led to seek the public good because it was in their self-interest to do so, not because they were disinterested devotees of the *res publica*. Decent individuals could be led to set their sights high enough to preserve a free and prosperous democratic order (Diamond, 1977).

Some Implications of Our System of Checks and Balances for the Exercise of Administrative Phronesis

We cannot take seriously the notion that administrators have a right to participate in rule unless we are prepared as teachers to place the problems of democratic government, as briefly sketched above, squarely before students and practitioners alike and to discuss the role that career administrators might play in ameliorating these problems. The need to do so is more urgent today than it has ever been in the past.

For one thing, our system of government has less institutional capacity for collective decision making than it has had previously. Over the last several decades, we have witnessed the rapid emergence of single-issue interest groups and democratic reforms of legislative bodies that have had the collective result of reducing the capacity of our institutions of government to rule—to mediate, to judge, and to choose among competing claims. Before he became a victim of single-issue politics in the 1980 elections, Iowa Senator John Culver observed that

> strident and self-righteous groups of voters are proliferating in number and narrowing in focus. . . . [F]or each narrow, self-defined lobby. . . the worth of every public servant is measured by a single litmus test of ideological purity. Taken together, the tests are virtually impossible for any officeholder who hopes to keep both his conscience and his constituency. (Drew, 1979, p. 45)

Democratic reforms at all levels of government have created more open access to government by a larger number of participants, but in doing so they have reduced the capacity of legislative bodies to reach a long-term working consensus. Such developments have not reduced the number of problems requiring attention or the number of decisions that government officials have to make. They have simply left career

administrators in the uncomfortable position of bearing a disproportion-
ate share of the burden of governing.

These problems have been further compounded by a deterioration in
a variety of mediating social structures that the framers of the constitutional order relied on to temper and soften some of the more abrasive
dynamics at work in a large commercial republic (Nigro & Richardson,
1987; Berger & Neuhaus, 1977). Schools, churches, and the families
were seen as important mediating influences that would help to transform the pursuit of raw self-interest into a broader and longer term
interest in the community as a whole. The decline in these mediating
structures has produced an expanding body of literature within the last
decade challenging the adequacy of the Lockean tradition with its
emphasis on the pursuit of enlightened self-interest.[4] This literature has
sought to recover a well-developed theory of community that has
existed alongside our predominant tradition of Lockean individualism.
The animating principle of this theory of community has been civic
virtue, or the "willingness of the individual to sacrifice his private
interests for the good of the community" (Wood, 1969, p. 68; Bellah,
Madsen, Sullivan, Swidler, & Tipton, 1986).

Since Lockean individualism does not supply "a convincing and
generally accepted theory of political obligation," there is little or no
moral basis upon which to appeal to others to sacrifice the pursuit of
self-interest for the larger public good (Morgan, 1976). In fact, our most
challenging and trying moments as a nation have found our political
leaders seeking to articulate a foundation for the American political
order that could overcome the defects of the founding edifice by sup-
plying some pillars capable of appealing to a sense of duty and of right
(Jaffa, 1959, chaps. XVI & XVII; King, 1970, pp. 111-131).

When the decline of our institutional capacity for collective decision
making is combined with the deterioration of the mediating role of the
various social institutions such as organized religions, the nuclear
family, and schools, we face a difficult challenge of self-government.
While it would be silly to lay the full burden of this challenge on career
administrators, it would be both foolish and silly to ignore the potentially constructive role they can play.

Unlike judges who are limited to specific cases and controversies,
career administrators can explicitly and legitimately go far beyond what
Donald Horowitz (1977) has called the "historical facts" in a case to
consider present and future "social facts." As with judges, this requires

a certain kind of temperament. Can it be assumed that the qualities of judgment upon which such a temperament rests are automatically acquired by career administrators through the daily routines of administering the public's business? In the case of judges, this entire maturation process is left pretty much to chance. We are reasonably safe in doing so with judges because there is a deep and broad tradition upon which to rely. It begins with the law school and the process of teaching individuals how to think like a lawyer. It matures gradually over time as lawyers and judges carry on a daily dialogue between the bench and the bar. This dialogue moves from the narrow focus on the particulars of a case to broader concerns involving the court as an institution and finally, at the appellate level, to a concern for broad constitutional principles.

Is there anything analogous at work at the administrative level? In fact, something similar to this process has been suggested by those like Wamsley (1987) and Kass who, (elsewhere in this volume) develop a theory of agency. Central to the theory of public agency is the notion that career administrators begin with an immersion into an agency's past history and move to a broader concern for the public interest. This occurs as a result of the need for the history and tradition of a given agency perspective to interact with the history and tradition of other agencies' perspectives. The danger of excessively narrow and parochial perspectives is tempered by the need to interact with other equally legitimate and sometimes competing agency claims. This process of ascension ends with a consideration of the broad constitutional order that frames the entire universe of discourse.

This habit of mind is not the usual portrait that is painted by students of the administrative process. Organizational theorists see self-seeking behavior that is frequently at odds with the organizational mission, while political scientists and sociologists see mainly co-optation by private interest groups. The difference between these various perspectives result from seeing administrators as prudential agents of a larger structure of constitutional authority.

But, as was discussed above, this structure of constitutional authority treats the public interest as problematic. Once this is understood and accepted by public administrators, they can acquire a perspective that will foster a variety of desirable qualities: tentative steps and experimental action, curiosity and dialogue about ends as well as means, the capacity to learn as well as respond, humility and skepticism about "grand designs," greater awareness of the unique responsibility and potential contribution of each individual to a national dialogue about the public interest, and, finally, a greater attentiveness to the word of public discourse.

CONCLUSION

The vision of administrative phronesis outlined above places an especially heavy burden on those of us in the educational arena. Unlike our judicial tradition we do not have a widely shared understanding of how the administrative process can and should work. In the meantime we cannot leave the emergence of this tradition to chance. We must actively participate in its creation.

The creation should begin by confronting administrators with the problematic character of democratic government. In doing so we will be forced to move beyond our overly narrow preoccupation with administrative corruption and wrongdoing to the construction of a more active governing role for administrators within our constitutional democracy. This will require that we cultivate an expanded vision of administrative competence that moves us beyond our traditional concerns for efficiency to broader concerns for administrative prudence, both functional and constitutional. If we accomplish little else in the aftermath of the bicentennial celebration of the founding of our Constitution and the centennial celebration of the founding of public administration, we will have taken an important first step in developing the distinctive and legitimate role that administrative phronesis plays in American governance.

NOTES

1. Also see Chayes (1976). For an excellent recent summary of the Critical Legal Studies Movement, see Goldstein (1988); also see Black, (1960), and Dworkin (1972).

2. For a useful summary of this literature see Quinn (1988), and Srivastva (1988).

3. See Storing (1981).

4. See Bailyn (1967); Wood (1969); Pocock (1975); Kendall and Carey (1970); McWilliams (1973); De Maio (1980); Yarbrough (1979); and Bellah et al. (1986).

REFERENCES

Aberbach, J.D., & Rockman, B.A. (1988, March/April). Mandates or mandarins? Control and discretion in the modern administrative state. *Public Administration Review, 48,* 606-612.

Bailyn, B. (1967). *The ideological origins of the American revolution.* Cambridge, MA: Belknap Press.

Bellah, R.M., Madsen, R., Sullivan, W.M., Swidler, A. & Tipton, S.M. (1986). *Habits of the heart: Individualism and commitment in American life.* New York: Harper & Row.

Berger, P., & Neuhaus, R. (1977). *To empower the people: The role of mediating structures in public policy.* Washington, DC: American Enterprise Institute.

Black, C., Jr. (1960). *The people and the court: Judicial review in a democracy.* Englewood Cliffs, NJ: Prentice-Hall.

Chandler, R. (Ed.). (1987). *A centennial history of the American administrative state.* New York: Free Press.

Chayes, A. (1976). The role of the judge in public law litigation. *Harvard Law Review, 89,* 281.

Cooper, T. (1987, July/August). Hierarchy, virtue, and the practice of public administration: A perspective for normative ethics. *Public Administration Review, 47,* 320-328.

Davis, K.C. (1971). *Discretionary justice: A preliminary inquiry.* Urbana: University of Illinois Press.

De Maio, G. (1980, August). *Religion, republicanism and the American founding.* Paper presented to the NEH/ASPA Seminar, Citizenship Ancient and Modern, Washington, DC.

Diamond, M. (1959). Democracy and the Federalist: A reconsideration of the framers' intent. *American Political Science Review, 53.*

Diamond, M. (1975a). The Declaration and the Constitution: Liberty, democracy, and the founders. In N. Glazer & I. Kristol (Eds.), *The American commonwealth* (pp. 39-55). New York: Basic Books.

Diamond, M. (1975b). The revolution of sober expectations. In *America's continuing revolution* (pp. 25-41). Washington, DC: American Enterprise Institute.

Diamond, M. (1979). Ethics and politics: The American way. In R. Goldwin (Ed.), *The moral foundations of the American republic* (2nd ed.) (pp. 39-72). Charlottesville: University of Virginia Press.

Drew, E. (1979). *The Senator.* New York: Simon & Schuster.

Dvorin, E., & Simmons, R. (1972). *From amoral to humane bureaucracy.* San Francisco: Canfield Press.

Dworkin, R. (1972). *Taking rights seriously.* Cambridge, MA: Harvard Press.

Farrand, M. (1937). *Records of the federal convention* (rev. ed., 4 vols.) New Haven, CT: Yale University Press.

Finer, H. (1941, Summer). Administrative responsibility in democratic government. *Public Administration Review, 1,* 335.

Frederickson, H.G., & Hart, D.K. (1985, September/October). The public service and the patriotism of benevolence. *Public Administration Review, 45,* 547-553.

Friedrich, C.J. (1940). Public policy and the nature of administrative responsibility. In *Public Policy* (3-24). Cambridge, MA: Harvard Press.

Fuller, L. (1978). The forms and limits of adjudication. In S. Goldman & A. Sarat (Eds.), *American court systems: Readings in judicial process and behavior* (pp. 51-52). San Francisco: W.H. Freeman.

Goldstein, L.F. (1988, March). *Indeterminacy and constitutional theory: A critique of CLS and its fellow-travelers.* Paper presented to the Western Political Science Association, San Francisco.

Goldwin, R. (1977). *The moral foundations of the American republic.* Charlottesville: University of Virginia Press.

Hart, D.K. (1974). Social equity, justice and the equitable administrator. *Public Administration Review, 34,* 3-11.

Hart, D.K. (1984, March). The virtuous citizen, the honorable bureaucrat, and public administration. *Public Administration Review, 47,* 116-117.

Horowitz, D. (1977). *The courts and social policy.* Washington, DC: Brookings.

Jaffa, H. (1959). *The crises of the house divided.* New York: Doubleday.

Kendall, W., & Carey, G.W. (1970). *The basic symbols.* Baton Rouge: Louisiana State University Press.

King, M.L., Jr. (1958). Pilgrimage to nonviolence. *Stride toward freedom.* New York: Harper & Row.

King, M.L., Jr. (1970). In H. Storing (Ed.) *What country have I* (pp. 111-131). New York: St. Martins.

Lewis, A. (1966). *Gideon's trumpet.* New York: Vintage.

Likert, R. (1961). *New patterns of management.* New York: Harper.

Long, N. (1962). *Polity.* Chicago: Rand McNally.

Lowi, T. (1979). (2nd ed.), *The end of liberalism: The second republic of the U.S.* New York: W.W. Norton.

Marini, F. (1971). *Toward a new public administration.* Scranton, PA: Chandler.

McGregor, D. (1967). *The professional manager.* New York: McGraw Hill.

McGregor, E.B., Jr. (1984, March). The great paradox of democratic citizenship and public personnel administration. *Public Administration Review,* 126-132.

McKeon, R. (Ed.). (1947). *Introduction to Aristotle* (Modern Library College ed.). New York: Random House.

McWilliams, W.C. (1973). *The idea of fraternity in America.* Berkeley: University of California Press.

Morgan, D.F. (1976, June). *Lincoln: Law, politics and public morality.* Paper prepared for Conference on Lincoln's Thought and the Present, Springfield, IL.

Morgan, D.F. (1987, November). Varieties of administrative abuse: Some reflections on ethics and discretion. *Administration and Society, 19,* 267-284.

Morgan, D.F., & Rohr, J.A. (1982, March). *Administrative discretion and bureaucratic statesmanship: Serving the public interest.* Paper presented to the American Society of Public Administration, National Conference, Honolulu, HI.

Morgan, D.F., & Rohr, J.A. (1986). Traditional responses to administrative abuse. In D. Hibbeln & D.H. Shumavon (Eds.), *Administrative discretion and public policy implementation* (pp. 211-232). New York: Praeger.

Nigro, L., & Richardson, W. (1987, September/October). Administrative ethics and founding thought: Constitutional correctives, honor and education. *Public Administration Review, 47,* 367-377.

Pocock, J.G.A. (1975). *The Machiavellian movement.* Princeton, NJ: Princeton University Press.

Pressman, J., & Wildavsky, A. (1973). *Implementation* (2nd ed.). Berkeley: University of California Press.

Quinn, R. (1988). *Beyond rational management: Mastering the paradoxes and competing demands of high performance.* San Francisco: Jossey Bass.

Robson, W. *Justice and administrative law: A study of the British constitution.* Westport, CT: Greenwood, reprinted from 1951 edition.

Rohr, J.A. (1978). *Ethics for bureaucrats: An essay on law and values.* New York: Marcel Dekker.

Rohr, J.A. (1986). *To run a constitution: The legitimacy of the administrative state.* Lawrence: University of Kansas Press.

Sedgwick, J.L. (1987, November). Of centennials and bicentennials: Reflections on the foundations of American public administration. *Administration and Society, 19,* 285-308.

Scott, W., & Hart, D.K. (1979). *Organizational America.* Boston: Houghton Mifflin.

Storing, H.J. (1981). What the anti-federalists were for. In H.J. Storing (Ed.), *The Complete Anti-federalists* (Vol. I). Chicago: University of Chicago Press.

Srivastva, S. (1988). *Executive integrity: The search for high human values in organizational life.* San Francisco: Jossey Bass.

Thach, C. (1969). *The creation of the presidency: 1775-1789.* Baltimore: Johns Hopkins University Press.

Thayer, F.C. (1978, May). Materialism and humanism: Organization theory's odd couple. *Administration and Society, 10,* 86-106.

Wamsley, G.L., Goosell, C.T., Rohr, J.A., Stivers, C.M., White, O.F., & Wolf, J.F. (1987). The public administrator and the governance process: Refocusing the American dialogue. In R. Chandler (Ed.), *A Centennial History of the American administrative state* (pp. 291-320). New York: Free Press.

Wildavsky, A. (1976). *Speaking truth to power: The art and craft of policy analysis.* Boston: Little Brown.

Wilson, W. (1941, December). The study of administration. *Political Science Quarterly, LVI,* 481-506.

Wood, G.S. *The creation of the American republic, 1776-1787.* Chapel Hill: University of North Carolina Press.

Yarbrough, J. (1979, January). Republicanism reconsidered: Some thoughts on the foundation and preservation of the American republic. *The Review of Politics, 41,* 61-95.

3

Discretionary Public Administration: Toward a Platonic Guardian Class?

CHARLES J. FOX
CLARKE E. COCHRAN

INTRODUCTION

Although there have always been advocates of increased administrative discretion, we detect a distinct swing in public administration literature reaffirming it. For convenience we will refer to the diverse advocates of this swing, along with selected intellectual forebearers as the "discretion school."[1]

Four proximate causes can be adduced to explain this renaissance. First, public administration reacted viscerally to the "bureaucrat bashing" of the Carter and Reagan years and such very real manifestations of it as the Civil Service Reform Act of 1978 and the vendettas carried out by Reagan political appointees (Rosen, 1986).

Second—and this reason is related to the first—public administration has gathered ammunition from political science findings and journalistic accounts of weaknesses in the fabric of legitimacy of its political accusers. The bureaucracy, after all, was not responsible for Watergate or the design flaws of policy in Southeast Asia. Moreover, the mythical accountability loop between "the people" and elected officials has been tarnished by the image selling of candidates, the influence of money, low voter turnout and high voter apathy, the disarray of political parties, and insufficient policy specificity of election campaigns (Ginsberg & Stone, 1986). Unquestioned obedience to superiors so chosen, or loyalty to the policies they pursue, is not a self-evident virtue.

Third, the effects of the ethics movement within public administration imply increased discretion. The American Society for Public Administration (ASPA) has debated and finally adopted a code of ethics. At the urging of the National Association of Schools of Public Affairs and Administration (NASPAA) courses in ethics are rapidly proliferating in MPA programs (Worthley & Grumet, 1983). It is implicit in the notion of ethical study and dialogue that public administrators have sufficient autonomy to apply what they have learned. Of course, it has been observed that the ethics movement is only a part of a more long-range evolution of public administration toward professionalism (Kearney & Sinha, 1988), which also entails enhanced administrative discretion.

Fourth, at a higher level of abstraction, second and third waves of iterations stemming from the New Public Administration movement have broadened the scope of organization theory in ways that outflank classical rational comprehensive modes of thinking. It is by now commonplace to reject the politics-policy/administration dichotomy. Further developments based on phenomenology, critical theory, and psychotherapy attack as well as the objective/subjective and fact/value dichotomies with which the former bifurcation is associated (Harmon & Mayer, 1986, pp. 282-388). At risk is the very lynchpin of administrative compliance: functional or instrumental rationality, the use of appropriate means to achieve politically determined ends.

If the political rhetoricians are wrong to bash bureaucrats, if their own legitimacy is questionable, if administrators are autonomously to apply ethical principles on behalf of the public good, and if they must themselves adduce ends for the means they control, are we not well on the way to government by administrators?

This chapter will explore this possibility by taking it to its logical and most profound extreme, which we take to be Plato's argument for a guardian class. We proceed by first explicating Plato's views. We will then contrast Plato with current views favoring administrative discretion. In the process of comparison, we believe an outline of a thoroughly credible case for discretion will unfold, especially in light of the seamy side of electoral representative democracy so recently displayed. This leads to a concluding section where the big question is joined: must we abandon government by (all) the people in order to save government of the people, and *for the people*?

PLATO'S GUARDIAN CLASS

Most contemporary arguments for administrative discretion pale before the kind of discretion allowed the guardians in Plato's description of the best possible *polis* in his *Republic*.[2] Therefore, the implications for democracy of discretion may be examined best from the vantage of its logical extreme. The guardians reveal the important strengths and limitations of broad administrative discretion. This section outlines the origin of the guardians and how they fit in Plato's understanding of justice, then their education is considered, and finally their tasks in a well-balanced *polis* are sketched.[3]

The guardians first appear in the ideal *polis* when the need for a specialized military class becomes apparent. The *öpolisò* constructed before that time was primitive, rural, and without luxuries. Glaucon, however, objected that such a city was fit only for pigs. Human beings need fine wines, sweet dishes, music, and other refinements of civilization. Since, however, the perfect *polis* has as a founding principle that each person must do only those tasks for which he (or, in the political system of the Republic, she) is best suited, there must be a warrior class to specialize in defending the luxuries of the *polis* from external enemies.[4] It is important to highlight this founding principle because of the idea that governance, like any other function, requires specialization and a concentration of effort and attention. This is similar to the views of contemporary discretionists who, at the extreme, maintain that the business of governance is too complex to be left to the whims of officials elected by only fragments of an inattentive citizenry.

The guardians must be both spirited and philosophic, so that they can effectively defend and know the fundamental needs of the *polis*. This combination of qualities is rare; therefore, the guardians need a special education.[5] Their primary education is in music and gymnastics. Under music is subsumed more than the narrower modern term, including song, rhythm, and harmony, but also stories, poetry, and drama. The kinds of music to which the young may be properly exposed must be strictly supervised so that they will hear only those designed to acquaint them with beauty, truth, justice, and virtues such as self-control and courage. Future rulers must not learn evil habits, self-indulgence or love of money. Gymnastics too is really training for the soul, as it disciplines the body and helps it to recognize true beauty (*Republic*, Book III).

The guardians and rulers are not economically superior classes. Indeed, they are to live in barracks like soldiers, to eat in common mess halls, and to process no property of their own and especially no gold, silver, or other precious things. Moreover, men and women are equal in these classes and have the same tasks. Children are to be raised in common, without knowing their mothers and fathers, thus ensuring unity in the *polis* (*Republic*, Book V).

Those most qualified to be rulers in the *polis* of the *Republic* receive a special form of higher education. In their teens and 20s, they are to be educated in geometry, arithmetic, astronomy, music, and solid geometry. All of these subjects are to be integrated with one another, so that the overview "reveals the kinship of these studies with one another and with the nature of that which *is* (*Republic*, p. 536c; see Book VII). The most difficult, and the most dangerous study is dialectic, the powerful tool of dialogue that allows those with the ability and strength of soul to become philosophers and to advance to the vision of the Forms or Ideas, especially the Form of the Good. Dialectic is studied from age 30 to age 35. Then the prospective rulers must return to the guardian class and learn to take orders, to serve the *polis* as soldiers. Only at age 50, when they are mature enough, are they brought to the vision of the Good and initiated into the class of rulers.

The purpose of this whole system is to secure the greatest possible benefit for the community as a whole (*Republic*, pp. 419a-420b, 465d). The community as a whole is happy, most importantly, because it is just. Each person in the community is performing his or her proper role; each is doing that one thing that fits and fulfills his or her whole life. Moreover, the general and special training has guaranteed that the rulers and their helpers, the guardians, are those most qualified to rule. They are the most virtuous of character, possessing bravery, wisdom, temperance, and justice. They are self-controlled, and they will not exploit the populace, at least partly because they are not allowed to possess income or property of their own.

Moreover, the rulers are the best educated and most intelligent of all the citizens. They know, and know how to realize, the needs of the political system as a whole. They are not partial to one class or section, and they distribute benefits and burdens equitably to themselves and others. Trained to respect and care for their fellow citizens of all classes, their goal is only what is best for all. In contemporary terms, they are guided by the "public interest" (Cochran, 1974).

And their discretion is complete. The rulers are to govern according to their best judgments. They are guided only by their knowledge of the highest things, by their own strengths of character, and by their training in mathematics and the other subjects of higher education. It would be ridiculous to subject such persons to the rule of law, for law, with its rigid prohibitions and directives, is insufficiently flexible for ever-changing circumstance.[6] Similarly, as pointed out in Schubert's classic explication (1957) of what he takes to be the position of "Administrative Platonists," politicians do not represent the general public interest, for they are caught up in contests for popular approval and in political games. The administrator, on the other hand and from the platonic perspective, possesses the objectivity to see and define the public interest and, at the same time, the technical skill to design and implement specific policies to advance the good of the community as a whole. The administrator must be a political person in the best sense of that term, aware of the wishes and desires of the public and able to articulate and fulfill them in ways that the public itself cannot.

Suitably adapted, then, Plato makes a good, indeed philosophically the best, case for administrative discretion in the public interest. The words *suitably adapted*, should be stressed, because Plato's Guardians have significantly different tasks appropriate to the well-functioning *polis*. In general terms, Plato's Guardians are much less technical than modern administrators. Citizens with the proper character—citizens who are honest, courageous, temperate, and just—will have little need for expert administrators to tell them what they can and cannot do. Indeed, the *Republic* contains a passage that satirizes the whole business of detailed legislation to prevent and punish wrongdoing. Socrates says: "Such men are surely the most charming of all, setting down laws like the ones we described a moment ago and correcting them, always thinking they'll find some limit to wrongdoing in contracts and the other things I was just talking about, ignorant that they are really cutting off the heads of a Hydra" (*Republic*, p. 426e; see pp. 425b-427c). For Plato, lawmaking and rule making are either useless or matters of common sense.

What, then, is it that Plato's Rulers do? They have only three very important tasks: to exclude riches and poverty from the *polis*, to keep the size of the *polis* small, and to forestall lawlessness by maintaining the system of education (*Republic*, pp. 421d-425b). All three tasks are concerned with the unity of the political system. Riches and poverty divide a *polis* and subject it to envy and civil strife. The rulers' job is to see to it that no one, least of all themselves, grows wealthy and that no one becomes poor. Growth beyond a certain size also means division within the political system. Therefore, the rulers must maintain the number of citizens at a moderate level, so that all might know one another and might come to see each other as brothers and sisters.

But most important is the maintenance of the system of education. For it is education, in both its broadest and its most basic sense, that determines the future of the political system. The educational system determines the character of citizens; it establishes whether virtues or vices will be the disposition of the citizens. The entire system of education is focused on shaping the souls of the young so that they become truthful, brave, loyal, self-controlled, thoughtful, just, and wise. With such qualities, the rulers have little else to do, for peace and harmony prevail. Without citizens like that, the *öpolisò* is doomed to no end of trouble—dishonesty, litigiousness, anger, violence, resentment, cheating, sexual excess, official corruption, and injustice. For Plato the rulers must have discretion because, to use George Will's (1983) phrase, statecraft is soulcraft.

COMPARING PLATO AND THE DISCRETION SCHOOL

This section compares Plato to what was identified earlier as the discretion school. To set up appropriate tension we first show how alarmed some of Plato's commentators are by his putatively elitist and antidemocratic views. Second, we conjecture the standpoint of discretion advocates. Third, we assess how close discretionists come to Plato on three issues: (a) how complete the discretion, (b) knowledge of the Good, and (c) character of administrators/guardians and the role of education in promoting it.

Plato as Apologist for Dictatorship

Karl Popper (1950) and others (see Thorson, 1963) are quite critical of Plato and, in Popper's term, the "historicist" spirit of which Plato is the founder. Popper, who in contemporary political science terminology might be regarded as a pluralist or incrementalist, calls himself an advocate of piecemeal social engineering. Accordingly, it is to him the height of arrogance to promote any grand philosophical scheme that pretends to universalism. Such schemes, including those of Hegel and Marx, are not only wrong but dangerous, even evil. They cause war and oppression in their grandiloquent names. The Platotonic claim to acquaintance with the Good, the Just, the True, the Beautiful, and the proper ways of achieving and maintaining them through appropriate political arrangements is anathema.

It follows from this line of reasoning that a Platonic state is at best paternalistic and at worst a totalitarian dictatorship. To these critics it is a very short step from philosopher king to Hobbes's leviathan. Further, there is no exit. Plato may be reasonably interpreted as advocating "communism of the family" (communal raising of children) only for the guardian class. If this is the best way to raise children, as Plato seems to believe, they will be better educated than children of the producing classes, thereby creating a self-perpetuating ruling class much like the *apparetchiki* bureaucratic class of Communist party members in the Soviet Union.

Standpoint of Discretionists

Is this where the discretionists are unwittingly heading? To circle in on this question, let us first attempt to conjecture about the standpoint of the discretionists.[7] A cynic once remarked that theory was little more than the attempt to draw credible demarcation lines between who one likes and dislikes. Suspending for a moment the ontology of "likes and dislikes," suppose there is some truth to the observation. Among the important things that discretionists like is their, may we say, "calling." The calling of discretionists is, as far as we can tell, universally that of professor, usually in schools, departments, or divisions that in one way or another touch upon public affairs/policy/administration. The authors of this chapter are no exceptions. Our mission, *raison d'etre*, is to educate, and be educated by, current or future career public servants. As professors expounding book knowledge against the experimental reality check of our in-service students, we are likely to form bounds of trust and mutual respect—"a social construction of reality" (Berger & Luckman, 1967). Given the intimacy, the shared vulnerability, and the inquisitiveness of seminar education properly done, wouldn't we transpose real human faces of good people onto what to others are faceless functionaries? Our image would differ greatly from bureaucrat-bashing politicians and from victimized or alienated clientele (Morgan,

1986). And we would try to share our insider image with misinformed others through the articulation of theory.

Teachers of public servants are virtually required to take a leap of faith that the techniques they teach to their classes will not be misused. The exploding variety of personnel techniques, for instance, are not "good" in themselves, as Taylor could naively assume in his day. Most personnel experts know that "Theory X" motivational techniques are oppressive and that "Theory Y" techniques can be manipulative. Yet all these techniques and more are parts of the curriculum. Most personnel experts would not give a loaded gun to a child nor teach how to oppress workers. So, we give all the techniques available and hope—we can do no other—that individuals to whom they are given will use a humane combination of them in the varied work situations in which they will find themselves.

We conjecture further that standpoint analysis gives a clue to why current discretionists differ from their "Administrative State" fore-parents. Students and associates of the latter were on, or were headed for, higher rungs of the hierarchy than can be expected of contemporary products of mass education. Thus Administrative State Theorists like Appelby (1952), Waldo (1984), Bailey (1964), and Fainsod (1940) could affirm discretion at the bureaucratic apex and hierarchical obedience the rest of the way down. Recent discretionists affirm discretion for their mid-level alumni and are compelled to question hierarchy itself (e.g., Thayer, 1973; Lipsky, 1980).

The point of the above is that discretionists would be hard-pressed to build an image of their co-constructors of reality as the elitist oppressors Plato's critics fear. Discretionists might willingly be pushed to an image of their friends as guardians of the public interest, especially when one compares a known cadre against not fully legitimate competitors: politicians and inattentive voters. But they would not, at least not wittingly, support the Platonic state at oppressive Leviathan. (The lesser evil of paternalism will be discussed below.)

So far we have briefly sketched Plato's view of the guardian class more or less following the sequence of the *Republic*, noted how his insights can be negatively interpreted, and explicated what we take to be the standpoint of the discretion school. We turn now to the question of how close to the Platonic position discretion theorists have ventured. In other words, we array discretionist writings according to categories derived from Plato.

Discretion Not Absolute

The intellectual context for discussions of discretion was set almost half a century ago by the polar positions of Carl J. Friedrich (1940), who favored considerable discretion, and Herman Finer (1941), who wished to eliminate it by an iron cage of rules and regulations (for an excellent discussion see Cooper, 1982). Friedrich stops short of Plato's view that external constraints (laws, regulations, etc.) are totally useless because people of poor character will find ways to get around them and people of good character do not need them. To Friedrich, external checks have limited utility, but the internal disposition to apply expertise on behalf of the public interest is vastly more important. Emphasis on internal dispositions leads most discretionists in the same direction as Plato: toward proper education (see Education and Character, p. 101).

Among public administration theorists, the band of legitimate debate has shifted decisively toward the Friedrich polar position for reasons discussed in the introduction to this chapter. Indeed, Friedrich may now occupy the center with the new poles occupied by Harmon (1974, 1981), who sometimes sounds as if he favors complete discretion, and Cooper (1982), who attempts a dialectical balance between external and internal constraints. Harmon's existential or proactive administrator has been criticized (e.g., by Cooper) for having no standard except the goodness that results from self-actualizing action. This may be a little unfair because self-actualizing may require appropriate "I-thou" face-to-face transactions between organizational members or between administrator and client. This, in turn, may well gather or channel ambient social norms and focus them in the phenomenological moment of encounter. Thus, for instance, such norms and dispositions as expressed in Bailey's classical exposition—acceptance of moral ambiguity, recognition of contextual forces that condition moral priorities, and fair-mindedness tempered by charity (see Bailey, 1964, for complete list)—may be entailed in the face-to-face encounter. Still, Harmon's proactive administrator may be very close to Plato's Guardians, who might not reject the idea that community norms are self-actualized through their self-actualization. The active locus or pump of the process remains the discretionary action of the subject administrator. Cooper, on the other hand, has linkages between responsiveness to *concrete* external constraints and internalized commitments to perform public duties well.

There is, in other words, more objectivity, materiality, and weight to Cooper's externalities than to Harmon's.

Another view that is close to at least a positive interpretation of Harmon's is that of Fox (1989). Arguing by analogy to the distinction between "used language and language-in-use" employed by various continental linguists, Fox contends that ethical space (discretion) is not truncated by external laws and regulations. Indeed, the more they proliferate, layer on layer, the more discretion increases as administrators simply use some chosen concatenation of rules to express their judgments. In other words, like a language, SOPs are more a means for autonomous creative expression than a damper.

Arrayed between these not-so-distant poles are the new public administration thinkers (e.g., Fredrickson, 1971), who recommend discretion based on considerations of equity. They would have public servants use discretionary actions with a bias toward the weak, inarticulate, and disorganized to counterbalance the unequal influence of the powerful, articulate, and organized. It is within this context that Henry Kass (1988; 1989; and this volume) is working on a theory of agency as a role or "position," which envelops normative constraints situated in the culture and articulated in the Constitution and republican values. He ends up close to Cooper in that linkages are sought between external and internal responsibility. Still, for all of these discretionists, internalization is the key to accountability, not the mechanical application of rules, regulations, and laws made elsewhere. They seem all to be moons within Friedrich's orbit.

The Blacksburg group is also working on a theory of agency (Wamsley, Goodsell, Rohr, Stivers, White, & Wolfe, 1987). While Kass's work is based on individual agency, the Blacksburg approach is more institutional. Through agencies as repositories "of specialized knowledge, historical experience, time-tested wisdom, and a degree of consensus about the public interest" (Wamsley et al., 1987, p. 301), they seek at least coequal status for what they call The Public Administration with other branches of government. At times they seem to go further and argue for agency supremacy. Agency legitimacy is achieved by (a) a continuity with tradition matched only by the judiciary, (b) a claim to be representative in both sociological and functional senses, and (c) constitutional grounds, especially civil servants' oaths of office to uphold the Constitution and the laws. But this is not the unmitigated supremacy of the guardian class: "The public administrator therefore should be both an analyst and an educator but not a philosopher-king or mandarin" (Wamsley et al., 1987, p. 316).

Most discretionists, then, shrink from fully embracing Plato's stance and try to accommodate a modicum of political and/or citizen influence. This leads us to the next Platonic category—knowledge of the Good. If administrators are to be proactive on behalf of the public interest, how can it be apprehended?

Knowledge of the Good

In Plato's works, the Good is nowhere clearly defined. Methods of approaching it are offered, but these are matters for the section Education and Character. Nonetheless, it is such knowledge on which the guardians base their claim to rule (Waldo, 1984). The Good defines the public interest. Similarly, contemporary discretionists would like to claim access to knowledge of the public interest equal, if not superior, to other actors, superior when other actors are excessively self-interested (Cochran, 1974; Schubert, 1957). What better way to affirm discretion than Plato's way?

Three views and one suggestive sketch emerge. The first view is based on Rawls's Theory of Justice (1971). The second two use a "regime values" approach but with divergent results. The suggestive sketch comes from the Blacksburg group. David K. Hart's (1984) work is used to explicate both views one and three. The work of John Rohr (1978) is used for view two.

Rawls, while not fully digested, has been understandably influential. Not all who follow him fully recognize the neo-Kantian foundations of his approach (similar, interestingly, to Friedrich, 1940) (e.g., Stackhouse, 1989), but his carefully reasoned attack on utilitarianism has eroded that position's previous hegemony.

Perhaps the best attempt to apply Rawls to public administration is that of David K. Hart (1974; see also Harmon, 1974). Hart wants to provide substantive ethical grounds for the New Public Administration's "equitable administrator," that is, the one who seeks to redress the imbalance of influence on behalf of the powerless. Once the Good has been persuasively demonstrated, it is a simpler task to apply it to concrete situations. In a nutshell, Rawls's Good is that equality in the distribution of social valuables should prevail and such inequalities that do exist are justified if and only if they benefit the least advantaged. (Such a distillation does great violence to the richness of Rawls.) Hart hopes to start a Kuhnian paradigm revolution in public administration ethics with this Rawlsian salvo. So, like Plato, knowledge of the Good is warrant for good deeds. Also like Plato's guardians, administrators would perform the tasks of preventing the destabilizing extremes of wealth and poverty. Unlike Plato, however, access to the Good is not exclusive to the administrator. Indeed, Hart's view is that social consensus on the Good is required so that the administrator may go about correcting inequalities unimpeded by annoying disagreement.

A second way to apprehend the Good is through regime values. This position would seem to have as much, or more, promise as the Rawlsian leap to disembodied, decultured, and ahistorical pure reasoning by which his principles of justice are established (see Hart, 1974, on The Original Position, p. 6). As expressed by their principal proponent, John Rohr (1978), regime norms are based on the *founding* of the nation and evolving constitutional interpretations. As Rohr points out, it is especially relevant to *public* administration and avoids the need to appeal to diverse and individually constituted personal ethics. Rohr argues that the Good, the public good/interest, can be wrung out of the Constitution and interpretations of it by the Supreme Court.

This may be interpreted as quite close to Plato, with Supreme Court justices playing the role of a council of philosopher kings, whose pronouncements are studied by the guardian class as guides for exercising their discretion. Further, Justices are the proper age and receive specialized training, as Plato requires of his rulers. Moreover, the Good is discovered by way of a dialectic between precedent and social evolution. Although errors (e.g., *Dred Scott*) are made from time to time, they are ultimately corrected; two steps forward, one step back, but the Good will out. It may be objected that what is known as The Founding is really a kind of mythical, yet fortuitous, codification of questionable natural law "verities" distilled from the Age of Enlightenment. Nonetheless, once such standards have been culturally accepted as a set of inviolable first principles, they do form standards, which all rationalist ethicists desire, and from which ethical reasoning can deduce appropriate behavior.

Interestingly enough, a decade after Hart's (1974) attempt to foment a Kuhnian revolution based on *egalité, fraternité*, and Rawls, he returns to the pages of the *Public Administration Review* recommending a counterrevolution. Hart, as contra, puts an entirely different gloss on regime values, which is also compatible with (at least some interpretations of) Plato, but not in the same way as we read Rohr's contribution.

Hart's argument proceeds in two stages. He first outlines a rather lofty standard of citizen virtue. He then piles on additional moral qualities expected of the "honorable" bureaucrat. Because we believe that Hart in this piece confirms the fears of Plato's detractors (see previous section, Discretion Not Absolute), care must be taken in assessing it.

Hart first asserts that human nature is unchanging. It is "divided between a predisposition toward moral behavior. . . and the passions . . ." (1984, p. 112). "Right reason" is required to bring out the former aspect and suppress the latter. Right reason requires effort, discipline, and education, but may also be employed to find "the truth about human nature [and] that truth should determine the requisite political forms" (p. 113). Since responsibility for virtue belongs to individuals, he rejects authoritarian paternalistic institutions and relies instead on the "presumption that individuals understand and are committed to the necessity of constant study, from history to philosophy, from aesthetics to poetry " (p. 114). In other words, American society is the guardian class writ large.

Hart then goes on to take two stances, each controversial in itself but also contradictory when juxtaposed. First, "government must be guided by a moral purpose: the realization of the American regime values ". . . requiring that all individuals know what those values are. . . ." That requires, in turn, that people "*do*" philosophy, which is understood as the *critical* evaluation of assumptions and arguments. "[A]ll citizens [are required] to subject these [natural law values of the American regime] to the most rigorous philosophical scrutiny. . . ." A lot to ask of every citizen. Second, on the very same page of Hart's text (p. 114), "[t]he virtuous citizen must *believe* [Hart's emphasis] that the American regime values are true. . . ." If so, however, why *do philosophy*? On the basis of this faith:

> whenever any situation compromises the regime values, the virtuous citizen is required to act immediately in defense of those values. Thus, when one encounters racism, sexism, the invasion of privacy, or some such, one must instantaneously oppose them. (Hart, 1984, p. 115)

To these citizen duties are added caring, moral entrepreneurism, and *noblesse oblige* for the honorable bureaucrat. But most importantly:

> They must never allow themselves to be party to the compromising of the
> regime values, whether through partisan decisions, economic considera-
> tions, presumed administrative efficiencies, or professional neutrality.
> (Hart, 1984, p. 115).

We have been sniping at the edges of Hart's argument, but a more
important point is yet to be made. It is precisely Hart's version (not
Rohr's) of apprehending the Good that most frightens Plato's detractors. With no disrespect to Hart's own motives, it is fanaticism to
suppose such a firm grip on natural law cum regime values cum the
absolute Good. The difference between Rohr's approach and that of
Hart is that Rohr holds out the form of the Good ahead of us as
something we are haltingly striving for, while Hart has it already
established, commanding certain behaviors. Rohr's Good entices and
seduces us onward. Hart's good is a demanding and jealous Good. What
may be seen as objectionable in Hart's use of regime values is the fixity
of it. They must be *believed* and then acted upon with not even a nod to
prudence required in real-life situations. In Hart's hands, regime values
become rigid external norms, established elsewhere, which ought to
control behavior. The trouble with this is that except for a few hints
about racism, sexism, and privacy, we do not know exactly how regime
values can be translated into behavioral guides. Furthermore, it is
interesting that the founders of the regime values were guilty of all those
things that Hart would have us so vigorously and righteously strike
down in their name: racism (they owned slaves), sexism (despite Abi-
gail Adams's plea to John—no vote), and invasion of privacy (the Alien
and Sedition Acts).

The less-developed suggestion for apprehending the Good or the
public interest comes from the Blacksburg group (Wamsley et al., 1987,
pp. 304-307). It can be covered briefly. The Blacksburg group thinks
that public interest may be approximated, if not defined, negatively, that
is, by successive loppings off of what it is not. It is not individual
interests, group interests, or aggregates of these in equilibrium. This
may be interpreted as quite Platonic as it closely resembles the actual
course of Platonic dialogues. The inquiry into justice, for instance, is
sought through a *via negativa*, in which successive approximations of
justice are rejected as genuine justice is pursued.

Education and Character.

If knowledge of the Good is the apex of the Platonic system, education as a way to climb to the top is a close second. Of course, education is an attractive solution to almost every problem; we should not forget that it is the solution to the Marxist problem of creating a postcapitalist humanity and has produced, in practice, indoctrination and reeducation camps. Two sides of education are important: the education of the educators (the guardians) and the educators' education of the citizens. To both Plato and many discretionists the two are dialectically related. As pointed out in the first section of this chapter and reinforced by the Hart (1984) essay, that we have otherwise criticized, good citizens make for good government and vice versa (e.g., tax compliance). Proper education creates both.

Space constraints require that the discussion of citizen education be limited to its effects on discretion. If discretionists are correct about the dysfunctions of representative political accountability, then public administrators are in some senses directly accountable to citizens (Frederickson, 1982, p. 502). It follows that their expertise is to be shared not just with legislators but with citizens themselves. Thus city planners hold neighborhood meetings to get citizen input before promulgating a master zoning plan. But they first inform those gathered about options, possibilities, and limitations. Education becomes a reciprocal relationship (Rohr, 1984, p. 139).

Also influential in discretionist literature is Lipsky's (1980) discussion of street-level bureaucrats. Lipsky assigns to bureaucratic discretion the education of clients to be clients. Since his category includes everything from police officers to intake workers to school teachers, the educational responsibilities of those occupations can hardly be understated. At issue is a fundamental choice in attitudes of bureaucrats. They can either act in such ways as to make themselves an elite with exclusive expertise, the road to technocracy, or try to empower clients to become full citizens. Like Plato, most discretionists believe the latter strategy has the best chance of promoting the Good.

More important in discretionist literature is educating the educators, for good (Platonic) reasons. As indicated above, discretionists, virtually by definition, follow the Friedrich fork of the Friedrich-Finer antimony. Relying on internal-subjective accountability as opposed to external-objective controls entails Plato's concern for developing the character traits of bravery, wisdom, temperance, and commitment to justice. Stephen K. Bailey's now classical essay honoring Paul Appelby is fully compatible with Plato in this regard (Bailey, 1964; see discussion of Harmon above).

Perhaps the most revealing discussion of educating administrators occurs in the debate over professionalism. Professionalism is a controversial subject because it has two very different connotations. To some it signifies petty self-serving, conducted behind the veil of unnecessary specialization, bogus expertise, and obscurantist jargon. Taken this way, professionalism is the very opposite of Friedrich's (1940) internal accountability. Of course, it is the avoidance of *external* accountability that is the crux of Frederick C. Mosher's (1982) disparagement of creeping professionalism in his virtually paradigmatic discussion of the "professional state." Critics of the seemingly irresistible momentum of the American Society for Public Administration for professional status for its membership, among which are some discretionists (e.g., Fischer & Zinke, 1989), fear precisely this elitist-protectionist aspect of professionalism.

To others, professional status for public administrators is a shield behind which administrators can do good while fending off the illegitimate missives of ideological political appointees.

A much more positive interpretation of professionalism has surfaced only very recently. While recognizing negative aspects of professionalism, these authors end up taking professionalism as a "calling." Most provocative is Terry L. Cooper's (1987) appropriation of Alasdaire MacIntyre's *After Virtue* (1984). Both positive and negative aspects of professionalism are accounted for by way of MacIntyre's concept of a practice. In a way that would surely be appreciated by Friedrich, MacIntyre distinguishes between internal and external goods of a practice. "External goods are those which can be achieved in many ways other then engaging in a particular practice." They include "money, prestige, status, position, and power" (Cooper, 1987, p. 322), clearly the more reprehensible aspects of professionalism.

Internal goods represent the positive aspects of a practice-profession. They conform to Friedrich's internal accountability and Plato's emphasis on character. "It is in the nature of internal goods that though they are produced out of competition to excel 'their achievement is a good for the whole community'" (Cooper, 1987, p. 322).

Professionalism, in the benign sense, is internalized duty to do well. It is a kind of performance ethic, close to a calling and the protestant work ethic, by which people (professionals) simply are called to do their best, for anything less would be embarrassing to them. It is ingrained pride in performance. Despite the contributions of established professions like law and medicine to the negative aspects of professionalism, one expects the positive aspects to prevail when one goes to the courtroom or hospital.

The most emphatic case for professionalism in public administration is made by Kearney and Sinha (1988). Using Moore's (1970) definition of *professionalism* they emphasize:

> adherence to a set of normative and behavioral expectations, usually embodied in a code of ethics. . . . A professional organization . . . created to enhance and protect the "calling" . . . education and training of exceptional duration . . . a service orientation; competent performance is related to client needs. . . . Members enjoy a degree of autonomy in decision making by virtue of their specialized knowledge, but they are restrained by their responsibility. (1988, p. 571)

If these sterling qualities are the essence of professionalism, they are greatly to be desired. According to Kearney and Sinha,

> There are four principal advantages of professionalism in government. First, it promotes bureaucratic responsibility and accountability through professional norms and standards. . . . Second, it serves as an antidote to the common ailments of bureaucracy. Third, professionalism aids cooperation and understanding between scientific and political estates. Finally, it provides an important source of intrinsic motivation for professional employees. (1988, p. 575)

If the positive assessment of professionalism prevails, it entails more humanistic curricula for professional schools. This is one of the motivations behind the ethics movement described in the introduction of this chapter. Any move in this direction, however, has a long distance to cover to change priorities from "education for" to Plato's "education of."

To sum up this subsection, it may be said that although education and character are important components of discretionist strategies, they fall far short of Plato's commitment to them. However, if recent writings on professionalism are prologue, education may be the vehicle by which Plato's Guardian class is more closely approximated. And, just as there seems to be a movement in medicine to educate patients, so too an educational component might be added to the relationships between public administrators and their citizen clients. Professional education that in some way incorporates the virtues and avoids the technicism, is then an important element in the discretionist strategy.

RESIDUAL DILEMMAS OF DESCRETION

We began by indicating that a swing toward discretion had become detectable in public administration literature. We then described Plato's extreme discretion model, and the third section compared Plato with the discretionists. Except for the dilemmas to be discussed below, it seems that collectively, if not in each case individually, a good and sophisticated case has developed for administrative discretion. Administrators will exercise discretion but not as much discretion as Plato's guardians because, if for no other reason, the institutional context within which they work is too complex and no one seems to be asking for *that* much discretion. Moreover, when internalized as second nature, regime norms, especially in the Rohr sense, discretion will have an effect. As education of administrative professionals catches up to the reality that neutral tool-wielding functionaries are not the appropriate product of the schools, we may inch toward more soulcraft, and the administrators so instructed may work to empower their sector of the citizenry. Despite the cogency of the discretionist vision, however, three residual issues or dilemmas remain to be addressed if discretion is to be advanced beyond its current standing. Yet to be answered are these potential objections: (a) excessive idealism, (b) paternalism, and (c) reintroduction of the policy/administration dichotomy. Our response suggests a mass elite.

The "Realist" Demur

It is not clear that discretionists, each working in his or her own corner of the vineyard and, of course, brought together as a school only by the imaginations of the authors of this chapter, have confronted or can confute the objections or possible objections to their views. Since

Charles Fox and Clarke Cochran count themselves as at least auxiliary members of the imagined school, such issues the ones that concern us most. One such critique was mounted by Schubert against the previous generation of discretionists or what he calls "administrative platonists" (Schubert, 1957). Like current discretionists, they (i.e., Fainsod, 1940; Redford, 1954; and Appleby, 1952) recognized various failings of traditional political accountability mechanisms and argued for administrators to fill the void. Schubert's (1957, p. 354) objection is that administrative platonists are reduced to blind faith in administrators, the only corrective being their own sermons:

> In effect, Fainsod, Redford, and Appleby tell us that the public interest would be realized if bureaucrats abjured administrative delinquency and obeyed the exhortations of these moralists, which may be paraphrased as:
> "Be clever!"
> "Be wise!"
> "Be good!"

So much for education and professionalization as fail-safe.

Schubert's acidic dismissal of administrative guardianship seems to be devastating. Still, as will be discussed below with regard to the concept of a mass elite, such guardianship may be better than the alternative of slavish attendance to merely electoral accountability.

Paternalism

The charge of paternalism is more difficult to duck. The question "Who the hell do you think you are?" has been tough for liberal-minded people ever since taking on the burden of being their brother's keeper. Doing good and being a do-gooder are very hard to separate. Still the opposite impulse—of "I got mine Jack" or "Let them stew in their own juice,"—is even more reprehensible. The trick to doing good, as many discretionists have acknowledged, is to do it through empowerment of the client. As Cooper has put it:

> [T]he ethical obligations of the public administrator are to be derived from the obligations of citizenship in a democratic political community. These obligations include responsibility for establishing and maintaining horizontal relationships of authority with one's fellow citizens, seeking "power with" rather than "power over" the citizenry. (1984, p. 143)

The good of Plato's Guardian class, ultimately, is to educate the souls of all citizens to recognize and receive the virtues. If, however, the citizens are simply uninterested, then we may have to live with the charge of paternalism (see subsection on mass elite below).

Reintroduction of Politics/Administrative Dichotomy

The present authors had not recognized the problem of reintroducing a politics/administration dichotomy until a student of one of us brought it up in seminar. We were discussing the Blacksburg manifesto (Wamsley et al., 1987) and the student objected: "but they are just reintroducing the politics/administration dichotomy except now from the administrative side."[8] The implications of this are truly Platonic. Instead of using the dichotomy to comfort democrats against administrative abuse of power, now it is used to insulate "real and integral governance by administrators" from the corrupting influences of politics understood as untrammeled and greedy self-interest (see Wamsley et al., 1987, p. 307). In other words, rather like the French political system before the Fifth Republic, political machinations were chaotic but benignly irrelevant because the bureaucratic corps were running the country. Electoral politics, which most people think of as *the* politics, become merely epiphenomenal noise. Used this way, the dichotomy becomes the contemporary stand-in for Plato's myth of metals.

Mass Elite

A conjecture was offered earlier in this chapter about the standpoint of discretionists. We cast them as educators in programs of public affairs whose constituency was current or future mid-level bureaucrats. Concern for the careers of these students and empathetic engagement in the problems they now, or will, face probably fills a significant portion of their mind space—we know that it does ours. Taking the part of mid-level public servants entails several positions that one tries in various ways to reconcile with other standard value commitments of generalized liberalism as articulated in regime norms. By far the most difficult reconciliation is between the public management point of view and democratic values. To a degree, we really do trust our students to pursue the public interest with more integrity, sensitivity, and, in the positive sense, professionalism than the officials that the electoral process produces. Thus we really are attracted to at least a moderate version of the guardian class *in our setting*. That setting is local government and we cannot claim to know the extent of its generalizability; that task must be left to individual readers. Moreover, the authors believe that there is such a thing as the public interest (Cochran, 1974) and that, while it may not be subject to a precise definition, we know it, or at least we know what it isn't, when we see it.

We came to our view of what can very well be considered elite rule only reluctantly. We would much rather endorse the views of the Evergreen Group (see Adams et al., this volume) and join in the quest for the full democracy they so attractively outline. Unfortunately, full democracy in the settings with which we are most familiar does not seem possible in the near or medium term. With important exceptions, the people are apolitical in any policy sense unless their own particularistic interests are involved. Electoral politics engages either those particularistic interests or policy-irrelevant social, cultural, and religious norms, none of which can claim more than a small point on the spectrum of the public interest. City councils are generally not much more than the decaying residues of once vibrant old-boy networks of localized petite bourgeois. Into this vacuum march professionally trained, sophisticated, socially aware, and virtuous public administrators (i.e., our students and colleagues). Better them, we say, than the existing alternative.

We think that this may be more democratic. Government of the people and for the people may, under current circumstances, be better pursued only by those who care enough to invest their best efforts; those who are involved, in the Burkean sense, in the deliberations—maximally informed and maximally disinterested deliberations over conditional futures.

For lack of a better term, we call the class of mid-level public servants with sufficient informational and organizational resources to engage in deliberations "the mass elite." It sounds like an oxymoron, but dialectical concepts must always suffer that accusation. It is an elite in the sense of the guardian class because its members are specially trained. But it is a mass in the sense that membership in it is not artificially denied, and its membership is at least minimally representative of race, gender, and religious affiliations of the population. We intend the label to evoke a relevant political and democratic community divorced not by intent but by intentionality from apathetic others. In a way that he would not embrace, we are pushed to the position of accepting Habermas's (1975) vision of a constricted public sphere. However lamentable its constriction may be, it does, if only in its own sphere, conform to Henry Kariel's admonition that we should accept as democratic "nothing less than a society all of whose members are active participants in an interminable process [of cooperative activity] and who would not mind such activity" (cited in Harmon & Mayer, 1986, p. 377). The facts of the matter are that most people are not interested in formal government. Perhaps it is arrogant of us to assume that they would be. Perhaps their fulfillment comes not from governing themselves in our sense of government, but from participation in all the other myriad forms of self-through-community-realization available to them including: dog clubs, recreational vehicle clubs, church activities, Little Leagues, fan clubs, and so on *ad infinitum*. It follows that the best that can be done is to assure as much democracy as possible in the sphere where the mass elite's projects are carried out. Thus they are an unwilling elite, but fortunately, they are not few. They are not at the top of formally charted hierarchies and thus do not support, as our discretionist forefathers did, top-down accountability. They are democratic within their sphere, which is the only sphere where they have solid influence. And they are democratic at the boundaries of their sphere as long as those who seek to enter it have the "communicative competence" (Habermas, 1975) to engage in the deliberations; that is, they must be sincere, not overly self-interested, willing to educate themselves, and willing to have their views subjected to the same doubt and questioning as is usual in deliberation.

How can the present authors be sure that our colleagues will and do exercise their discretion in ways that further the public interest? We can't; at least we can't altogether. But basically they seem to be accountable to each other through informal norms of association and through more formal trade associations and active alumni associations. In other words, there is a network of professional city administrators who are in regular communication with each other, and through this network peer norms are expressed and reinforced. These administrators seem to take very seriously their stewardship (see Kass, this volume) of the public interest. On behalf of it, and as the permanent governments and repositories of institutional memories and the possessors of policy expertise, they do sometimes co-opt and manipulate their putative elected betters—the city councils who are part-time, poorly paid, and usually quite temporary. Bad laws that stubborn city councils nonetheless pass are not implemented or are implemented very half-heartedly. The major influence of city councils is the negative one of reluctance to tax, thereby keeping city administrators on a rather short resource leash. But councils do not generally concern themselves with the line items in the budget. The tenure of the city managers with whom we are familiar is generally as long as they wish to make it. Turnover is very low.

We may be idealizing what we perceive to be the case in our setting, and we cannot speak with confidence of other governmental settings. Two additional factors make our comparison of our colleagues with Plato's Guardian class salient. The first is the size of the governmental components in our setting. West Texas towns are not metropolises. They get no larger than 200,000. Most are considerably smaller than that. The relatively manageable size of the administrative structure means that they do not become huge impersonalized mechanisms with highly differentiated and isolated departmental structures. It is usually the case that everybody knows everybody else and what everybody else is doing. Therefore, our towns and their administrative structures share some of the features of the *polis*. Second, the issues of city management are not the global ones confronting larger American governmental units. Compared to the charge of the Environment Protection Agency, say, or Health and Human Services, the ratio of tame to wicked problems (Harmon & Mayer, 1986, chap. 1) favors the tame. We recognize then, that our diminutive guardian class may not work everywhere. Nevertheless, we suspect that it is not atypical of local politics and administration in many parts of the United States.

As is evident, the authors of this chapter count themselves among the discretionists. One of them in particular has views very close to the Harmon extreme of discretion. But we pause before the magnitude of the conclusion that Plato and Aristotle reached so long ago. To them, democracy was mob rule with tendencies toward the rule of the demagogue. In trying to carve out theoretical space for administrative discretion contemporaneously with the disenfranchisement of good sense in the electoral process, we have come upon precisely the problematic for which Plato recommended a guardian class. Have we, then, ceased to be the democrats that we had always regarded ourselves as being?

NOTES

1. As exemplars of the current discretion school we use primarily the works of Terry L. Cooper (1987, 1984, 1982); H. George Fredrickson (1982, 1971); Charles J. Fox (1989); Michael M. Harmon (1981, 1974); David K. Hart (1984, 1974); Henry Kass (1989;

and this volume); Richard C. Kearney and Chandah Sinha (1988); Michael Lipsky (1980); John A. Rohr (1984, 1978); and the Blacksburg Group (Wamsley et al., 1987). First-generation discretionists, advocates of the administrative state, include Paul Appelby (1952), Dwight Waldo (1984), Stephen K. Bailey (1964), Emmette S. Redford (1954), Merle Fainsod (1940), and Carl J. Friedrich (1940).

2. In this discussion of Plato's theory of discretion in the guardians, the Greek term *polis* is used in order to avoid misleading assumptions that Plato was talking about cities or states in the modern sense. Though *polis* is often translated *city-state*, such a term is even more misleading in the modern context. Our discussion refers to political units with some independence at whatever level of the American political system. The term *polis* can perhaps best be taken to refer to the people as a whole within a unified political system, whether at the national, state, or local level.

3. Qualifications are in order at this point. First, we do not pretend to a full explication of the role of the guardians in Plato's political theory. Second, the *Republic* itself is not Plato's last word on politics and administration. Later dialogues, particularly *Statesman* and *Laws*, provide a wealth of additional material qualifying what might be said here about the guardians in the *öRepublicò*. We shall only refer occasionally to these dialogues. Finally, and most importantly, what we offer here is a conventional, nearly literal, interpretation of the *Republic* and the significance of its guardians. Other and deeper interpretations substantially challenge this approach and have a great deal to recommend them. In particular, note the interpretations of Bloom (1968) (following Leo Strauss) and Voegelin (1975).

4. See especially *Republic*, pp. 372a-376c. (All citations of the *Republic* are from the Bloom translation, references are given by Stephanus page numbers to facilitate comparison with other translations.)

5. Though Plato does not specifically say so, it seems that all citizens must receive this same early education, for the guardians are to be selected according to their special talents from the pool of all young persons, who, therefore, must have the same basic education. Plato explicitly includes women in the guardian class; see especially *Republic*, Book V, pp. 449a-454d.

6. *Statesman*, pp. 294-303. (Citations of the *Statesman* are to the B. Jowett translation.) The regimes described by Plato in the *Statesman* and in the *Laws* are governed by the rule of law, but Plato clearly regards them as second best to the rule of the philosopher directly, without the mediation of law.

7. A standpoint or *standpunkt* analysis is roughly based on phenomenological epistemology (see Fox, 1980; in press, for explication and further references), an interpretive methodology that stands or falls, essentially, on the degree to which readers find it *prima facie* evident when presented to them. See also Denhardt (1984, pp. 159-163). It is also consistent with the sociology of knowledge tradition.

8. We owe this point to Monica Gibson, MPA, May, 1988, Texas Tech University.

REFERENCES

Appelby, P.H. (1952). *Morality and administration in democratic government*. Baton Rouge: Louisiana State University Press.

Bailey, S.K. (1964, December). Ethics and the public service. *Public Administration Review, 24*, 234-243.

Berger, P.L., & Luckman, T. (1967). *The social construction of reality.* Garden City, NY: Doubleday.

Bloom, A. (1968). Interpretative essay. In A. Bloom (Trans.), *The Republic of Plato* (pp. 305-436). New York: Basic Books.

Bloom, A. (Trans.). (1968). *The republic of Plato.* New York: Basic Books.

Cochran, C.E. (1974, May). Political science and "the public interest." *Journal of Politics, 36*, 327-355.

Cooper, T.L. (1982). *The responsible administrator: An approach to ethics for the administrative role.* Port Washington, NY: Kennikat.

Cooper, T.L. (1984, March). Citizenship and professionalism in public administration. *Public Administration Review, 44*, 143-151.

Cooper, T.L. (1987, July/August). Hierarchy, virtue, and the practice of public administration. *Public Administration Review, 48*, 320-328.

Denhardt, R.B. (1984). *Theories of public organization.* Monterey, CA: Brooks/Cole.

Fainsod, M. (1940). Some reflections on the nature of the regulatory process. In C.J. Friedrich & E.S. Mason (Eds.), *Public Policy* (pp. 320-322). Cambridge, MA: Harvard University Press.

Finer, H. (1941, Summer). Administrative responsibility in democratic government. *Public Administration Review, 1*, 335-350.

Fischer, F., & Zinke, R. C. (1989, November). Public Administration and the code of ethics: Administrative reform or professional ideology? *International Journal of Public Administration, 12*, 841-854.

Fox, C.J. (1980, September). The existential-phenomenological alternative to dichotomous thought. *Western Political Quarterly, 33*, 357-379.

Fox, C.J. (1989, November). Free to choose, free to win, free to lose: The phenomenology of ethical space. *International Journal of Public Administration, 12*, 913-930.

Fredrickson, H.G. (1971). Toward a new public administration. In F. Marini (Ed.), *Toward a new public administration* (pp. 309-331). Scranton, PA: Chandler.

Fredrickson, H.G. (1982, November/December). The recovery of civism in public administration. *Public Administration Review, 42*, 501-508.

Friedrich, C.J. (1940). Public policy and the nature of administrative responsibility. In C.J. Friedrich & E.S. Mason (Eds.), *Public Policy*. Cambridge, MA: Harvard University Press.

Ginsberg, B., & Stone, A. (Eds.). (1986). *Do elections matter?* Armonk, NY: M.E. Sharpe.

Habermas, J. (1975) *Legitimation crisis.* T. McCarthy (Trans.) Boston: Beacon Press.

Harmon, M.M. (1974, January/February). Social equity and organizational man: Motivation and organizational democracy. *Public Administration Review, 34*, 11-18.

Harmon, M.M. (1981). *Action theory for public administration.* New York: Longman.

Harmon, M.M., & Mayer, R.T. (1986). *Organization theory for public administration.* Boston: Little, Brown.

Hart, D.K. (1974, January/February). Social equity, justice, and the equitable administrator. *Public Administration Review, 34*, 3-11.

Hart, D.K. (1984, March). The virtuous citizen, the honorable bureaucrat, and "public" administration. *Public Administration Review, 44*, 111-120.

Jowett, B. (Trans.) (1937). *The statesman, Vol. 2.* New York: Random House.

Kass, H. (1989, November). Exploring agency as a basis for ethical theory in American public administration. *International Journal of Public Administration, 12*, 949-969.

Kearney, R.C., & Sinha, C. (1988, January/February). Professionalism and bureaucratic responsiveness: Conflict or compatibility. *Public Administration Review, 48*, 571-579.

Lipsky, M. (1980). *Street level bureaucracy: Dilemmas of the individual in public service.* New York: Russell Sage.

MacIntyre, A. (1984). *After virtue* (2nd ed.). Notre Dame, IN: Notre Dame University Press.

Moore, W.E. (1970). *The professions: Roles and rules.* New York: Russell Sage.

Morgan, G. (1986). *Images of organization.* Beverly Hills, CA: Sage.

Mosher, F.C. (1982). *Democracy and the public service.* (2nd ed.). New York: Oxford University Press.

Popper, K.P. (1950). *The open society and its enemies.* Princeton, NJ: Princeton University Press.

Rawls, J. (1971). *A theory of justice.* Cambridge, MA: Harvard University Press.

Redford, E.S. (1954). The protection of the public interest with special reference to administrative regulation. *American Political Science Review, 48*, 1107-1108.

Rohr, J.A. (1978). *Ethics for bureaucrats: An essay on law and values.* New York: Marcel Dekker.

Rohr, J.A. (1984, March). Civil servants and second class citizens. *Public Administration Review, 44*, 135-150.

Rosen, B. (1986, May/June). Crisis in the U.S. civil service. *Public Administration Review, 46*, 217-214.

Schubert, G.A., Jr. (1957). "The public interest" in administrative decision making: Theorem, theosophy, or theory? *American Political Science Review, 51*, 346-368.

Stackhouse, S.B. (1989, November). Upholding justice in an unjust world: A practitioner's view of public administration ethics. *International Journal of Public Administration, 12*, 889-912.

Thayer, F. (1973). *An end to hierarchy! An end to competition: Organizing the politics and economics of survival.* New York: Franklin Watts.

Thorson, T.L. (Ed.). (1963). *Plato: Totalitarian or democrat.* Englewood Cliffs, NJ: Prentice-Hall.

Voegelin, E. (1957). *Order and history, vol. III: Plato and Aristotle.* Baton Rouge: Louisiana State University Press.

Waldo, D. (1984). *The administrative state* (2nd ed.). New York: Holmes & Meier.

Wamsley, G.L., Goodsell, C.T., Rohr, J.A., Stivers, C.M., White, O.F., & Wolfe, J.F. (1987). The public administration and the governance process: Refocusing the American dialogue. In R.P. Chandler (Ed.), *A centennial history of the American administrative state* (pp. 291-317). New York: Free Press.

Will, G. (1983). *Statecraft as soulcraft: What government does.* New York: Simon & Schuster.

Worthley, J.A., & Grumet B.R. (1983, Spring). Ethics and public administration: Teaching what "can't be taught." *American Review of Public Administration, 17*, 54-67.

4

Stewardship as a Fundamental Element in Images of Public Administration

HENRY D. KASS

INTRODUCTION

The major purpose of this chapter is to argue that no matter what image or metaphor is used to think of the role played by American public administrators in our political system, that image must be built on the concept of stewardship if it is to be accepted as legitimate by the American public. The word *stewardship*, as used here, means the administrator's willingness and ability to earn the public trust by being an effective and ethical agent in carrying out the republic's business.

Pursuit of this argument takes on a certain urgency when one notes the legitimacy crisis currently facing the American political system, particularly its administrative component (Fiorina, 1983). While one can argue that the administrative state has never been overly popular in the United States, the recent criticism of public administration has reached what Kaufman (1981) characterized as "pandemic" levels.

Mitchell and Scott (1987) have offered a thesis similar to the one advanced in this chapter to explain Kaufman's pandemic. They argue that the recent cynicism about American government rests less on traditional "bureaucratic bashing," or loss of faith in our institutions, than on skepticism concerning the stewardship of public leaders, including public administrators. Ominously, they go on to argue that the present loss of faith in the legitimacy of our leadership may yet result in a loss of legitimacy for the republic itself.

Their thesis, and the one to be explored in this chapter, suggests a sharp departure from the concept of legitimacy embodied in the dominant technocratic and cybernetic image (Zinke, Chapter 7) of the American public administrator. As viewed through this image, the legitimate use of administrative authority requires only that it be efficient and effective in pursuit of the goals articulated by the political elites that dominate the state. By contrast, legitimacy resting in stewardship requires that efficiency and effectiveness be informed by, and subordinated to, the ethical norms of justice and beneficence. Thus, stewardship encompasses the traditional administrative norms of efficiency and effectiveness and subordinates them to the general ethical norms.[1]

Consequently, to say that the republic is confronted with a legitimation crisis occasioned by a failure of stewardship implies a good deal more than to say this crisis has been caused by lapses in technocratic expertise. When one argues that administrators have failed as technocrats, one accuses them of being inefficient, ineffective, and ultimately unproductive. While these charges are serious in their own right, accusations that administrators have failed as stewards of the public trust are even more serious. This is because they imply those concerned are being accused of unjust acts and lack of care for their constituents. In short, they are indicted for an ethical as well as a technical default in bearing the trust delegated to them by the republic.

Examining this thesis will require four steps. First, the term *stewardship* will have to be defined and analyzed more fully if it is to become more than a cliche based on a brief definition. Since stewardship is really acting for someone else in a trustworthy manner, it really refers to the status of being a good *agent* for the other. Thus, it is possible to develop an administratively applicable definition of *stewardship* by reviewing the general ethical theory that governs agency, the "acting for" relationship in society.

Second, since agency is a normative social theory, found most prominently in commercial law (Meecham, 1914; Ferson, 1954; Pollock & Maitland, 1968), it will be necessary to relate it explicitly to government and public administration. In order to do this, the general theory of the associational state advanced by Tussman (1960) will be used.

Third, based on this analysis, *stewardship* will be defined and its practice described. At the same time, the impact on the state of the failure to practice public stewardship will be summarized.

AGENCY THEORY: A BRIEF OVERVIEW

Developing the theory of agency to establish the nature of stewardship will require two steps. First, it will be necessary to sketch, within the severely constricted limits of this chapter, a normative theory of agency.[2] Then, this theory will have to be applied to the unique conditions imposed by the public sector.

It is important to note at the inception of this study that the basis for the normative theory discussed here is the fundamental social relationships and institutions engendered when one person acts for another. Thus, while the chapter will not ignore the extensive literature on this subject developed by commercial law, it will in no way confine itself to the commercial applications of this potentially seminal social concept.

Agency developed out of the need to have free individuals represent one another's interests in an economically and socially specialized society like our own. In earliest times, those who acted for others were normally family dependents or bound servants who, in a real sense, were mere extensions of a *pater familias*. Agency originally arose out of the needs of unrelated, free individuals to serve and be served by others. In particular, agency as a social relationship responded to a free individual's demand to retain considerable, personal, and moral autonomy while working on behalf of others (Pollack & Maitland, 1968; Meecham, 1914).

With the growth of politically liberal, economically specialized societies in the West, agency provided a way to manage the multiple interdependencies created by extensive economic and technical specialization without sacrificing the reliability of the agent or the individual autonomy so often prized in these societies. Viewed in another way, agency was one of the few institutions in such a world that sought to ameliorate the alienation and lack of trust that characterizes a society of strangers with few organic bonds to one another. The ethics of agency allowed the isolated and specialized person in a pluralist society to trust, in Tennessee Williams's words, "the kindness of strangers." Specialized individuals, heavily dependent on one another, could give and receive basic services without experiencing exploitation as recipients or loss of freedom as providers. In this sense, modern agency became liberal, industrial society's substitute for the bonds of family, community, and servitude, allowing free, atomic individuals to serve other similarly situated individuals.

In passing, it should also be mentioned that modern agent has expanded the meaning of the "acting for" relationships in society to include organizations as well as individuals. Whereas both servitude and agency originally contemplated a social relationship between individuals, modern agency enlarges the meaning of the terms *principal*, *agent*, and *third party* to include collectives (particularly complex organizations) as well.

As a social relationship, agency is engendered when an agent acts for a principal in such a way as to impact a third party. To effectuate a successful agency relationship, the agent must substitute its capacities for those lacking in the principal so that the welfare of the principal is achieved. In this sense, adequate substitution of agent capacity for principal capacity lies at the heart of the agency relationship. When adequate substitution cannot be honestly and effectively achieved, agency fails.

In order to understand the nature of the substitution, it is also necessary to emphasize that agency is essentially a social relationship and principal, agent, and third party are all roles that the same individual or collective can play sequentially or simultaneously. Moreover, the principal and agent roles will vary with the type(s) of capacity that the principal lacks and seeks in the agent. For example, a principal that can make judgments, but is incapable of acting on its own behalf, seeks an agent that can literally carry out its explicitly stated will. In short, in such cases the principal seeks a *functionaire*.

However, when the principal has neither the capacity to judge nor act on its own behalf, it needs an agent that can be trusted to act as a plenipotentiary. Such an entity is usually termed a *fiduciary*. Both the fiduciary and functionaire could generically be termed agents. Yet, they play considerably different roles vis à vis the principal because of the principal's differing capacity to judge and act in various situations.

While agency is an extremely useful social relationship, the potential disparities of power and lack of traditional familial and communal ties among the actors can also give agencies, principals, and even third parties unparalleled opportunities to misuse and exploit one another. As might be imagined, the potential for injustices being committed in an agency relationship increases in a number of ways when the power of the state is involved.

Agents can take advantage of a principal's ignorance of their work and/or inability to monitor their activities and misuse their trust. Arrow terms the first situation "the hidden information problem" and the second "the hidden action problem" (Arrow, 1984, p. 38). However, principals can also abuse an agent's trust, endanger an agent physically, and most important, deny an agent's ethical autonomy by requiring it to do things that the agent believes are harmful or unjust to others. Third parties can be grievously injured by the conduct of agents, either acting in collusion with the principal or by themselves. However, third parties can also conspire with either principals or agents to abuse the trust of the others who are involved in the relationship.

This vulnerability problem represents the major blockage to achieving a successful and ethical agency relationship; unless vulnerability is overcome, agency is too dangerous an arrangement to enter into on the scale required by modern society, no matter how valuable a social relationship it is. It is not surprising, then, that a body of ethical theory, still largely reflected in commercial law (Meecham, 1914; *3 American Jurisprudence*, (2nd ed.), 1986; Ferson, 1954), has grown up to deal with this issue. One could also argue that the numerous professional codes found in contemporary society (including that of the American Society for Public Administration) also addressed themselves to the vulnerability problem in a variety of ways, ranging from assuring potential principals of the professional's competence and ethicality as an agent to stating agent rights over and against the demands of an unfair or unscrupulous principal.

Underlying the laws and codes that address agency one can discern a system of ethical norms which attempt to reduce the vulnerabilities associated with agency. Observance of those ethical norms literally makes it possible to conduct agency as a social relationship. Moreover, when a person or collective acts consistently in accordance with these norms, *even when it is extremely difficult to reconcile and effectuate them*, they can be designated a good agent or what will hereafter be called a *steward*.

This system of ethical norms consists of a set of related general and special obligations (Hart in Quinton ed., 1967; Nelson, 1975; Fishkin, 1982). The general obligations are those of just and beneficent treatment (Frankena, 1973), and presumably these are owed by all members of humankind to one another. The special obligations apply these general norms to the specific roles and relationships created by agency itself and are to be judged by how well they reduce the vulnerabilities associated with agency through assuring that those involved in the relationships observe the tenets of justice and beneficence.

The special norms of agent are of two sorts, *fiduciary* norms and *agent integrity* norms. Fiduciary norms call upon the agent to do the good for the principal that it has pledged to do. In other words, they direct the agent's beneficence to the service of a particular principal. Consequently, they lie at the heart of the agency relationship. If fiduciary norms go unobserved for reasons other than fidelity to general obligations of justice and beneficence, the very fabric of the agency relationship is rent asunder.

The first fiduciary norm requires that the prospective agent commit itself to effective realization of the principal's interest, even when doing so requires a sacrifice of its own interest and welfare. The second major fiduciary norm is an important corollary to this pledge. It requires a would-be agent to represent its capacity to act on behalf of the principal both accurately and honestly, even when it is to the benefit of the agent to misrepresent the facts. Together, these norms obligate the agent's commitment and capacity to the service of the principal's interest.

Agent integrity norms provide an important constraint on the treatment of individuals who either act directly as agents or who are associated with organizations exercising agency. These norms ensure that the rights of individuals to just and beneficent treatment as human beings are not abrogated simply because they are bound to a principal by the fiduciary norm. Agency norms that protect the agent's personal integrity range from the principal's obligation to honor contracts with its agents to requirements that the principal not place an agent involuntarily in harm's way.

This analysis suggests something about the nature of a good agent that will bear heavily upon the latter sections of this chapter. First, a good agent observes the fiduciary norms. In essence, this requires it to be both efficient and ethical. The agent must achieve the principal's interest and welfare and be ethical in the process of doing so.

Second, individual agents are allowed to have, and are required to exercise, a personal conscience. Moreover, in order to ensure that they are not intimidated in the exercise of conscience, the principal is not allowed to impugn the agent's individual safety and well-being.

These thoughts lead to two other comments before completing this discussion. The ethical system just outlined attempts to answer one of the most serious objections leveled against using agency as a basis for a theory of social and political ethics. It is often contended that agent norms are really means to instrumentalize an individual or organizational agent and make it little more than an amoral tool at the principal's disposal (Pitkin, 1967). Thus, the agent becomes bound to do the principal's bidding no matter how unethical it may be from the larger, social standpoint. Those who hold this viewpoint contend that the agency relationship actually short-circuits the agent's individual or organizational responsibility as an ethical actor. It opens the way for the actor to justify even heinous acts done in the principal's name as a faithful pursuit of the principal's interest and welfare.

However, a cursory glance at the ethical system outlined above indicates that it is not susceptible to this criticism. The fiduciary norms are clearly limited by overriding considerations of justice, beneficence, and respect for the agent's own personal or organizational integrity. All the specific norms of agency are basically applications of universal justice and beneficence norms to agency settings. All specific norms, including fiduciary norms, are judged by how well they effectuate these universal obligations in agency. When the fiduciary norms are used to justify unjust acts or harm done to others, they fail to support these universal norms and meet this test. By the same token, when an agent is required to make unethical commitments in order to retain its position, the specialized norms of agent integrity are violated. Thus, as long as the actors in agency choose to observe the ethical system just described, the relationship can be valuable to those who depend upon it, without it being used as a rationale for this exploitation of the parties involved or society at large.

Second, as noted, while agency was originally contemplated as a relationship between two persons, it has increasingly involved complex organizations acting as either agents or principals. In some minds, this has nullified the entire ethical aspect of the representative, since ethical action is seen beyond the capacity of the complex organization (Ladd, 1970). From this standpoint, not only are government organizations incapable of observing an ethical system like agency, they stand in the way of individual employees doing so if their actions are not deemed in the organization's interest.

Following arguments originally posed by Goodpaster, Matthews, and Matthews (1982), it is contended that government organizations not only can act ethically as agencies, they should be treated as such and are also capable of supporting the ethical agency of their individual employees. This argument is based on the view that organizations can take what Frankena (1973, 1980) called "the moral point of view." Taking a moral point of view and acting on it requires two things: (a) rationality—that is, the ability to frame one's projects and understand their implications for others, and (b) respect for others as ends in themselves, which leads one to refrain from treating them unjustly and harmfully.

It is well known that organizations are quite capable of acting rationally (Simon, 1976), and it is now understood that they can culturally endorse as well as enforce value systems involving, among other things, respect for humans as ends in themselves (Smircich, 1983a, 1983b). Therefore, it is not too much to expect that public organizations be able to take a moral point of view and act ethically as agents or, for that matter, use the social control systems at their disposal to encourage individual employees to do so as well (Wamsley, Goodsell, Rohr, Stivers, White, & Wolfe, 1987).

It also might be argued that since we can talk about the ethicality of an organization, we can also talk about its integrity as an entity. Thus, it might be possible, under some circumstances, to extend the protection of the agency integrity norm usually reserved for individuals to organizations. This would be especially true when a principal tries to have an organization violate its institutional commitment to justice and beneficence in the name of the fiduciary norms.

AGENCY THEORY: APPLICATION TO THE PUBLIC SECTOR

With this general sketch of the agency theory complete, there remains the task of applying this concept to the public sector. It is to this task that we now turn using Joseph Tussman's (1960) analysis of agency and its role in the associationally based state. As Tussman suggests, agency is central to the modern theory of the state. He views the democratic state as an association formed to pursue the common interests of the participants. Put another way, the state is an association the function of which is to manage the most common, crucial interdependencies in a society to the common advantage of those involved.[3] Indeed, the management of these interdependencies is seen as so important that the collective membership of the association voluntarily submits to these powers even when this demands subordination of their own individual and factional interests.

Tussman argues that there are two basic roles played by individuals and groups in the association. One of these is the role of *members*, in which participants in the associated state receive the benefits of having their shared interdependencies managed and interests pursued. The other role is that of *agent*, in which participants of the association are required to act on behalf of the shared interests of the members of the state. As these observations indicate, it is difficult to conceptualize the role of member without the role of agent, because the benefits that accrue to membership can only be realized through the action of agency. It is very important to note here that unlike most human principals, an associated principal is virtually unable to act at all without agency of some sort. Thus, an association like the state has no capacity to act outside of the agency relationship. It is always and ever fully dependent on its agents to do its business.

Therefore, agency is literally the active impulse of the associated state. Without agency, the state is impotent and the *res publica*, the common business of the people, goes undone. It can therefore be said that agency is central, not peripheral, to the very existence of the modern, democratic state.

In its public sector application, agency shares the basic purposes, mechanisms, and problems that characterize the general social concept of agency just discussed. Public agency, like all agency, is essentially an ethical system that allows groups and individuals with few organic social ties and of widely disparate powers to serve and act on behalf of one another without the stronger actors exploiting the weaker ones. In the case of the public sector, agency is designed to prevent those who have been empowered to act on behalf of the associated state to exploit that association and its members for their individual and collective interest. Correspondingly, it also protects the personal integrity and dignity of individual agents from abuse by members or other agents of the state.

The mechanism used to establish agency in the public sector is similar to that used on society at large. Agency is largely set up to facilitate one entity acting faithfully in the interests of another without unilateral or mutual exploitation in the process. Accordingly, this requires an identifiable principal and an identifiable agent or set of agents.

In the democratic state, the principal is variously identified as "the people," "the republic," or even "the taxpayers." In any case, it is ascribed a coherent identity as some sort of social body. The agents of the state become all those who act on behalf of the state through any kind of decision-making institution. Thus, agents of the state may run the gamut from electors, through legislators and professional administrators, to elected chief executives. These agents act through decision-making "tribunals" (Tussman, 1960). These tribunals are normally organized around some functional division of labor (e.g., electoral, legislative, executive, judicial, etc.) and their actions are both internally and externally coordinated. Further, the actions of tribunals are both set forth and limited by an established set of basic rules and the laws flowing from those rules. The resultant organization can be termed variously "the state" or "the government."

This theory poses two serious problems, one common to all agency-based concepts and the other unique to employing the notion of agency in a pluralist democracy such as our own. The common problem is the familiar conundrum of vulnerability. However, in the public sector it increases in force geometrically because of the great power placed in the hands of public agencies. One may empower his or her plumber to fix the sink, but it is another matter to empower a second lieutenant to fire an atomic cannon in one's defense. Indeed, one can argue that much of the so-called legitimation crisis in modern American politics has roots in citizens' realistic fear that public agents can abuse individuals, groups, and one another while justifying themselves in terms of service to the public and its welfare.

As in the operation of any other form of social agency, the fiduciary and agent integrity norms (interpreted in terms of general norms of justice and beneficence) play the major role in alleviating the problem of mutual vulnerability in the republic. However in the political system these norms operate through constitutional and governmental institutions. For example, the fiduciary norms are translated into systems of "political interest articulation," elector and administrative accountability, and, most important, agent acculturation. The agent integrity norms become enforced not only through political and social acculturation, but in terms of civil service regulations, union contracts, and judicial appeals systems. The ultimate norms of justice and beneficence enter the democratic system through its basic constitution via the "equal protection" and "due process" provisions. These are then enforced not only through the judicial system, but also through legislation and administrative practice as well.

The second serious problem associated with employing agency as an ethical system in the public sector lies in the nature of pluralistic democracy. In such a pluralist political system, it is thought unrealistic to use the agency ethic as a standard of public service because it is felt impossible to identify a public principal with a coherent identity or interest (Aberbach & Rockman, 1988). Pluralists hold that modern, technologically complex societies are composed of diverse, specialized publics, with equally diverse interests (Bentley, 1908; Truman, 1955). It is held that the closest one can approach a coherent public principal or interest in such a society is the fleeting, ever changing accommodations made among contending interests in a political "group process."

The agent ethic is sorely compromised in such a political environment because agency depends upon the existence of a principal with a discernible interest for the agent to serve. Put another way, it is impossible for an agent to observe the fiduciary norms unless it can know the public principal and its interest. If the fiduciary norms are unenforcible in an authentic manner, then agency, as an ethical system, is rendered totally useless. While it is impossible to address this issue fully within the limits of this chapter, it is necessary to sketch some answer to this objection in order to present the agency ethic as a viable basis upon which to judge the legitimacy and worth of administrative leaders in this country.

The sum and substance of the argument made here to counter pluralist objections to agency is this: As long as the public principal is sought in the group process and the kaleidoscopic publics and public opinions associated with that process, the pluralists are right. No legitimate basis upon which to identify a unitary public principal or its interest will be found.

However, if attention is shifted to the basic political association and process that gives coherence to the pluralist political system itself, we may be able to find the principal and interest we seek. This argument will be pursued here briefly.

Even pluralists like Truman (1955) are forced to admit that what separates a pluralist system from a state of Hobbesean anarchy is that the pluralist system is based in a political association formed to conduct the business of the people to their common advantage. In short, the most pluralist of political systems must still rest on the assumptions of interdependence, common advantage (Tussman, 1960), and shared political rules of the game (Truman, 1955), which underlie any republic.

Thus, the republican association manages the interdependencies, promotes the common interests, and provides the political processes that make the pluralist political system possible. Take these away and one has political chaos rather than a political system. Even the pluralist polity must rest in a shared sense of association and community or it is more an open warfare than a civilized politics.

Pluralism, for all its seeming diversity, thus rests on the unity of association and a common civic undertaking—in short, the unity that characterizes the republic. Consequently, if one focuses on the common association that supports a civil and civilized pluralism, one will find in the republic both the identity of the principal and the principal's interest necessary to support an operational agency ethic.

Because the republic is the association upon which even the pluralist political system is based, it possesses three distinct advantages over diverse publics and interests as a candidate for the public principal. First, thinking of the republic as the principal in the political system focuses the agent's attention on what it really serves: the shared interest in managing the social interdependencies that form the *raison d'etre* of the republican association.

Second, focusing on the republic, the agency is directed to the region in which the pluralist political dialogue bears most directly on the public interest. Thus, the agent can see past the buzz and noise of pluralist politics, with its shifting policy agendas, "hot buttons," and "windows of opportunity" (Kingdon, 1984), to focus on the republic, its constitution, and, most important, the themes present in the continuing dialogue over its nature and purpose. As agents review and conduct this dialogue, they are afforded insights into the fundamental regime values (Rohr, 1978) which the republic seeks to realize as a political association. In turn, the agent's relatively easy access to this dialogue makes it possible to gain a working understanding of the basic values that ought to shape considerations of the republic's interest and welfare.

Third, the very nature of the republic suggests some criteria with which to judge how well an agent's actions serve this body. As noted, the republic is an association to manage the most important interdependencies among the members of a society. Therefore, an agent's success can be reckoned by how well it enables the members of society to recognize the true nature of their interdependencies, grasp the issues that these interdependencies raise, and facilitate the joint resolution of those issues in the political process.

Consequently, one need not abandon agency in a pluralist system. One need simply recognize that underlying pluralism, like any other political form, is a social system and an associational consensus that allows that system to operate successfully. It is this association and the consensus it represents that constitutes the real principal and interest to be served by the public agent.

Looking over the arguments just presented suggests the place of the agent relationship in government, particularly the government of the democratic republic. Basically, agency sets forth the role expectations placed upon those who would act for the republic. Like any role system, it links expectation through self-image to action (McCall & Simmons, 1978). In this way, the norms of agency present in society, and the constitutional limits upon which the American republic is based, are instilled in the personal and organizational images of its agents. Here the values inherent in both agency and constitution help shape the actions of the agent. Agency thus links the abstractions of ethics, constitution, self, and organization to the concrete daily practice of those public agents who serve us.

With the public sector theory of agency outlined, it is now possible to address the two major questions that lie at the heart of this chapter. First, what constitutes being a good public agent—that is to say a *steward* of the republic? Second, when public agents fail to exercise stewardship, what is the impact on the republic and its legitimacy?

One could simply say that stewardship is a form of agency in which the agent acts as well as possible in another's place. This definition of stewardship, of course, begs the question of exactly what is entailed in "acting as well as possible in another's place." However, using the theory of public agency just sketched, it may be possible to provide some plausible answers to this question.

The theory of agency suggests that excellence in agency is indicated by a resolution (or at least significant amelioration) of the vulnerability problem. From the agent's point of view, the resolution of the vulnerability problem turns on the degree to which the principal and third parties trust the agent. Therefore, stewardship can only be achieved by an agent after it is trusted by other parties in the relationship. It can now be seen why Mitchell and Scott (1987) insist that stewardship ". . . is based on the notion that administrators must display the virtues of trust and honorableness in order to be legitimate leaders" (p. 448). In short, an agent earns its popular designation as a steward and its legitimacy by deserving the trust of others.

Yet, how does an agent prove worthy of this trust? How does one practice agency so as to earn the trust of others in the agency relationship? Here, agency norms themselves suggest two key criteria. First, agents must consistently realize the fiduciary norms in practice by effectively achieving the welfare of the principal. Second, they must achieve the principal's welfare without significant injustice or harm to others. In other words, the steward is an agent who practices in such a way as to be both *effective* and *ethical*.

Since these criteria are often in conflict with one another, being a good steward is extremely difficult in practice. However, if an agent is to be deemed capable of exercising stewardship, it must be able to reconcile, or rise above, these conflicts in ways that it can justify publicly on sound ethical grounds. As important, the would-be public steward must practice its agency in those ways that will ensure that protection of individual rights is not seen as failure to honor its fiduciary obligation to the republic, or conversely, realization of the republic's welfare is not interpreted as despotism at the expense of the individual.

The essential element in realizing these goals lies in what can be called the *disciplines* of stewardship. These disciplines are well known to most public administrators because they encompass the familiar internal control of personal responsibility for one's actions and the external control of accountability to others for one's conduct. In fact, most modern administrative systems employ these concepts in combination with one another. By admitting them as the disciplines that form a good agent, one simply recognizes the dominant role agency plays in modern, administrative life.

The internal discipline of responsibility requires the agent to commit itself personally or organizationally not only to the fiduciary norms, but also to the limits placed on them by the general norms of justice and beneficence. In this way, the agent assumes the arduous obligation of avoiding both the misuse of the power it has been granted and misrepresentation of its capacity to serve the principal. Further, the agent obligates itself to discriminate between the principal's interest and welfare and the rights of others to justice and beneficence.

In terms of fostering the legitimacy of powerful public agents, the discipline of responsibility is crucial. The misuse of power for the agent's personal, professional, or organizational ends erodes the institutions of the republic. This is so because the misuse of power normally involves ignoring or circumventing the limits placed on the agent by republican institutions. Misrepresentation of agent capacity, whether undertaken to enhance the agent's political position or to please the ambitions of the principal itself, normally results in the failure to perform as promised. This failure, in turn, undermines faith in the public agent's credibility and competence. Consistent violations by individual public agents, even if done in the name of the republic's welfare, ultimately raise the average individual's sense of vulnerability to the great power he or she has placed in this entity and adversely affects the legitimacy of both the agents involved and the republican association.

Yet, to rely solely on the agent's sense of responsibility is to rely on the agent's self-control alone, a course of action that poses several problems. Even the best of internal resolves can falter in the face of the powerful political pressures faced by most public agents. Moreover, internal disciplines, such as responsibility are largely self-referential; that is, the agent sits as judge and jury on its own actions. Thus, the internal disciplines of responsibility must be joined by external disciplines of accountability.

The key to exercising this external control is to require that public agents exercise their powers only when, where, and how they are constitutionally and legally allowed to do so by the republic. In essence, this means requiring agents to work through (or in the case of organizations often to constitute) a legitimate tribunal of the republic. Among the constraints republican tribunals place on public agency are requirements that agents: (a) confine their actions to constitutionally and legislatively defined public purposes, (b) submit their decisions for review and possible disallowance by constitutionally superior tribunals, (c) observe constitutional guarantees of individual due process and equal protection in their practice, and (d) be fiscally and managerially accountable for their actions to the membership of the republic (Tussman, 1960).

Finally, it must be remembered that external disciplines of accountability, no matter how difficult they are to enforce in practice, give members of the republican association a sense of immediate control over the actions of their agents. This sense contributes immensely to lessen the average individual's feeling of vulnerability to the agents he or she has empowered and accordingly increases the legitimacy of both agents and state in the eyes of the individual.

Having reviewed what constitutes the practice of stewardship, now let us turn to the question of what happens to the republic when its agents fail to achieve a consistent stewardship of its affairs. This failure behaves somewhat like a chain reaction or, perhaps more accurately, a self-enforcing cycle. It starts when agents fail to exercise the disciplines that promote stewardship. That is, they ignore the norms of agency and circumvent the tribunals of the republic.

These actions, if consistent enough, undermine the faith in the agent's competence, vision, and honesty. In short, the agent's credibility is destroyed. Failed credibility leads to failed trust, whether it is warranted by the agent's impotence or avarice.

As the credibility of public agents declines by virtue of their failures to conduct the *res publica*, either honestly or successfully, the vulnerability problem emerges with a vengeance. Now those who act as members of the political association fear the very individuals and organizations they have delegated to act as their agents. Honest agents come to fear dishonest ones and competent agents are vilified by incompetent ones (for example, Warren Hastings).

At length, the republic becomes impotent, or worse yet, at war against itself. It either cannot act because it lacks effective agents, or it acts through agents so self-serving that every action they take on the republic's behalf only serves to destroy the association in whose name it is taken.

At first, these events may only erode confidence in the agents themselves. However, because the republic cannot act for itself the failure of its agents is seen eventually as the failure of republican institutions (Mitchell & Scott, 1987; Lipset & Schneider, 1983). Put differently, a legitimacy crisis for the agents of the republic, if unchecked, becomes a legitimacy crisis for the republic itself.

STEWARDSHIP AND PUBLIC ADMINISTRATION

With the review of public agency and the concept of stewardship complete, it is now possible to return to the thesis of this chapter, that stewardship must be the foundational element in the image of the public administrator if public administration hopes to be regarded as a legitimate part of the American political system. The previous sections of this chapter have attempted to show that the exercise of stewardship is the fundamental factor in supporting the legitimacy of the public agent and the republic it serves. This is because stewardship signifies the achievement of both effectiveness and ethicality on the part of the agent and it is these twin elements that undergird both the agent's and the republic's legitimacy in the eyes of the public (Lipset & Schneider, 1983; Mitchell & Scott, 1987).

It was argued that the failure of stewardship eventually brings about the failure of the republic itself. Since the republican association can only act through its agents, their failure to exercise stewardship becomes literally the republic's failure to act effectively or ethically.

Since stewardship rests on observing the norms and disciplines of agency, images of public administrators that ignore or obscure these norms and disciplines rightly occasion public suspicion. Indeed, it often appears that those who advocate such images actually seek to avoid the self-sacrifice, responsibility, and accountability associated with the exercise of stewardship and by doing so absolve themselves of the twin burdens of effectiveness and ethicality. As a result, the legitimacy of public administration as an element in the political system is seriously undermined.

The imagery used to conceptualize public administration and public administrators in this volume is undoubtedly rich, ranging from "Platonic Guardians" through "balance wheels" to "information processors." However, any of these images that ignores agency and stewardship in the American setting does so at its own risk, or more properly, the risk of its legitimacy. Consequently, as we judge the usefulness and validity of each image, we could do worse than to apply the criteria of good agency—stewardship—to the images we evaluate.

NOTES

1. Throughout this chapter, justice and beneficence will be used as the two norms upon which ethical practice and the moral perspective rests. For a justification of this approach, see Frankena (1973, particularly Chap. III).

2. This section of the chapter draws heavily on several bodies of literature. First, since the concept is drawn from civil law, particularly commercial law, it is useful to review the entry "Agency" in *3 American Jurisprudence* (Editors, 1986). Compare this with the use of "agency" in the public sector in *63A American Jurisprudence*, "Public Officers and Employees" (Editors, 1984). Useful volumes of commentary on commercial agency are Meecham (1914) and Ferson (1954). The history of agency can be found in several sources: Holmes (1920); Pollock and Maitland (1968); McConnell (1966); and Editors, "Agency", in *Encyclopedia Britannica Macropaedia* (1986).

The concept of agency has been broadened in recent years by applying it to economics, business, administration, and political science. See Ross (1973); Jenson and Meckling (1976); Pratt and Zeckhauser (1984); Mitnick (1975, 1984a, 1984b); and Moe (1984). The most comprehensive bibliographical essay on the development of agency theory in the social sciences known to the author is found in Mitnick (1984a).

3. For a full discussion and justification of Tussman's association theory of the state see Tussman (1960, Chap. 1). An alternative view of the associated or contract-based state is offered by Rawls (1971).

REFERENCES

Aberbach, J.D. & Rockman, B.A. (1988, March/April). Mandates and mandarins? Control and discretion in the modern administrative state. *Public Administration Review, 48*, 606-612.

Arrow, K. (1984). The economics of agency. In J.W. Pratt & R.J. Zeckhauser (Eds.), *Principals and agents: The structure of business.* Boston: Harvard Business School Press.

Bentley, A.F. (1908). *The process of government.* Chicago: University of Chicago Press.

Editors. (1986). Agency. In *Encyclopedia britannica macropaedia* (Vol. 1, 15th ed.) (pp. 145-146). Chicago: Encyclopedia Britannica.

Editors. (1986). Agency. In *3 American jurisprudence* (2nd ed.) (pp. 495-892). Rochester, NY: Lawyers Co-operative.

Editors. (1984). Public officers and employees. In *63A American jurisprudence* (2nd ed., sect. 7, p. 670; section 13, p. 667). Rochester, NY: Lawyers Co-operative.

Ferson, M. (1954). *Principles of agency.* Brooklyn: Foundation Press.

Fiorina, M.P. (1983, March/April). Flagellating the federal bureaucracy. *Society, 20*, 66-73.

Fishkin, J.S. (1982). *The limits of obligation.* New Haven: Yale University Press.

Frankena, W.K. (1973). *Ethics* (2nd ed.). Englewood Cliffs, NJ: Prentice-Hall.

Frankena, W.K. (1980). *Thinking about mortality.* Ann Arbor: University of Michigan Press.

Goodpaster, K.E., Matthews, J.R., & Matthews, J.B. (1982, January/February). Can a corporation have a conscience? *Harvard Business Review, 60*, 132-141.

Hart, H.L.A. (1967). Are there any natural rights? In A. Quinton (Ed.), *Political philosophy.* Oxford: Oxford University Press.

Holmes, O.W. (1920). Agency. In *Oliver Wendall Holmes: Collected papers.* New York: Harcourt, Brace.

Jenson, M.C., & Meckling, W.H. (1976, October). Theory of the firm: Managerial behavior, agency costs and ownership structure. In J.W. Pratt & R.J. Zeckhauser (Eds.), *Journal of Financial Economics, 3*, 305-360.

Kaufman, H. (1981, January/February). Fear of bureaucracy: A raging pandemic. *Public Administration Review, 41*, 1-9.

Kingdom, J.W. (1984). *Agendas, alternatives and public policies.* Boston: Little, Brown.

Ladd, J. (1970, October). Mortality and the ideal of rationality in formal organizations. *The Monist, 54*, 488-516.

Lipset, S.M., & Schneider, W. (1983). *The confidence gap: Business, labor and govern-ment*. New York: Free Press.

McCall, G.J., & Simmons, J.L. (1978). *Identities and interactions: An examination of human associations in everyday life* (rev. ed.). New York: Free Press.

McConnell, J.P. (1966). *Law and business patterns and issues of commercial law*. New York: Macmillan.

Meecham, F.R. (1914). *A treatise of the law of agency* (Vol. 1). Chicago: Callaghan.

Mitchell, T.R., & Scott, W.G. (1987, November/December). Leadership failures, the distrusting public and prospects of the administrative state. *Public Administration Review, 47*, 445-452.

Mitnick, B. (1975). *The theory of agency: The fiduciary norm*. Paper prepared for the 1975 annual meeting of the American Sociological Association, San Francisco.

Mitnick, B. (1984a). *Agency problems and political institutions*. Paper prepared for the 1984 annual research conference of the Association for Public Policy Analysis and Management, New Orleans.

Mitnick, B. (1984b). *The bureaucrat as an agent*. Paper prepared for the 1984 Annual Meeting of the American Political Science Association, Washington, DC.

Moe, T.M. (1984). The new economics of organization. *American Journal of Political Science, 28*, 739-777.

Nelson, W.N. (1974). Special rights, general rights and social justice. *Philosophy and Public Affairs, 3*, 410-430.

Pitkin, H.F. (1967). *The concept of representation*. Berkeley: University of California Press.

Pollock, F. & Maitland, F.W. (1968). *The history of English law before the time of Edward I* (2nd rev., Vol. II). Cambridge, U.K.: Cambridge University Press.

Pratt, J.W., & Zeckhauser, R.J. (1985). *Principals and agents: The structure of business*. Boston: Harvard Business School Press.

Rawls, J. (1971). *A theory of justice*. Cambridge, MA: Harvard University Press.

Rohr, J. (1978). *Ethics for bureaucrats: An essay on law and values*. New York: Marcel Dekker.

Ross, S.A. (1973, May). The economic theory of agency: The principal's problem. *American Economic Review, 62*, 134-139.

Simon, H.A. (1976). *Administrative behavior: A study in decisionmaking processes in administrative organizations* (3rd ed.). New York: Free Press.

Smircich, L. (1983a). Concepts of culture and organizational analysis. *Administrative Science Quarterly, 28*, 339-358.

Smircich, L. (1983b). Studying organizations as cultures. In G. Morgan (Ed.), *Beyond method: Strategies for social science research* (pp. 160-172). Beverly Hills, CA: Sage.

Truman, D.B. (1955). *The government process: Political interests and public opinion*. New York: Knopf.

Tussman, J. (1960). *Obligation and the body politic*. New York: Oxford University Press.

Wamsley, G. Goodsell, C.T., Rohr, J.A., Stivers, C.M., White, O.F., & Wolfe, J.E. The public administration and the governance process: Refocusing the dialogue. In R.C. Chandler (Ed.), *A centennial history of the American administrative state* (pp. 291-320). New York: Free Press.

5

Images of Administrative Reason and Rationality: The Recovery of Practical Discourse

JAY D. WHITE

Since scientific management and bureaucratic organization theory were introduced, the rationalization of administration has been a persistent concern of theorists and practitioners alike. Two assumptions have fueled this concern. One is that improvements in administrative thought and action can lead to improvements in administrative processes, especially decision making. The other is that there is no better way to improve administrative thought and action than to make them more rational.

Although several definitions of *rationality* exist for public administration (Dunn, 1981), most of them are related to the theory of instrumental reason. The theory says that thought is rational to the extent that it follows the rules of deductive inference to calculate the correct means to a given end, and that action is rational to the extent that it follows a prescribed set of rules to coordinate means to a given end (Horkheimer, 1974). This image of reason and rationality seems appropriate for administrators because it typifies the act of getting things done.

Unfortunately, the instrumental image fails to account for other modes of thought and action involved in identifying and choosing means and ends. It ignores the fact that people participate in the determination of the ends they seek and the means they employ to achieve them. The instrumental image treats means and ends as being given to the decision maker, without the decision maker becoming involved in their development. Thus this image of administrative reason and rationality fails to explain the logic of envisioning means and ends and the rational basis for choosing them.

Decisions about what ends to pursue and what means to use are matters of political, legal, and moral judgment that fall in the realm of practical discourse. Practical discourse involves discussion, debate, deliberation, and argumentation over what is true or false, good or bad, right or wrong, and what should be desired. Administrators regularly engage in practical discourse. Unfortunately, they are not guided by an understanding of the type of reasoning involved in such discourse or by an understanding of the criteria for judging the rationality of practical thought and action. The bulk of administrative theory treats practical thought and action as being intuitive or subjective, and therefore non-cognitive, nondescribable, or nonrational. Consequently, little attention is paid to the process of determining means and ends in the context of practical discourse. Little is known about the logic of the normative, political, and moral judgments that administrators make.

Fortunately there are alternative theories of reason and rationality that account for the determination of means and ends. Interpretive reasoning describes the type of thought and action involved in understanding what means and ends are available to a decision maker. The rationality of interpretive reasoning depends upon the achievement of a successful dialogue among decision makers. Critical reasoning describes the type of thought and action required to make a choice among competing means and ends. The rationality of critical reasoning depends upon whether or not a chosen course of action leads to opportunities for growth and development. Both theories can be derived from hermeneutics, legal theory, and critical theory. If the logic of interpretive and critical reason developed in these philosophical traditions is accepted, practical discourse can be recovered as a legitimate ground for efficient, effective, and ethical administration.

This chapter points out the structural limits of the rational model as a mode of instrumental reason. Then, by way of legal theory, hermeneutics, and critical theory, an outline of a more comprehensive image of administrative reason and rationality is provided. This image recovers the importance of practical discourse in administration and gives legitimacy to administrative decisions and actions based on interpretation and critique.

THE STRUCTURAL LIMITS OF THE RATIONAL MODEL

Administrative decision making is popularly described by the rational model of decision making. It says that when faced with a problem, the decision maker should: (a) identify the goals, values, or objectives that will guide the decision; (b) rank order them according to their importance; (c) identify the alternative courses of action for dealing with the problem and the consequences of each; (d) weigh the costs and benefits of each alternative and its consequences; and (e) choose the alternative that maximizes the attainment of the appropriate goal, value, or objective (adapted from Anderson, 1979). Critics have pointed out that the comprehensive search process required by this model is often impractical, impossible, or undesirable (Simon, 1957; Lindblom, 1959; Etzioni, 1967), but in all alternative formulations, the inherent means-ends logic of thought and action remains the same.

The rational model is common in economics, political science, administrative theory, organization theory, and organizational behavior. Its intellectual origins are found in Aristotle's syllogism, Hobbes's definition of "modern reason" as the "reckoning of consequences" (1974), the classical economists' model of "economic man," Dewey's discussion of *How We Think* (1910), and Simon's phases of decision making (1965). The rational model permeates our bureaucratic form of social organization, dominates our economic system, and characterizes models of political behavior. It is also the "proper" mode of reasoning frequently taught in courses on policy-making, policy analysis, program evaluation, budgeting, financial management, organization theory, and organization behavior.

The rational model is a form of instrumental reasoning. It focuses on the coordination of means to ends or the following of rules to achieve ends. It involves both thought and action. The hallmark of instrumental thinking is the ability to deductively calculate the correct means to an end, with "correct" usually meaning the most efficient or effective way of accomplishing something. The hallmark of instrumental action is the ability to follow a prescribed set of rules or procedures to bring about an end. The rationality of instrumental thinking is determined by whether or not the correct means are identified. The rationality of instrumental action is determined by whether or not the correct end is actually achieved.

Argyris (1973) noted that the rational model is limited in its ability to capture a broad range of administrative reality. It does not account for emotional behaviors that are not immediately goal directed for either the individual or the organization, for example, psychological withdrawal or defensiveness. Such behavior does take place in organizations, but it is considered irrelevant even though it may contribute to or detract from individual development and organizational performance. Emotional behavior is irrelevant because it does not fit the rational structure of the model. Simon (1973) argued against Argyris that such behavior is dealt with by theories of motivation. By implication such theories augment the rational model, but they are not actually a part of the model itself.

There is a more fundamental limitation of the rational model. It does not explain the logic of how decision makers recognize problems, identify goals and alternatives, and choose among differing goals and alternatives. There is no philosophical, as opposed to behavioral, explanation of how the decision maker does this. As a result much of administrative thought and action is left unexplained from a philosophical perspective.

The rational model does not explain this broader range of administrative thought and action because it is derived from Aristotle's syllogism. The syllogism takes the following logical form: The end to be sought is X; actions of Y sort tend to achieve X; Z is an action of Y sort; therefore if X is desired then Z should be done. If the steps in the rational model of decision making are simplified, they reduce to a major premise (a problem to be solved), a minor premise (an action to solve the problem), and a conclusion (an injunction to act). The syllogism will tell you what course of action is deductively correct, but it will not tell you if your actions are right because the value statements contained in it may be wrong or inappropriate. In other words, there is nothing within the logical structure of the syllogism to tell a decision maker what end to value and what alternative has consequences to value over those of other alternatives. These judgments must be made outside the syllogism, based on some other mode of reasoning. Because the logical structure of the rational model is derived from the syllogism it cannot, by itself, tell the decision maker what end to seek or which means to choose. Thus the very structure of the rational model limits the rationality of administrative decision making.

Both Argyris (1982, 1985) and Simon (1983) have recognized the importance of reasoning in administrative situations, but they have had difficulty breaking away from a scientific perspective to envision alternative forms of rational thought and action. Simon still clings to instrumental thought and action, but speaks of reason in terms of behavioral images of creativity and intuition. Argyris has tried to describe non-instrumental thought and action in psychological terms.

Simon was aware that other modes of thought and action are involved in determining means and ends. In his response to Argyris he gave reason a prominent place in the design of the future. He said:

> In my Appollonian world, reason is the handmaiden of freedom and of creativity. It is the instrument that enables me to have peak experiences unimaginable to my cat or my dog. It is the instrument that enables me to dream and design. It is the instrument that enables me and my fellow men to create environments and societies that can satisfy our basic needs, so that all of us—and not just a few—can experience some of the deeper pleasures of sense and mind. And because we depend so heavily upon reason to create and maintain a humane world, we see the need to understand reason better—to construct a tested theory of reasoning man (1973, p. 352).

This appeal to reason seems misplaced because Simon's tested theory of reasoning man is limited to instrumental choice.

Simon's full image of reason is not captured in the rational model. There is nothing within the rational model that allows for peak experiences, dreams, and the pleasures of sense and mind. Simon imagined a much broader conception of reason than the mere coordination of means and ends. Of particular importance are efforts by people to make sense of their organizational environment and to derive meaning about their lives. Simon sensed this when he claimed that: "Reason plays a dual role, then, in social institutions. It is a tool that enables those institutions to act effectively toward goals. And it is also the instrument of thought through which Man sees the world and his own life, understands them, and invests them with meaning" (1973, p. 353). Calling reason an instrument and a tool retains the image of instrumental reason, but the other role for reason that Simon envisions is clearly an interpretive and critical task requiring practical discourse.

Simon has attempted to sort out the role of reason in *Reason in Human Affairs* (1982). He says: "We see that reason is wholly instrumental. It cannot tell us where to go; at best it can tell us how to get there. It is a gun for hire that can be employed in the service of whatever goals we have, good or bad" (1983, pp. 7-8). He concedes that there is something called the intuitive model of reasoning which "postulates that a great deal of human thinking, and a great deal of the success of human beings in arriving at correct decisions, is due to the fact that they have good intuition or good judgment" (1983, pp. 23-24). But true to his attachment to scientific inquiry, he maintains that the intuitive model of reasoning is "in fact a component of the behavioral model" (1983, p. 35). For Simon, reason is not some philosophical view of human mental capabilities but a behavioral reality, even though that reality is predicated on a philosophical image of reason and rationality. By sticking to his behavioral vision, Simon fails to see that the logic of other modes of reason, not necessarily intuitive reason, can be articulated.

Argyris has developed such concepts as Model I and Model II behavior, double-looped learning, organizational learning, and reflexivity (Argyris, 1982; Argyris & Schon, 1978). These concepts are an extension of his concern with noninstrumental modes of behavior such as spontaneity, feelings, intuition, creativity, sensitivity, defensiveness, openness, self-development, and competence acquisition. He believes that by giving an account of how these human qualities operate in organizational settings, they may be legitimized as appropriate forms of behavior even though they are not immediately goal directed or instrumental. He also believes that there are some similarities between his theories and the philosophical traditions of hermeneutics and critical theory but prefers to continue the development of his theories at the level of psychology (see Argyris, Putnam, & Smith, 1985).

Reason can be described and explained in behavioral and psychological terms as Simon, Argyris, and others do. But reason can also be described and explained philosophically as interpretive and critical modes of thought and action. The philosophical perspective is more fundamental because it provides the logical models of thought and action upon which to develop behavioral and psychological theories. Researchers wedded to positivism have ignored the philosophical perspective. This is ironic because the logical model upon which their theories are based is a philosophical image of instrumental reason. Unfortunately that image is limited in its ability to describe and explain a broader range of rational thought and action. A logical reconstruction of interpretation and critique can broaden the administrative image of reason and rationality. One avenue is through the logic of legal reasoning.

LEGAL REASONING

The theory of legal reasoning describes the logical processes lawyers and judges use to reach decisions about the facts of a case, the meaning of relevant laws and the applicability of laws to the facts at hand. The logic of legal reasoning provides a stepping-stone to interpretive and critical reasoning because legal reasoning is an exemplary case of both.

Levi (1949) described the logic of legal interpretation as reasoning by example, or from case to case. "It is a three-step process described by the doctrine of precedent in which a proposition descriptive of the first case is made into a rule of law and then applied to a next similar situation. The steps are these: similarity seen between cases; next the rule of law inherent in the first case is announced; then the rule of law is made applicable to the second case" (pp. 1-2). This three-step process shows that reasoning by example is referential and circular rather than linear as in instrumental syllogism.

The process of legal reasoning is the ability to find similarity and difference among the facts of the case and the meaning of relevant law. Cardozo (1960) describes such reasoning as "a process of search, comparison, and little more" in which: "Some judges seldom get beyond that process in any case. Their notion of their duty is to match the colors of the case at hand against the colors of many sample cases spread out upon their desk. The sample nearest in shade supplies the applicable rule" (p. 20). The process of searching, comparing, and matching colors depicts interpretive reasoning. The decision to choose one statement of facts over another or to apply a rule of the law to the case at hand involves critical reasoning.

Administrators are in the same place as lawyers and judges. They go beyond the limits of instrumental reasoning to employ reasoning by example, or interpretation to determine what ends should be sought and what actions should be taken. Like lawyers and judges they are in the business of making choices about what is true or false, good or bad. Experience suggests this is done on the basis of reasoning by example. Since administrators and judges (or lawyers) are human beings, there is no a priori reason to believe that their reasoning processes are any different; only the contexts differ.

Administrators reason by example to make sense of what is going on. For example, suppose an experienced personnel director is faced with a probationary employee who has not performed to expectations. How does the personnel director decide what to do about the employee? The director compares this situation to previous situations as a guide to decision making. In effect, he (or she) asks and answers the following questions: What are the facts of this situation? Are they similar to other situations? What was done in those situations? Should the same thing be done in this situation?

Suppose the probationary employee claims he is going through a divorce, the emotional stain of which is effecting his work, and that he is now seeking counseling and hopes it will help his job performance. He asks for an extension of his probationary appointment. The director may first want to determine if these statements are true. Then he may reflect on previous situations to see what was done in the past. Suppose he recalls a situation in which an employee was placed on probation because a drinking problem was interfering with job performance. The employee sought help from AA, is now performing up to expectation, and is off probation. Are the facts of the situation similar enough to extend the present employee's probationary period to be both fair to the employee and to help preserve a potentially useful employee? The director must decide if the precedent for the prior situation should be employed in the current situation.

Organizations have policies to handle decisions. They function in the same way as laws. In the example, the personnel director could turn to the policy and procedures manual to interpret the meaning of a relevant policy statement and its applicability to the present situation. Suppose the policy stated that extensions of probationary periods can be given under conditions of extreme but temporary personal hardship that affect an employee's performance. The director must now decide if this policy applies to the current situation. Is a divorce an extreme but temporary personal hardship? The director will answer this policy question according to his own beliefs and values just as judges would interpret the law according to their own beliefs and values.

This example can be extended into administrative practice by recognizing that organizational policies, procedures, and rules are not conceptually different from formal laws. Fundamentally, they are all statements about what people should or should not do. Administrators are called upon to interpret policies in making decisions about what ends should be sought and what means should be chosen. Like judges, administrators interpret the intent of those who established a policy. They look to the history of the policy to determine its purpose and scope. Then they apply their interpretation of the policy to the situation to see if it fits or, to paraphrase Cardozo, to see if the colors match. If they do, a choice will be made. If they don't, the administrator may go in search of a different interpretation of the policy or perhaps a different interpretation of how the policy was applied in a previous situation.

Administrators determine the facts of a situation, interpret the meaning of policies and procedures as well as past events or cases, and apply those interpretations to the facts at hand. They reason like lawyers and judges. They engage in a similar, if not identical, form of the interpretive and critical reasoning that have traditionally been associated with practical discourse.

INTERPRETIVE AND CRITICAL REASONING

The logic of interpretive and critical reasoning and rationality can be briefly reconstructed from the hermeneutics of Gadamer, Ricoeur and others; the critical theory of Marcuse and Habermas; and Fay's efforts to develop a critical social science based on the analytical philosophy of language.

Interpretive reason is the referential process of coming to understand the ends and rules of thought and action. It is the process by which we make sense of the world around us; by which we come to understand and relate to the shared norms, rules, meanings, and expectations that constitute the fabric of our social existence. We are constantly interpreting the events and objects we encounter on a daily basis, even though we may not be self-consciously aware of the special type of thought and action that this requires. The need for interpretation arises when we encounter something we do not understand, something that is unfamiliar to us, something that is out of the ordinary, or something that is contrary to what we believe to be true or good.

The structure of interpretive reasoning is expressed by the hermeneutical circle which describes the rational process of understanding. According to Palmer (1969) "Understanding is basically a referential operation: we understand something by comparing it to something we already know." It is a circular process in which "The circle as a whole defines the individual part, and the parts together form the circle" (p. 87). Kisiel explains:

When we read a book or view an abstract painting, a survey of some of the parts gives us an initial sense of what the whole is about, and this anticipation of the whole in turn determines the significance of the parts.

In and through this shifting emphasis between parts and whole, we gradually develop an interpretation of the whole in terms of its parts, and of the parts in terms of the whole. (p. 276)

Thus interpretation involves a mediation between universals and particulars, which ultimately leads to understanding upon which action takes place.

Like the rational model and instrumental reasoning, the hermeneutical circle is a logical reconstruction, one that illustrates the nature of reasoned thought and action that goes into understanding something. In contrast to the instrumental image that depicts reason as being deductive and linear, the hermeneutical circle depicts interpretive reason as being referential and circular. It is much closer to the actual situation of thinking than an instrumental deduction (Kisiel, 1972, p. 276).

The connection between legal reasoning and interpretation has been noted by hermeneutic theorists. Ricoeur (1971) considers H.L.A. Hart's account of the logic of legal reasoning a paradigmatic statement of the circle of interpretation. Gadamer considers legal judgment to be an exemplary case of hermeneutical interpretation (1975, p. 297). Bernstein (1983) agrees with Gadamer that: "the judge does not simply 'apply' fixed, determinate laws to particular situations. Rather the judge must interpret and appropriate precedents and law to each new, particular situation. It is by virtue of such considered judgment that the meaning of the law and the meaning of the particular case are codetermined" (pp. 147-148). The same can be said of administrators. They do not simply apply organizational policies to existing situations, but rather interpret the meaning of policies in light of interpretations of existing and possibly future situations. Thus the meaning of policy and the meaning of a particular situation are codetermined in the referential process of interpretation.

In the previous example, the personnel director had to interpret the meaning of organizational policy on extending probationary periods and the meaning of the situation. The policy stated that extensions will be given under extreme but temporary personal hardships that affect an employee's performance. The director's interpretive task is to determine the meaning of "extreme but temporary hardships." Interpretation is not done in a vacuum. From experience, the director has his own sense of what the words *extreme*, *temporary*, and *hardship* mean independently and when they are strung together. But interpretation does not stop with a generalized understanding of the meaning of the policy.

It proceeds to a consideration of the particular situation which has its own local means in the words *divorce, emotional strain, counseling,* and *job performance.* The director looks for a match between the meaning of the policy and the meaning of the situation. Logically, there is a codetermination of meaning in the decision to grant or deny the extension.

Reasoning by example to make legal decisions is not limited to interpretation. Indeed, the codetermination of meaning requires a choice among conflicting interpretations. The legal process involves making critical judgments of fact and value. Legal reasoning embodies "the ways in which lawyers and judges combine their beliefs about facts, events, and conditions in the world (beliefs about the actuality of things) with their moral beliefs and values (beliefs about right and wrong) to make legal choices" (Carter, 1979, p. 4). Such critical choices focus on conflicting interpretations of the facts of a case and the meaning of a relevant law. Either an event happened or it did not. Either a fact is relevant or it is not. One interpretation of the law will always be found to be better than another, even if after the choice has been made, a third and better interpretation may be found. The choice of one interpretation over another is the critical element in legal reasoning as well as administrative reasoning.

As Marcuse (1960) put it, critical reasoning is "the power of negative thinking," which is inherently dialectical (p. vii). It involves recognizing that things are not what they appear to be and must therefore be understood differently, and recognizing that things are not what they ought to be and must therefore be changed for the good of those involved. Critical reasoning is concerned with both truth and goodness. Critique occurs at the moment of misunderstanding and signals the needs for interpretation. It also occurs at the moment of understanding when that which is understood is either accepted or rejected as being true or false, good or bad. Critique makes interpretive reasoning dialectical.

The logical structure of critical reasoning is the process of self-reflection: the ability to see one's self in relation to one's situation or point of attention, be it a material object, another person, or a concept. "It is the special quality of being oriented toward something and also being aware of one's self in that orientation" (Denhardt & White, 1982, p. 166). This self-reflective turn allows one to judge the truth or desirability of one's relationship to things or events in one's environment, and may compel one to act in ways to change that relationship.

The critical aspect of the personnel director's decision is to choose one interpretation of the policy and/or the facts of the situation over another. Thus the director must decide if the employee is telling the truth and whether the policy regarding the extension of probationary periods applies to the situation. Making this decision is a self-reflective process expressed by the question: "Where do I stand in relation to what the employee is telling me?" A mental image is formed in which the director sees himself in relationship to the employee, against a background defined by his knowledge of the situation and experience with similar and different situations. The director's job is to either maintain this relationship by affirming its truth (or goodness) or to negate the relationship by claiming it to be false (or bad). The director must critique the situation to decide what to believe, what to value, and what actions to take based on those beliefs and values. In critical reasoning, this self-reflective turn is required to either accept or reject the relationship. Without critical self-reflection it would be impossible to choose among differing interpretations.

PRACTICAL DISCOURSE

Instrumental, interpretive, and critical reasoning require a domain of practical discourse—the opportunity to discuss and determine collectively the efficacy of relevant beliefs, values, means, and ends. Instrumental reasoning takes place within a highly restricted domain of discourse because the means and ends are treated as given to the decision maker. Discussion is limited to the choice of the best means to a given end. Interpretive and critical reasoning require a wider domain of discourse because these modes of reason are directed at what one should believe and value and at what ends should be sought and what means are available. The idea of practical discourse is ancient, but it has relevance today in spite of fears that a growing technocratic consciousness has robbed us of our ability to reason about normative, political, and moral questions (Marcuse, 1964; Habermas, 1970).

Practical discourse involves dialogue among decision makers about the rightness of the ends to be sought and the means to achieve them. Dialogue involves communication, argumentation, deliberation, persuasion, and choice. The goal of practical discourse is the attainment of a mutual understanding of peoples' beliefs and values. Mutual understanding does not necessarily mean accepting another person's beliefs and values, but rather understanding what those beliefs and values are and why others hold them, and vice versa.

There is fear that the rationalization of administration and society will lead to the inability to engage in practical discourse and to make normative, political, and moral judgments. Gadamer tells us:

> In a scientific culture such as ours the fields of *techne* and art are much more expanded. Thus the fields of mastering means to pre-given ends have been rendered even more monological and controllable. The crucial change is that practical wisdom can no longer be promoted by personal contact and the mutual exchange of views among citizens. Not only has craftsmanship been replaced by industrial work; many forms of our daily life are technologically organized so that they no longer require personal decision. In modern technological society public opinion itself has in a new and really decisive way become the object of very complicated techniques—and this, I think is the main problem facing our civilization. (1975a, p. 313)

Marcuse (1964) and Habermas (1970) have expressed similar concerns. They fear a society in which decision making is reduced to the selection of means to given ends and a population that is unable to address the truth or goodness of the means and ends. This can happen when we blindly adhere to the rational model of administrative decision making.

By itself, instrumental reasoning is not the culprit. Without it nothing would get done. The condition that Gadamer, Marcuse, and Habermas fear is not the result of instrumental reasoning, but rather the inability to engage in interpretive and critical reasoning, and that occurs when the domain of practical discourse is severely narrowed. Interpretive and critical reasoning provide for the identification and choice of means and ends. These modes of reasoning presuppose the existence of a domain of practical discourse in which the right means and ends can be selected.

The ability to say that the right means and ends have been selected is intimately tied to practical discourse. The rationality of interpretive reason is predicated on achieving a successful dialogue among decision makers in which a mutual understanding of means and ends is achieved. Agreement about what ends to pursue and what means to use to achieve them is not always possible, but a mutual understanding of what those means and ends are can be achieved if dialogue occurs. Dialogue is the ideal regulative concept to judge the rationality of interpretive reason.

The rationality of critical thought and action depends upon whether or not a chosen end and course of action lead to opportunities for growth and development. Critical reason also depends on dialogue. Self-reflection presupposes the ability to engage in discourse with others and with oneself to determine if certain norms, rules, values, policies, laws, or beliefs are restricting the freedom of individuals to grow and develop. We cannot choose to change our situation if we find it oppressive unless we first come to an understanding of our situation. Fay (1975) recognizes this when he states that the goal of a critical social science is "to enlighten the social actors so that, coming to see themselves and their social situation in a new way, they themselves can decide to alter the conditions they find repressive" (p. 103). The enlightenment of actors can only take place within a domain of practical discourse over the efficacy of the situation. Through self-reflection and dialogue, critique is rational if the actors come to an understanding that their situation is untenable and take action to change it. This is the regulative ideal for the rationality of critical reason.

IMPLICATIONS

Recognizing the importance of practical discourse and the role of interpretive and critical reasoning in administration has implications for research and education.

Researchers no longer have to rely solely upon the rational man model of instrumental decision making to build theories of administrative action. The logic of interpretive and critical reasoning offers equally useful models for the analysis of administrative decision making and the development of alternative theories of administrative action. As in the case of the rational model, these models can be used to develop a body of knowledge about how administrators interpret situations and make critical judgments of fact and value. They also articulate modes of thought and action that are more fundamental to administration than are instrumental reason and rationality.

Interpretive and critical reason can also stand as models for interpretive and critical research (White, 1986). A researcher can use the model of an administrator as an interpreter to answer questions such as: How does the administrator interpret his or her situation? What are his or her beliefs about the situation? What norms, values, or socially shared meanings are important to the administrator and how do they influence his or her actions? What are the symbolic forms—words, images, symbols, institutions—that administrators use to represent themselves to one another? These are only some of the questions that a researcher would ask to interpret administrative action.

Some of the recent research into organizational cultures implicitly assumes an interpretive model both of research and of the subjects being studied (Allaire & Firsirotu, 1984). This is particularly true in the case of studies that focus on the meaning of stories, symbols, and myths (Smith & Simmons, 1983), and studies that self-consciously use a semiotic approach (Barley, 1983) or fashion their methodology after the work of the noted anthropologist Geertz (1973). Geertz refers to the logic of cultural interpretation as "a continuous dialectical tacking between the most local of local detail and the most global of global structure in such a way as to bring both into view simultaneously," and claims that in "hopping back and forth between the whole conceived through the parts [that] actualize it and the parts conceived through the whole [that] motivates them, we seek to turn them, by a sort of intellectual perpetual motion, into explications of one another" (p. 239). This is an accurate description of the logic of interpretive studies of organizational culture. It is also analogous to Cardozo's (1960) discussion of legal interpretation as the matching of colors and Levi's (1949) three-step process.

True critical reasoning is more difficult to find in administrative research. There are some explicit examples in organization theory and behavior (e.g., Denhardt, 1981, 1984; Diamond, 1984; LaBier, 1983; Levinson, 1981; and Maccoby, 1976) as well as in policy analysis, planning, and public administration (e.g., Forester, 1982a, 1982b, 1984). The logic of critical reasoning is implicit in other administrative studies. Argyris's and Schon's (1978) theory of organizational learning describes how organizational actors can, if given the opportunity, change the norms and values that determine their behavior through double-looped learning that is analogous to critical self-reflection. As the logic of critical reason acquires more legitimacy, more critical research may follow.

Educators face issues of how to develop students' abilities for interpretive and critical reasoning. One possibility is to require a law course to learn how to reason by example, but there is no guarantee that any particular course will teach legal reasons. Another is to emphasize the case method of instruction. This might work well if the cases allow the students to compare the case at hand with prior cases to develop their ability to reason by example—to employ interpretation and critique. Learning how to improve interpretive and critical reasoning capabilities is a challenge.

Conventional teaching practices conform to the logic of instrumental reason. Weber (1958) observed that modern education takes on the rational bureaucratic structure of domination. This is evident in some typical teaching conditions and practices. Class sizes are large and getting larger. There may be as many as 50 students in a graduate course, maybe more in an undergraduate course. Lecturing is usually the primary mode of instruction. Certainly seminar discussions are out of the question given the size of the classes. Thus the instructor is placed in the position of giving information about a subject matter, or possibly carrying on a conversation with him- or herself in front of the room. If time permits, answers to students' questions merely tell them whether they correctly understood the readings or what the instructor said. The meaning and significance of the material for the students' lives is rarely explored in a dialogue that could lead to a greater understanding of the subject matter and one's self. Evaluation of student learning is often based on correct answers to questions that demonstrate that the student knows what the text or instructor has to say about a subject. Rationalized testing procedures such as true/false and multiple choice questions do not allow students to explore and state the meaning of the subject matter in terms of how they see themselves as present or future administrators.

This list can go on, citing more of the negative aspects of typical teaching conditions. Critics (Rogers, 1969; Freire, 1973) point out that very little real learning takes place under these conditions and with these practices. *Real learning* is described as a greater understanding of not only the subject matter but also of one's self in relation to the subject matter. Emerging from this understanding of the relationship between subject matter and one's self are new opportunities for action. Self-reflective learning can change the way one lives his or her life (Fay, 1977). Such learning is interpretive and critical rather than instrumental.

Taking learning to a more global scale, consider Habermas's (1975) belief that "the fundamental mechanism for social evolution in general is to be found in an automatic inability not to learn (p. 15). He raises the question of whether or not we have reached a stage of sociocultural development where instrumental reason has created a climate of "not-learning" rather than "learning" because of a shrinking opportunity for dialogue. He distinguishes between two levels of learning: nonreflexive and reflexive. In nonreflexive learning, statements of fact and value are "naively taken for granted and accepted or rejected without discursive consideration" (p. 15). Reflexive learning requires discussion of beliefs and values, which ultimately results in their acceptance or rejection based on argumentation. His perscription is "the institutionalization of practical discourse [which] would introduce a new stage of learning for society" (p. 16).

There is some reason to believe that interpretive and critical reasoning are being fostered. The pages of *Teaching Political Science*, the *Organizational Behavior Teaching Journal*, and the proceedings of the public administration teaching conferences are filled with reports on the use of case studies, administrative journals, mock assessment centers, classroom simulations, group exercises, data feedback instruments, and student self-assessments to improve the educational experience. The extent to which such techniques create a domain for practical discourse will determine the opportunity to develop a student's capacity for interpretive and critical reasoning.

These reports of alternative teaching techniques may be motivated by stated dissatisfactions with typical teaching techniques, and the primary justifications for using these techniques have come from the psychological literature. Reasons for using these techniques have not been presented from a ground of interpretive and critical reasoning. Since rational thought and action is a central theme in administration, and since rationality can be extended to include interpretation and criticism, a stronger justification for experimenting with different teaching techniques can be developed using reason as a base. If there are to be substantial changes in typical teaching conditions and practices, some rational justification must be offered to support those changes.

SUMMARY

This chapter has presented a critique of instrumental reason found in the rational model of administration and has developed a more comprehensive theory of administrative reason and rationality that incorporates interpretive and critical modes of thought and action. In order to support these alternative modes of reason and rationality, the importance of practical discourse must be recognized and recovered in administration. It is only through practical discourse that we can arrive at the ends we seek and the means we choose to achieve them.

REFERENCES

Allaire, Y., & Firsirotu, M. (1984). Theories of organizational culture. *Organizational Studies, 5*(3), 193-226.

Anderson, J. (1979). *Public policy making.* New York: Holt, Reinhart, & Winston.

Argyris, C. (1973). Some limits of rational man organizational theory. *Public Administration Review, 33*(3), 253-268.

Argyris, C. (1982). *Reasoning, learning, and action: Individual and organizational.* San Francisco: Jossey-Bass.

Argyris, C., Putnam, R., & Smith, D. (1985). *Action science.* San Francisco: Jossey-Bass.

Argyris, C., & Schon, D. (1978). *Organizational learning.* Reading, MA: Addison-Wesley.

Barley, S. (1983). Semiotics and the study of occupational and organizational cultures. *Administrative Science Quarterly, 28,* 393-413.

Bernstein, R.J. (1983). *Beyond objectivism and relativism: Science, hermeneutics, and praxis.* Philadelphia: University of Pennsylvania Press.

Carter, L. (1979). *Reason in Law.* Boston: Little, Brown.

Cardozo, B. (1960). *The nature of the judicial process.* New Haven, CT: Yale University Press.

Diamond, M.A. (1984). Bureaucracy as externalized self-system: A view from the psychological interior. *Administration and Society, 16,* 195-214.

Dernhardt, R.B. (1981). *In the shadow of organization.* Lawrence: Regents Press of Kansas.

Denhardt, R.B. (1984). *Theories of public organization.* Monterey, CA: Brooks/Cole.

Denhardt, R.B., & White, J.D., (1982). Beyond explanation. *Administration and Society, 14,* 163-171.

Dewey, J. (1910). *How we think.* New York: D.C. Heath.

Dunn, W.N. (1981). *An introduction to public policy analysis.* Englewood Cliffs, NJ: Prentice-Hall.

Etzioni, A. (1967, December). Mixed scanning: A third approach to decision making. *Public Administration Review, 27,* 385-392.

Fay, B. (1975). *Social theory and political practice.* London: George Allen & Unwin.

Fay, B. (1977). How people change themselves. In T. Ball (Ed.), *Political theory and praxis* (pp. 200-238), Minneapolis: University of Minnesota Press.

Fay, B. (1987). *Critical social science.* Ithaca, NY: Cornell University Press.

Forester, J. (1982a, Winter). Planning in the face of power. *Journal of the American Planning Association,* 67-80.

Forester, J. (1982b). The policy analysis-critical theory affair. *Journal of Public Policy, 2*(2).

Forester, J. (1984). Bounded rationality and the politics of muddling through. *Public Administration Review, 44*(1), 23-32.

Freire, P. (1973). *Education for a critical consciousness.* New York: Seabury Press.

Gadamer, H.G. (1975a). Hermeneutics and social science. *Cultural Hermeneutics, 2.*

Gadamer, H.G. (1975b). *Truth and method.* New York: Seabury Press.

Gadamer, H.G. (1977). *Philosophical hermeneutics.* Berkeley: University of California Press.

Geertz, C. (1973). *The interpretation of culture.* New York: Basic Books.

Habermas, J. (1970). *Toward a rational society* (J. Shapiro, Trans.). Boston: Beacon Press.

Habermas, J. (1971). *Knowledge and human interests.* Boston, Beacon Press.

Habermas, J. (1973). *Theory and practice.* Boston: Beacon Press.

Habermas, J. (1975). *Legitimation crisis.* Boston: Beacon Press.

Hobbes, T. (1974). *Leviathan* (M. Oakeshott, Ed.). New York: Macmillan.

Horkheimer, M. (1974). *Eclipse of reason.* New York: Seabury Press.

Kisiel, T. (1972). Scientific discovery: Logical, philosophical, or hermeneutical. In D. Carr & E. Casey (Eds.), *The phenomenological horizon* (pp. 263-284). Chicago: Quadrangle.

LaBier, D. (1983). Emotional disturbances in the federal bureaucracy. *Administration and Society, 14*(4), 403-448.

Levi, E.H. (1949). *An introduction to legal reasoning.* Chicago: University of Chicago Press.

Levinson, H. (1981). *Executive.* Cambridge, MA: Harvard University Press.

Lindblom, C.E. (1959, Spring). The science of "muddling through." *Public Administration Review, 19*, 79-88.

Maccoby, M. (1976). *The gamesman.* New York: Simon and Schuster.

Marcuse, H. (1960). *Reason and revolution: Hegel and the rise of social theory.* Boston: Beacon Press.

Marcuse, H. (1964). *One dimensional man.* Boston: Beacon Press.

Palmer, R. (1969). *Hermeneutics.* Evanston, IL: Northwestern University Press.

Ricoeur, P. (1971). The model of the text: Meaningful action considered as a text. *Social Research, 38*, 529-562.

Ricoeur, P. (1974). *The conflict of interpretation.* (D. Idhe, Ed.). Evanston, IL: Northwestern University Press.

Rogers, C. (1969). *Freedom to learn.* New York: Bobbs-Merrill.

Simon, H.A. (1957). *Administrative behavior.* New York: Free Press.

Simon, H.A. (1965). *The shape of automation for men and management.* New York: Harper & Row.

Simon, H.A. (1973). Organizational man: Rational or self-actualizing. *Public Administration Review, 33*(4), 346-353.

Simon, H.A. (1983). *Reason in human affairs.* Stanford, CA: Stanford University Press.

Smith, K., & Simmons, V. (1983). A Rumpelstiltskin organization: Metaphors on metaphors in field research. *Administrative Science Quarterly, 28*, 377-392.

Weber, M. (1958). The rationalization of education and training. In H. Gerth & W. Mills (Eds.), *From Max Weber.* London: Oxford University Press.

White, J.D. (1986). On the growth of knowledge in public administration. *Public Administration Review, 46*, 15-24.

6

The Responsible Actor as "Tortured Soul": The Case of Horatio Hornblower

> In every truth the opposite is equally true. For example, a truth can only be expressed and enveloped in words if it is one-sided. Everything that is thought and expressed in words is one-sided, only half the truth; it all lacks totality, completeness, unity. When the Illustrious Buddha taught about the world, he had to divide it into Sansara and Nirvana, into illusion and truth, into suffering and salvation. One cannot do otherwise, there is no other method for those who teach. But the world itself, being in and around us, is never one-sided.
>
> (Herman Hesse, *Siddhartha*)

INTRODUCTION

In 1804, with the Peace of Amiens having broken down and war between England and France renewed, Horatio Hornblower, Commander of H.M. Sloop Hotspur, *engaged his small ship in his country's desperate and protracted blockage of French seaports, thwarting the Emperor Napoleon's plans for invasion. During an incident near Brest* Hotspur *drew heavy fire from a French shore battery while attempting to rescue survivors from a companion vessel that had just been sunk. After the rescue, but still within enemy range,* Hotspur's *main topmast backstay was severed and fell to the deck with a loud thump not three yards from*

Hornblower's feet. The damage had been done by the impact of a live shell that had yet to explode . . .

> and there on the deck, death, sizzling death, was rolling towards him; and, as the ship heaved, death changed its course with the canting of the deck, in a blundering curve as the belt round the shell deflected its roll. Hornblower saw the tiny thread of smoke, the burning fuse one-eighth of an inch long. No time to think. He sprang at it, as it wobbled on its belt, and with his gloved hand he extinguished the fuse, rubbing at it to make sure the spark was out, rubbing at it again unnecessarily before he straightened up. (Forester, 1962, p. 283)

Hornblower, whose courage and cunning had already made him a hero in the eyes of his crew and something of a legend among others of the British blockade fleet, impatiently ordered onlooking crewmen back to their duties when, "as if some Gorgon's head had turned them all into stone" (Forester, p. 283), they gaped at their captain in slack-jawed amazement in the wake of his seemingly calm, even casual heroics.

With characteristic understatement, Hornblower reported in the most minimal of terms Hotspur's *rescue operation to his superior, one Captain Chambers. Some weeks later Chambers's own report to the Admiralty appeared in the Naval Chronicle, as was then the custom in such matters, and would be read widely thereafter by the British public. Its last sentence read:*

> Captain Hornblower informs me that Hotspur *suffered no casualties although she was struck by a five-inch shell which did considerable damage aloft but which fortunately failed to explode. (p. 286)*

On reading Chambers's account, Lieutenant Bush, Hornblower's admiring second-in-command, strenuously protested the omission of any mention of Hornblower's daring action.

> "'Tisn't right, sir. 'Tisn't fair. 'Tisn't fair to you, sir, or the ship."
> "Nonsense, Mr. Bush. What d' you think we are? Actresses? Politicians? We're King's officers, Mr. Bush, with a duty to do, and no thought for anything else. Never speak to me again like this, if you please, Mr. Bush. . ." (p. 287)

whereupon Hornblower abruptly dismissed his subordinate.

It was horrible to see Bush shamble out of the cabin, hurt and depressed. The trouble with Bush was that he had no imagination; he could not envisage the other side. Hornblower could—he could see before his eyes at that moment the words he would have written if Bush had had his way. "The shell fell on the deck and with my own hands I extinguished the fuse when it was about to explode." He could never have written such a sentence. He could never have sought for public esteem by writing it. Moreover, and more important, he would scorn the esteem of a public who could tolerate a man who would write such words. If by some chance his deeds did not speak for themselves he would never speak for them. The very possibility revolted him, and he told himself that this was not a matter of personal taste, but a well-weighed decision based on the good of the service; and in that respect he was displaying no more imagination than Bush.

Then he caught himself up short. This was all lies, all self-deception, refusal to face the truth. He had just flattered himself that he had more imagination than Bush. More imagination, perhaps—but far less courage. Bush knew nothing of the sick horror, the terrible moment of fear which Hornblower had experienced when that shell dropped. Bush did not know how his admired captain had had a moment's vivid mental picture of being blown into bloody rags by the explosion, how his heart had almost ceased to beat—the heart of a coward. Bush did not know the meaning of fear, and he could not credit his captain with that knowledge either. And so Bush would never know why Hornblower had made so light of the incident of the shell and why he had been so irascible when it was discussed. But Hornblower knew, and would know, whenever he could bring himself to face facts. (pp. 287-288)

Any dissection of this episode, especially one littered with theoretical categories and pretensions to psychological insight, surely runs the risk of spoiling the fun of reading about Hornblower, whose deeds speak so eloquently for themselves and whose tortured ruminations afterward seem to invite sympathy more than analysis. Indeed, I fear it likely that Hornblower himself might summarily dismiss speculations of the sort that follow as "bombast and fustion," epithets he usually reserved for fatuous poems by the likes of Lord Byron.

The reasons for Hornblower's appeal, warts and all, as a literary hero make him an ideal exemplar for the subject of this essay, namely, what I shall term here the theory of *countervailing responsibility*. Hornblower is a paradigm of the responsible actor precisely because his deeds and reflections so vividly embody the ambiguous and even contradictory meanings of the word *responsibility*. Where academic writing about the subject typically strives for consistency, justification, and closure by means of the impersonal tools of logic or precedent, Hornblower struggles unendingly to understand the meaning of his own responsibility amid the unpredictable and often terrible circumstances in which he must act. That his creator, C.S. Forester, never endows his protagonist with anything approaching complete self-understanding makes Hornblower believable by reminding us of our own capacity for self-deception. What Forester does not allow his captain to realize is that his struggle to comprehend his own internal contradictions is evidence not of his wretched failings, as he supposes, but of his heroism.

Hornblower's adventures will be used to illustrate both a particular theory of responsible action and a way of thinking about theorizing as a means to inform it. Each of these aspects is related to the other. Since various meanings of the word *responsibility* stand in inevitable tension with one another, it is misleading to equate responsible action in its fullest sense with *correct* action. Action that is deemed correct from the standpoint of one meaning might very well be incorrect or irresponsible from the standpoint of another. Thus a theory of responsibility cannot reasonably be expected to provide correct answers about how to act or even to delimit the range of possible courses of action that could be classified as being responsible. Rather, in view of the contradictory meanings of *responsibility*, a theory about it can at the most provide a framework for reflection within which various meanings of the word can be assessed in relation to the concrete circumstances they are intended to illuminate.

A principal thesis of this chapter holds that the purpose of theorizing should be to foster reflective conversation about "what to do next" and also about what we have been doing as retrospectively revealed to us. Bad theorizing, then, stops conversation and in so doing stops social process more generally, since the latter is chiefly, if not exclusively, comprised of conversations, both oral and written, with others and with ourselves. The terms of these conversations should be both general enough to have wide-spread salience, but also specific enough that differences between, say, good and evil, health and sickness, and so forth are, at least in the abstract, unequivocal. Thus, I shall stipulate that ordinary virtues, while they may vary both in their relative priority among individuals and in the ways in which their relevance to actual situations may be interpreted, are nonetheless likely to have virtually universal salience to those, which includes most of us, who even occasionally reflect upon questions of right and wrong, good and evil.

Further, for any virtue or moral principle that we might mention, it is possible to identify what I shall term a *countervailing* virtue with which the first stands in tension (Hampden-Turner, 1971). Although this assumption falls short of being self-evident, the notion of countervailing virtues is familiar enough to most of us. Beginning with high school civics class, for example, we have been taught that liberal democracy is a process for mediating trade-offs between the competing values of liberty and order (or, from a somewhat different perspective, between liberty and equality). What is less often made clear, however, is the corollary idea that serious harm results from an exclusive emphasis on one as opposed to the other of these two values. Each value or virtue may generate its own pathologies unless it is held in tension with its partner. Liberty, unless checked by the virtue of order, produces chaos; while order that is not countervailed by liberty results in oppression.

While I believe that this formulation has much common-sense appeal, it is usually grasped only partially owing to our tendency—which is evident in conversations that have broken down or stalled—to be oblivious to the pathologies of our own preferred virtues. In addition, by unconsciously projecting our own fears onto others, we often interpret opposing virtues exclusively in terms of their pathological or "shadow" side. The advocate of unbridled liberty, that is, regards oppression as the sole alternative to *his* preferred virtue, while the champion of order regards chaos as the only option to *hers*.

COUNTERVAILING MEANINGS OF ADMINISTRATIVE RESPONSIBILITY

The idea of countervailing virtues depicted in Table 6.1 will be expanded in the discussion that follows in order to summarize three definitions of *responsible action* as well as their countervailing relationships to one another. The three meanings of *responsibility*, for which there is substantial normative support in the public administration literature, embody differing senses of the virtuous; but all three exhibit two generic pathologies that become manifest unless each meaning is countervailed by the other two (see Table 6.2). Each definition of responsibility, then, constitutes both a primary meaning as well as a countervailing meaning to both of the others.

TABLE 6.1: Virtues, Pathologies, and Countervailing Virtues

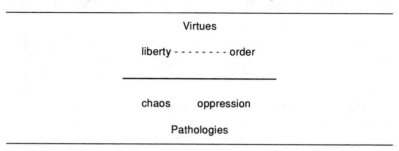

Political Responsibility

The combined legacies of Woodrow Wilson (1941), Max Weber (1947), and Herbert Simon (1976) provide the theoretical basis for the most familiar and influential conception of responsible action in American public administration discourse. Wilson's insistence on the separation of politics (policy formulation) from administration (implementation) parallels Weber's distinction between ends and means implied by the legal/technical mode of rationality embodied in the bureaucratic form of social organization. Drawing from logical positivism, Simon later offered an influential epistemological basis for Wilson's dichotomy by arguing for a radical analytical distinction between values and facts, with value judgments constituting the stuff of politics and factual judgments comprising the domain of administration. These three dichotomies—politics and administration, ends and means, value and fact—combined to provide an easily grasped and unambiguous normative conception of the administrator's proper role in democratic[1] government, namely: The administrator has both a moral duty and a legal obligation to enforce laws and implement policies enacted by democratically elected representatives, who give authoritative voice to the public will.

Organizationally, the separation of politics from administration thus dictates that administrators are hierarchically subordinate to elected representatives. That is, organizational arrangements, which usually approximate the bureaucratic form described by Weber, should be devised so that rewards (e.g., promotion, pay, job security) and penalties be meted out in order to ensure that administrators comply with a policy's rules and intent. Their compliance defines whether administra-

TABLE 6.2: Countervailing Meanings of Administrative Responsibility

Meaning of Responsibility	Pathologies	Countervailing Meanings
Political: Action that is accountable to or consistent with objectives or standards of conduct mandated by political or hierarchical authority	Opportunism: Sycophantic obedience (or passivity) motivated by personal gain or political expedience	Professional
	Reification of Authority: Obedience resulting from the apprehension of authority as a compelling force that determines behavior, such that personal responsibility is disclaimed or lost to conscious awareness	Personal
Professional: Action that is informed by professional expertise, standards of ethical conduct, and by experience rooted in agency history and traditions	Goal Displacement: Covertly controlling the policy process and enhancing agency power through the assertion of professional expertise	Political
	Impersonality: Dealing with people impersonally as cases, irrespective of unique needs or contexts	Personal
Personal: Action that is informed by self-reflexive understanding; and emerges from a context of authentic relationships wherein personal commitments are regarded as valid bases for moral action	Narcissism: Posturing about personal values in order to deny the legitimate constraints of authority	Political
	Confluence: Flouting professional standards by overpersonalizing decisions in order to justify incompetence or avoid confrontation	Professional

tors have acted in an accountable manner, and conformity to the letter and intent of a policy allows administrators to be "called to account" for their actions or inaction. Political (or hierarchical) responsibility is thus synonymous with accountability, which, in addition to being enforceable through legal sanctions, also carries with it a moral imperative that is embedded both in the democratic ethos of the broader society and in the value system of public administrators (Finer, 1941).

An important parallel to the idea of accountability is the notion of efficiency. If, through legitimate political processes, value judgments about the proper ends of the state have been enacted into law, the responsibility of administrators is not simply to implement the law in a dutiful manner, but to do so with the least possible expenditure of resources. Efficiency, defined as the ratio of expenditures to results, is thus an instrumental value, and discretion by administrators is properly limited to judgments about the means (for Simon, "factual judgments") by which efficiency may be best achieved, not to the desirability of the ends themselves.

Professional Responsibility

The emergence of this second category of responsible action may be attributed to a growing awareness of the limitations of accountability as a sufficient practical and normative guide for administrators. In its earliest form, professional responsibility simply entailed the avoidance of wrongdoing, especially action intended to reap personal or political gain for the administrator. Such phrases as "the doctrine of neutral competence" (Sayre & Kaufman, 1960) and "a passion for anonymity," for example, suggest an image of the administrator as a selfless professional who shuns the limelight in the course of dutiful service. From this view professional and political responsibility are complementary, rather than countervailing. The virtues (as well as the pathologies) of each serve to reinforce the other.

By the early 1940s, however, the notion of the professional as a neutrally competent technocrat was challenged by a growing recognition of the breakdown of the policy/administration dichotomy. The blurring of the distinction between policy-making and implementation meant that administration necessarily entailed discretionary judgments, not only about technical matters, but also about values. The complexities of modern government, according to Carl J. Friedrich (1940), who championed this view, required that administrators be attentive to public opinion, as well as professional knowledge and ethics, in their interpretation of legislative intent.

At an analytical level the dichotomies between ends and means, values and facts were also shown to be problematic. Ends, as Weber (1947) himself noted, are inevitably shaped by the institutional means originally designed for their attainment. More generally, ends are shaped by social processes, which in turn are profoundly affected not only by institutional norms, but also by social practices embedded in language forms and cultural traditions. Thus questions about values are not limited, as in the earlier conception of political responsibility, solely to ends, but also to the means—or processes—that produce them. Questions about means, in other words, are inherently political questions. The consequence of this for public administration was the recognition that bureaucracy, around which debates had been earlier limited to whether or not it was efficient, was a political force in its own right, a source of values.

Friedrich's advice that administrators exercise discretion in the implementation of policy seems, in retrospect, to alter only modestly the traditional notion of political responsibility, especially when contrasted with a later challenge to it offered by John Rohr (1984). Friedrich chiefly made a virtue of necessity, arguing that the inherent generality of policy, coupled with the idiosyncratic nature of the cases to which it is applied, makes administrative discretion unavoidable. By implication, responsible discretion (i.e., professionalism) entails reflection about ethical standards and public opinion as they bear on the judicious application of the general to the specific.

Rohr, on the other hand, seeks to establish for public administration a vital role as a participant in the political process, having a constitutionally legitimate claim to share in governing. In his analysis of the doctrine of separation of powers, Rohr cites both the language of the Constitution itself, as well as *The Federalist Papers* and other historical documents, in order to show, first, that public administration is not prohibited from active involvement in legislative and judicial functions. But more affirmatively, in view of the framers' wish that legislation reflect an intimate appreciation of public sentiment, the subsequent evolution of American political institutions has revealed administrative agencies to be often more representative of and responsive to that sentiment than the legislative branch. Support for this assertion, Rohr says, is found in the sheer numbers of administrators compared to legislators; the emergence of "street-level bureaucracies," where the contact between government and citizen is most immediate; and in the fact that administrative agencies, more so than legislatures, are specialized repositories of knowledge, experience, and historical commitments that are invaluable (as well as constitutionally legitimate) sources for the generation and even advocacy of policy alternatives. Apart from the affirmative role that agencies should (and do) play in formulating policy, Rohr's analysis also supports a more limited but no less crucial role for administrators, namely, saying "no" to, or actively contesting within legal limits, orders and policy proposals of their political masters.

From Rohr, and to a lesser extent from Friedrich, it is possible to infer a conception of administrative responsibility—one that is consonant with American political tradition and thought—that confers upon administrators an autonomous status as professionals. Professional responsibility does not reject or diminish political responsibility; but these two conceptions of responsibility do stand in counterpoint to one another, like a conceptual separation of powers in which the excesses of opposing virtues may be tempered by one another.

Opportunism

By *excesses* I am speaking mainly of the pathological, shadow side of any one meaning of responsibility, which may emerge unless a countervailing meaning is asserted. One of the two generic pathologies of political responsibility is opportunism, for which the countervailing meaning is professionalism. The simplest and most passive form of opportunism is merely to do nothing unless given a direct order that is unambiguous. Doing nothing qualifies as obedience only in the negative sense of not disobeying authority and qualifies as opportunism when its motive is to stay out of trouble. Whether inaction so motivated produces its intended result, however, is another matter. While doing nothing might frequently go unpunished, it may also be viewed by one's superiors as failing to take initiative. But action, too, entails risk; so the administrator who ponders, if only for self-interested reasons, whether to act in the absence of clear and authoritative instructions may want to consider Hornblower's rule that it is better to get into trouble for doing something than for doing nothing.

Opportunism may also be expressed more actively in sycophantic obedience to one's superior's every whim, through ostentatious or at least highly visible acquiescence to orders. Dickens's Uriah Heap is the fictional prototype of the sycophant, in whom the virtue of loyalty is grotesquely transformed into the vice of obsequiousness. A more contemporary, and for our purposes here a more illustrative, example of the opportunist is John Dean, counselor to President Nixon during the Watergate affair. Dean's own account (1976) of his actions during Watergate shows how his loyalty to Nixon, when accompanied by ambition borne of personal insecurity and unconstrained by a sense of professional responsibility, resulted in a most venal form of opportunism. Dean not only complied with illegal orders, but also failed to do what a good lawyer is supposed to do: namely, to provide, from a detached professional vantage, information and advice that, even if unpleasant, might check the momentarily unwise or imprudent exercise of political authority.

Professionals are those who, in Aaron Wildavsky's (1979) phrase, "speak truth to power." But they are helped to perform this role when it is acknowledged to be legitimate by both the profession and the public. It should be emphasized, however, that speaking truth to power is only in the most extreme cases, such as whistle-blowing, an act of contesting political authority. Rather, for public administrators it involves primarily the assertion of expertise, professional detachment, and experience grounded in agency tradition in an active and, if need be, forceful dialogue with elected officials (Wamsley, Goodsell, Rohr, Stivers, White, & Wolfe, 1987).

Goal Displacement

If every virtue has its vice, we should temper an appreciation of professional responsibility by recognizing its shadow side, namely, that of goal displacement. *Goal displacement* will be defined here as the tendency of professionals to seek personal gain by disguising political action under a veneer of neutral or technical competence. To a degree, at least, it is an act of deliberate bad faith, and, whether or not the assertion of its presence is justified in any particular case, it is reflected in a profound public distrust both of bureaucracy and the professions. Thus, although Rohr (1984) may be able to produce convincing arguments on constitutional grounds for public administration's legitimate status as a governing institution, skeptics will be quick to note that bureaucratic self-interest might well displace the public interest as a motive for administrative action. Government agencies are concentrations of professionals, whose expertise, according to this argument,

serves chiefly to make even less visible and more insidious the appropriation of political power by the bureaucracy. There seems to be a
common sentiment behind George Bernard Shaw's observation that
"all professions are conspiracies against the laity" and Sayre and Kaufman's (1960, p. 404) contention that New York City bureaucrats invoked the doctrine of neutral competence as a cynical ruse to further
their own ends.

Professionals, as well as the agencies they populate, participate in the
political process, not in the open discourse about the public interest that
Rohr recommends, but as either powerful interest groups pursuing their
own parochial ends or captives of the interest groups whom they are
intended to regulate. This is the essence of Theodore Lowi's (1969)
influential critique of "interest group liberalism," in which powerful
interests, including government bureaucracies, have steadily and invis-
ibly usurped from the Congress the responsibilities for articulating the
public will and translating it into national policy. The consequence of
interest group liberalism is nothing less than the loss of the popular
sovereignty.

Lowi's critique, however, is more persuasive than is his proposed
remedy, which consists chiefly of urging Congress both to reassert its
traditional role as formulator of national policy and to shift back to the
Congress the locus of public discourse about it. Public agencies could
then resume their traditional role as dutiful implementors of congres-
sionally defined national purpose. Despite the obvious merit of his
critique, Lowi's proposed solution seems to amount to reestablishing
the policy/administration dichotomy, greatly oversimplifying the problem of administrative accountability by ignoring the inevitability of
political judgments made in the name of administrative discretion.
Lowi's mistake is in believing that the problem of public accountability
can be solved by granting to the Congress the exclusive right to participate in the discourse, which only serves to drive underground, out of
public view, the necessary involvement of government agencies in the
formation of national policy. The solution, for Rohr, is not to exclude
agency participation in policy-making, but to legitimate and make more
visible their participation in the national discourse about it.[2] Both Rohr
and Lowi would agree as to the real dangers of agency manipulation of
the policy process through either covert dealings with interest groups
or self-serving claims of neutral competence. Rohr, however, interprets
the doctrine of separation of powers in such a way that the pathologies
that are always latent in the exercise of professional responsibility by

administrators may be countervailed by, rather than (as with Lowi) narrowly subordinated to, the requirement of political responsibility. In subordinating the professional to the political to the degree he does (and assuming that it were possible to begin with), Lowi's solution appears to leave little possibility that the pathologies of political responsibility can be countervailed by the wisdom, experience, and commitment of professionals.

Personal Responsibility

To this point, the discussion of the tensions between political and professional responsibility has summarized the debate about administrative responsibility as it is typically framed in the public administration literature. Specifically, the standard debate depicts administrators, and others with whom they must contend, as consciously rational actors aware of what they are doing and why they are doing it. They are, in other words, decision makers and goal seekers who strategize and sometimes even deceive, but they can also reason in good faith both about the right thing to do in a particular situation and in a general, abstract way about the moral basis for their actions.

In the standard debate, responsibility is assumed to be an attribute of the decision—not, at least primarily, of the actor who makes it. A decision is deemed to be responsible as judged by its consequences, its consistency with a normatively preferred principle, or its having been arrived at by the judicious weighing of competing principles. From the decision frame of reference, then, we may speak of actors as being responsible only in a derivative sense, that is, insofar as their decisions produce desired consequences or conform to preferred principles.

The idea of personal responsibility is comprehensible only by shifting the frame of analysis from the decision to the more generic realm of action. From this latter frame of reference, responsibility may be seen as a quality that inheres in the actor, rather than in decisions. From the standpoint of the personal, decisions are responsible in a derivative sense; that is, as manifestations of action taken by responsible actors.

Personal responsibility essentially involves an awareness of both the existence and the social and psychological limitations of one's role as agent or cause of one's action. It may be understood as a relational notion in two important respects. First, personally responsible action is self-reflexive, which means that the actor monitors the flow of his or her inner life so as to be aware of the relation of consciously intended actions and the less visible, deeper projects of the psyche that are reflected in those actions. In Jungian terms, to be self-reflexive is to be aware of the dialectical relation between conscious will and unconscious energy, to realize that knowing of the manifest content of action can reveal only a partial understanding of it. Self-reflextivity means that people "retroflectively consider unconscious material as it appears in their actions and otherwise in their lives generally" (White, 1990, p. 216). Because access to the unconscious can never be immediate and direct, self-reflexivity cannot be deliberately willed by asserting "shoulds" and "oughts." It can be prompted and encouraged, however, by fostering "disinterested curiosity," a "friendly collaboration" (White, p. 216) between the conscious and the unconscious that is marked by an attitude of acceptance, rather than denial or judgment, toward one's spontaneous acts, including seemingly inexplicable slips of tongue or pen or embarrassments.

Personal responsibility derives its moral nature from its self-reflexive character. By *moral* I am not referring to correctness as measured by adherence to a principle or an objective standard. Rather, the moral nature of personal responsibility inheres in the actor's status as agent of his or her actions, for which responsibility cannot ultimately be lodged outside him- or herself in, for example, a higher authority or learned principles of conduct, no matter how sincerely they may be felt or persuasive their intellectual justification. This should not be read as an indictment of principled thought, but as a caution against the belief that principles can be in any decisive sense authoritative. Rather, principles serve as valuable, yet fallible, symbols both for framing the emergent and unique contexts of action and for self-reflexively questioning one's psychological or emotional stake in those contexts.

In the absence of such a self-reflexive understanding the latent pathology of principles is manifested in their reification. This reification occurs when the actor overobjectifies principles by unconsciously divorcing them from their original, affective source in the psyche or by incorporating them whole, as memorized instructions from others. The reification of principles is a profound act of forgetting, in which the project of knowing oneself is truncated in the narrower interest of self-justification. It amounts to a kind of intellectual Eichmannism, in which responsibility is projected onto what have come to be regarded as compelling abstractions, reducing morality, as Edward Whitmont (1982, p. 90) has put it, to petrified legalism. Even a passionate belief in principles exhibits an inauthentic passion when they are invoked as compelling explanations or justifications of action, rather than as symbols that are used self-reflexively.

The pathology of principles is evident not only in self-justification, but also in self-condemnation, which in a similar manner inhibits self-reflexivity and thus personal responsibility. When we reify our principles (which in truth are usually someone else's), our failure to live up to them leads only to a feeling of guilt, requiring constant absolution from others, rather than to reflective self-understanding. To be self-reflexive about principles entails an attitude of self-acceptance in order to probe the role that they play in our inner lives, allowing us to see splits between who we wish to be and aspects of ourselves that, for the present, we deem to be unacceptable. As Whitmont describes it:

> While unavoidable as a first step in individuation, this split needs bridging over once an ego is established. Only through perceiving one's transgression as "missing the point" (the original meaning of the Hebrew *chato* and the Greek *hamartia* which came to mean "sin") rather than as reprehensible sin, can the individual personality liberate itself from rigidity and continue the course of its evolution. (p. 91)

By permitting us access to the inner world of the actor, the episode from *Hornblower and the Hotspur* with which this essay began aptly illustrates how the idea of personal responsibility alters and enriches our understanding of political and professional responsibility. Recall Hornblower's private reflections after he had dismissed Lieutenant Bush from his cabin. In the first of the two paragraphs, we read how Hornblower, the consummate professional, refuses to allow his sense of duty to degenerate into a craven attempt to curry favor with his superiors. Although his loyalty to the service is virtually absolute, Hornblower exhibits an acute appreciation of how it might have been contaminated by opportunism had he followed Bush's advice to trumpet his own bravery. His professionalism is further evident as he defends as being for "the good of the service," rather than a matter of personal taste, his insistence that his deeds must speak for themselves. This is not because Hornblower has a passion for anonymity. Indeed, because he despairs of languishing for the rest of his career at the middling rank of commander, Hornblower desperately hopes for the kind of notoriety that he could so easily have achieved.

So far, Hornblower's internal dialogue neatly encapsulates the tensions between duty and integrity, political responsibility and professional responsibility. But just when the reader is prepared to bestow accolades on him for his selfless and professional devotion to duty, Hornblower pronounces himself a coward and his rationalization of his action a fatuous self-deception. Although Hornblower, as usual, overstates the case against himself, he nonetheless instinctively knows that beneath the noble expression of principle lurk the demons of his psyche that only he knows about—and, even then, only when he has the courage to "face facts." While Hornblower no doubt exaggerates in believing that his prior analysis was "all lies," he would have been right to conclude that it contained only partial truths. Rational discourse can at most contain only part of the truth, the virtue of which is transformed into the pathology of rationalization unless it is understood, if only incompletely, in the context of one's deeper project of personal development. Being able to probe the relation between the intellectual content of one's principles and the less visible role they serve in sustaining one's emotional life constitutes the essence of the idea of self-reflexivity. To be personally responsible is to face facts, however unpleasant, so as to avoid self-deception and self-justification. For Hornblower this reflexive capability is evident in his awareness that his reason for omitting any mention of his valor was at least as much to conceal from himself his own cowardice as it was a sober expression of his professional integrity.

Personal responsibility is essentially a psychological notion, rather than a matter of moral courage that can be consciously willed. Thus when people speak of taking or accepting personal responsibility for their actions, the idea is inevitably distorted. Taking and accepting connote conscious intention, rather than self-reflexive awareness. Similarly, being personally responsible should not be confused with acting on the basis of one's personal values. Personal values, because they are intellectual constructions, differ little from professional or political values, regardless of how sincerely they may be felt. They are authentic only to the extent that the person self-reflexively understands them in the context of their relation to the psychological purposes they serve.[3]

The second relational aspect of personal responsibility derives from its social character. Action takes place in or presupposes a social context, which is to say a context of human relationship. Action is necessarily interaction and is distinguished by its emergent and unpredictable quality rather than, at least principally, its rationally planned quality. The more intimate the relationship, as for example in a face-to-face encounter, the more it may be mediated by the unique contingencies of the moment rather than governed by general, impersonal categories of appraisal and objectified principles of correct behavior. Such categories and principles, to be sure, may and do influence the encounter, but they increasingly seem to be gratuitous, contrived, and inappropriate as the unpredictable dynamic of the encounter unfolds. While they may be appropriate and even necessary in less intimate contexts, principles serve as barriers to an authentic relationship by distancing actors from one another.

In gestalt psychology, the use of principles as barriers to relationship is defined as a form of introjection, the "swallowing whole of other people's ideas, judgments, and styles" (Herman & Korenich, 1977, p. 52), which can never be fully assimilated. In social relationships, introjects have the effect of stifling authentic feelings and thus block genuine contact with others by functioning as "screens or walls of alien material blocking a free exchange of ideas and feelings" (p. 54). When this happens the relationship is regulated, rather than allowed to take its natural course. The result is that actors calculate their action toward one another so that what was once, or might otherwise have become, a relationship is transformed into a transaction between self-interested, atomistic selves. Mutual commitment and understanding are replaced by the individual calculation of utility. Although cooperation may occur under such circumstances, it is, as Arendt (1958) draws the distinction linguistically, "in order to" achieve a goal rather than "for the sake of" the relationship itself.

To be personally responsible is to act on the basis of a commitment to—out of a feeling of responsibility for—another person and to recognize that commitment as a valid basis for moral action. Action based on personal commitment to another does not deny the legitimacy of principled thought, but it does suggest that the latter serves mainly to frame the context within which action occurs, not to determine in any final sense its content or outcome.

Self-reflexivity and human relationship, the two cardinal elements of personal responsibility, both presuppose the other. The quality of self-reflexivity, wherein actors engage in an open and flexible dialogue between their outer and inner worlds, depends fundamentally on the quality of the relationships that bound and provide them a social context. Action takes place in a context of intersubjectivity in which meaning is mutually negotiated, constituted, and revised. In the absence of relation with others, there could be no action toward which to direct self-reflexive attention. Self-reflexivity is an interiorized form of intersubjectivity that presupposes a prior and ongoing relation with others in order that it may avoid being stranded on the "reef of solipsism," to borrow Sartre's phrase. Not only must others be present, but present in relationships that are characterized by mutual commitment and caring. Self-reflexivity is fragile, elusive, and at best a partially successful effort at self-understanding. It may easily degenerate into defensiveness and self-justification unless the sincerity and good will of one's partner in the relationship are implicitly felt.

Conversely, authentic relationships based on mutual commitment need self-reflexive participants having a strong sense of independence and individuality in order that that commitment not be transformed into cloying sentimentalism or collusion in one another's "craziness," to use the current idiom. Mutual commitment requires independent, self-aware agents capable of confronting the other with unpleasant facts or an alternative perspective. Thus self-reflexivity and commitment to the other as a person stand in seemingly paradoxical relation, as countervailing aspects of personal responsibility—each potentially pathological unless complemented by the other.

Personal Responsibility as a Countervailing Meaning

The tensions between political and professional responsibility, including the two pathologies for which each meaning countervails the other, are explicable within a framework of discourse that views actors as self-aware, rational beings. The four remaining pathologies of responsibility, two of which are covered in this section and two in the next, involve differing aspects of the notion of personal responsibility. The introduction of the personal as a countervailing meaning to the first two, however, involves more than just the addition of a third meaning of responsibility. Instead, it represents a confrontation between opposing conceptual frameworks, in which the belief that action is exclusively the product of rational decision is radically augmented by a psychological perspective that seeks to understand action in terms of its unconscious origins and its role in the personal development of the actor.

The Reification of Authority

Earlier, I discussed the pathology of principled thought as a type of reification in which other people's beliefs are swallowed whole rather than assimilated. Principles, that is, are used nonreflexively, precluding the possibility of their playing a developmental role in mediating the relation between conscious thought and unconscious energy. When this happens the actor's sense of agency is lost to conscious awareness with the result that decisions are compelled by principles rather than freely made. Responsibility is lodged in principles—and subsequently in the decisions that seem ineluctably derived from them—rather than in the actor.

Reification more generally may be seen as an alienated mode of consciousness in which people lose sight of their authorship of the social world by apprehending "the products of human activity *as if* they were something else than human products—such as facts of nature, results of cosmic laws, or manifestations of divine will" (Berger & Luckmann, 1967, p. 89). The reification of the social world is made possible, and to a degree even inevitable, whenever it is established and then regarded as an "objective reality," paradoxically existing apart from—or so it seems—the ongoing human production of it. Institutions and roles, because they appear to be among the most objectively "real" of social artifacts, are especially prone to reification—both by their inhabitants and by those whose lives are touched by them. As Berger and Luckmann describe it,

> [T]he basic "recipe" for the reification of institutions is to bestow on them an ontological status independent of human activity and signification. . . . Through reification, the world of institutions appears to merge with the world of nature. It becomes necessity and fate, and is lived through as such, happily or unhappily as the case may be.
>
> Roles may be reified in the same manner as institutions. The sector of self-consciousness that has been objectified in the role is then also apprehended as an inevitable fate, for which the individual may disclaim responsibility. The paradigmatic formula for this kind of reification is the statement "I have no choice in the matter, I have to act this way because of my position"—as husband, father, general, archbishop, chairman of the board, gangster, and hangman, as the case may be. This means that the reification of roles narrows the subjective distance that the individual may establish between himself and his role-playing. The distance implied in all objectification remains, of course, but the distance brought about by disidentification shrinks to the vanishing point. (pp. 90-91)

Institutions and roles are, of course, bound by authority, which means that their reification also necessarily involves the reification of authority. When authority is reified—that is, when orders are interpreted as automatically compelling obedience—personal responsibility is disclaimed or simply lost to conscious awareness. Thus when authority is reified it would be inaccurate to say that people choose or decide on rational grounds to obey authoritative instructions because the possibility of conscious choice—that is, to obey or not to obey—is precluded by a reified mode of consciousness.

While the pathology of reified authority finds its most grotesque expression in recent history in the case of Adolph Eichmann, it should be remembered that Arendt's (1963) account of his trial reveals the ordinariness, not of the terrible consequences of his acts, but of the mindset that permitted him to act as he did. Eichmann did not decide, at least as we are usually led to understand acts of deciding. To qualify as a meaningful act, a decision must presuppose both a self-conscious awareness of what one is doing and the availability of alternative courses of action from which to choose. To ignore the psychological impediments to self-aware choice makes impossible any meaningful distinction between the virtue of loyalty (accountability) and the pathology of blind obedience.

Moreover, it is probably useless to assert consciously held moral values or principles of ethical conduct to countervail the reification of authority. Reification is by definition an unconscious process, which is likely to be reinforced rather than eliminated through attempts at persuasion through rational arguments about values and principles. These may have some limited value in countering the reification of authority, but only when they are understood self-reflexively, permitting the actor to comprehend his or her part in producing, sustaining, and contesting authoritative relationships. The essential point, however, is that it is self-reflexivity, rather than rational thought and judgment, that enables the dereification of authority. In so doing, personal responsibility countervails the second pathology of political responsibility.

Impersonality

In Max Weber's description of the ideal-typical bureaucracy (1947), the norm of impersonality in decision making not only promotes efficiency of operation, but also helps to assure that decisions will be made impartially, free of bias and favoritism. As Weber knew, however, impersonality cuts two ways, its pathology revealed in the pervasive depersonalizing of organizational relationships that accompanied the rationalization of social life spawned by the bureaucratic age.

Professionalism is closely linked to the norm of bureaucratic impersonality owing to the belief that competence may be measured by standards of performance (including, but not limited to, efficiency criteria) that transcend particular persons. Professionals are trained to deal with the general, with differentiations limited to impersonal categories, on the expectation that generalized knowledge will be appropriate to the aggregate of cases to which it is applied. Robert Biller (1979), however, cogently describes the paradox of professionalism in the context of a diverse and heterogeneous clientele.

> What must be remembered is that professionals always have knowledge about "answers" derived from that aggregation of knowledge which the profession has codified. Persons, in this sense, are quite opposite from professionals. Persons tend to experience increasingly unique problems and opportunities that produced for them the need to seek out the specialized services of professionals. At the interface between persons and professionals, each brings quite opposite though symmetrical definitions. The professional brings *answers* codified from knowledge developed from the common experiences of many persons. The person brings *questions* that are uniquely contextuated in a lifetime's increasingly particularized experiences. . . . Persons are different with respect to their unique biological and social histories. (p. 158)

From the standpoint of Biller's analysis, impersonality no longer embodies the virtues of impartiality and fairness when its intended beneficiaries experience their problems and opportunities in unique and idiosyncratic ways. Under these conditions the impersonality of professionalism becomes pathological by neglecting the unique character of the problems that individual clients experience. When clients are treated professionally in this fashion, the likelihood that a relationship may evolve in which the professional and the client might jointly define the latter's problems and agree upon appropriate courses of action is replaced by the professional's unilateral imposition of problem definitions and solutions. Clients (or patients) are treated as cases, and success is defined according to criteria decided upon by the profession. (The extreme example of this is the announcement by the physician that even though the patient died on the operating table, the surgery was a technical success.)

To countervail the pathology of professional impersonality requires an appreciation of the second cardinal feature of personal responsibility, namely, that commitment to another person constitutes a valid basis for moral action. This entails more, however, than simply a moral injunction that professionals ought to make decisions on the basis of such commitments. These commitments presuppose a context of authentic relationship in which action unfolds in unpredictable ways, producing outcomes that reflect, in Mary Parker Follett's (1940, p. 65) phrase, the "law of the situation." Relationships, even when they are characterized by disparities in expertise and authority, are more than "decision-making arrangements" for arbitrating preconceived interests. Rather, relationships are contexts for action in which interests are created and revealed through the process of interaction itself. Decisions, like interests, emerge from social process; they are not consciously made in the conventionally rational sense. From this perspective, responsibility is no longer an attribute of the decision, but of people who are authentically engaged in social process. Responsibility, in the sense that Follett uses the word,

> is possible only by active and reflective participation in the social process by which collective purposes unfold. Responsibility, here, does not mean adherence to an objective standard of truth arrived at through abstract intellectual thought nor obligation to a superordinate source of authority. Rather, in the personal sense that Follett intends, it refers to the self-understanding and self-realization that individuals experience when they invest their emotional energies in collaborative endeavors. (Harmon & Mayer, 1986, p. 343)

Pathologies of the Personal: Narcissism and Confluence

The pathologies of personal responsibility derive from the neglect or absence of either of its two defining elements: self-reflexivity and authentic relationship. These two elements may be seen as dialectically related, so that the presence of one to the exclusion of the other renders each pathological. Although I shall argue later in this chapter that political and professional responsibility can be seen as countervailing the pathologies of the personal, the two elements of personal responsibility internally countervail one another (see Table 6.3).

TABLE 6.3: Personal Responsibility as Countervailing Virtues and Pathologies

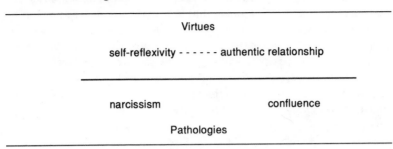

Virtues
self-reflexivity - - - - - - authentic relationship

narcissism	confluence
Pathologies	

Narcissism

In the absence of authentic relationship, self-reflexivity is transformed into the pathology of narcissism. Among the characteristics of narcissism that Christopher Lasch identifies is "pseudo self-insight" (1979, p. 33), rooted in the self-absorption of an inflated ego desperately fending off the anxiety of being alone in the world. Narcissism, which Lasch notes derives more from self-hatred than self-admiration, is a ubiquitous feature of the present age in which the bonds of "outmoded" authority have been cut loose, leaving individuals "free" to act on impulse, pursuing instant gratification and happiness.[4] The tragedy of narcissism inheres in its fear of intimacy, which is to say of authentic relationship. In the absence of intimacy the social context that enables true self-reflexivity is therefore denied and pretensions to it reduce to mere posturing. Personal values become nothing more than hollow slogans of autistic self-absorption.

It is no coincidence that the narcissistic personality both fears intimacy and, at the same time, rejects tradition, history, and authority. An appreciation of the past, as well as a concern with the future, presuppose the presence of relationship, whereas narcissistic gratification is atemporal, ahistorical, and oblivious to (even contemptuous of) cultural tradition. Intimate relationship is, if not exactly a microcosm of historical and cultural association, at least a precondition of it. And authority, however it may be abused, appears to play an essential role in the preservation of a human community and historical continuity.

The pathology of narcissism—which in organizations is expressed in posturing about personal values in order to deny the legitimate constraints of authority—is therefore countervailed externally by political responsibility, that is, through the assertion of political authority and requirements of public accountability. Authority and accountability, despite their own pathologies, serve as macrolevel analogues to the more intimate level of face-to-face relationship. They are healthy, even necessary, so long as they embody legitimate historical commitments and cultural traditions and are pathological when they are asserted as objective, incontrovertible truths. The narcissist, by bringing all authority into disrepute, is fundamentally incapable of knowing the difference.

Confluence

In the absence of self-reflexivity, authentic relationship degenerates into the pathology of confluence. In gestalt psychology, confluence describes relationships in which people lose their individual identities, the apparent benefit of which is a sense of stability, comfort, and predictability. Ironically, the pathology of overextended confluence is evident in people who, having lost their sense of individual identity, also lose "their capacity for real contact with one another" (Herman & Korenich, 1977, p. 74). Authentic relationship thus has a seemingly paradoxical quality involving, simultaneously, unity and separation.

Confluence, rather than sustaining and enriching the relationship, actually aids in destroying it. In order to retain and revitalize the relationship "confluence needs to be broken intermittently by differentiation" (p. 74), which means that individuality must be reasserted. This reassertion requires, in the terminology of this essay, a self-reflexive awareness of the limitations and possibilities of relationship insofar as it may affect one's own development and sense of individuality.

Confluence is the pathological partner of narcissism. Where narcissism sacrifices relationship in order to sustain a false image of independence, confluence sacrifices independence (enabled by self-reflexivity) to a false sense of relationship. Authentic commitment to the other is thus reduced to collusion—or, in Jerry Harvey's (1974) metaphor, a "trip to Abilene." As a result, superficial harmony spuriously passes for relationship, and its real purpose is to disguise the person's anxiety about an autonomous moral existence.

Where political responsibility symbolizes the virtue of unity around a common project, professionalism symbolizes the integrity of one's individuality in the face of pressures to collude in collective pathologies, such as "groupthink". Professional responsibility, that is, may be seen as a macrolevel analogue to self-reflexivity at the level of the personal. As such, professionalism may externally countervail the pathology of confluence, which is evident organizationally in decisions that are inappropriately personalized—for example, through dubious claims about wanting to avoid hurting another's feeling—when objectivity or confrontation is really needed.

CONCLUSION: THE PRIMACY OF PERSONAL RESPONSIBILITY

The symmetry with which the three meanings of responsibility (along with their six pathologies) are displayed in Table 6.2 may give the misleading impression that the political, the professional, and the personal are to be accorded equal normative standing. I should like to disabuse readers of this by noting that the idea of personal responsibility, because it is grounded in the preferred, more encompassing frame of analysis of action (including its unconscious as well as conscious aspects) rather than in rational decision, is foundational among the three conceptions of responsibility. This is not to diminish the importance of political and professional responsibility, but it does suggest that assessments of their crucial roles in informing responsible action should be grounded in an appreciation of the emergent and unpredictable nature of social action as well as the intimate connection of action to the project of human moral development. Rather than further explicating arguments made earlier, this last section of the chapter will illustrate the intuitive plausibility of this conclusion by recounting a final episode in the Hornblower saga.

Several weeks after the incident of the live shell, Hornblower was summoned to the flagship of Admiral Cornwallis, commander of the Channel blockade fleet, to discuss orders, which he would soon thereafter receive formally in writing, to sail alone to the neutral port of Cadiz, in Spain, to deliver dispatches to the British consul there. Upon returning by launch to the Hotspur, *Hornblower was informed by a chagrined Lieutenant Bush that his steward, Doughty, had been charged with mutiny and thrown into the ship's brig for striking a superior officer.*

Doughty, despite his lowly rank of ordinary seaman, had often taken advantage of his position as the captain's steward, regarding himself as exempt from the chain of authority that rigidly enforced discipline aboard ship and to which all officers and men of the Hotspur *(save Doughty) gave unquestioning obedience. Doughty, while skilled and dutiful in attending to Hornblower's personal needs, was ill-suited for life in the British navy, whose stern discipline was coupled with a rough-and-tumble daily existence. Doughty's loyalty was to his captain, not to the service, which Hornblower grew grudgingly to appreciate. Himself a product of humble origins and having even now very meager resources, Hornblower was grateful for (though somewhat ashamed of) whatever small luxuries Doughty's employ afforded him. A bond of friendship had implicitly formed between the two men, insofar as their differences in rank permitted it and despite Hornblower's inability to acknowledge the fact even to himself.*

During Hornblower's absence to confer with Admiral Cornwallis, Doughty had been assigned to a working party of other seamen to take on stores aboard ship.

> *Taking stores on board at sea was a job for all hands, and even when they were on board there was still work for all hands, distributing the stores through the ship. Doughty, in the working party in the waist, had demurred on being given an order by a bosun's mate, Mayne by name. Mayne had swung his "starter," his length of knotted line that petty officers used on every necessary occasion—too frequently, in Hornblower's judgment. And then Doughty had struck him. There were twenty witnesses, and as if that were not enough, Mayne's lip had been cut against his teeth and blood had poured down. (p. 297)*

Hornblower, who knew the Articles of War by heart, was instantly aware of the consequences of Doughty's act. Striking a superior officer, even a bully like Mayne who sadistically abused his authority, was punishable by nothing less than death upon conviction by a court martial comprised of other ships' captains, several of whom were aboard ships of the fleet clustered together close by. Within the hour Doughty would be tried and condemned, and by morning would be hanging from one of the yardarms of the Hotspur.

As Hornblower grimly pondered the inevitability of Doughty's execution, a messenger from Cornwallis's flagship delivered to the Hotspur *a pact of sealed orders, which Hornblower quickly opened. The first sentence read: "Sir: You are requested and required to proceed immediately in H.M. Sloop* Hotspur *under your command to the Port of Cadiz (p. 298)." Hornblower fixed his gaze on the word "immediately"—a word that would postpone Doughty's doom—and abruptly gave orders to set sail for the three-week voyage to Cadiz, out of sight of his fellow captains who would have served as members of the court martial. In Cadiz, however, there would be other British captains available for the same purpose.*

On reaching Cadiz, Hornblower ordered Doughty's incompetent replacement, Bailey, to prepare a special meal for the consul, who was to dine with him aboard ship that evening. When Bailey stumblingly offered some thoroughly inadequate suggestions for the meal (as Hornblower knew he would), in feigned disgust Hornblower ordered Bailey out of his sight and testily instructed Bush to bring Doughty out of confinement to prepare a proper meal. Later, alone with Doughty in his cabin to discuss the menu and dinner arrangements, Hornblower idly interspersed comments about other foreign ships also in port—especially those carrying flags of nations with which England was not at war. He made particular note of the presence of the U.S.S. Constitution, which was anchored a short distance away. Hornblower then asked, " 'By the way, Doughty, can you swim?' Doughty did not raise his head. 'Yes, sir,' his voice was hardly more than a whisper. 'Thank you, sir' " (p. 308).

Hornblower left and went to the quarterdeck to receive his guest, who was just stepping onto the gangway. Later, at the end of their conference in the chartroom, the consul regretfully declined Hornblower's invitation for supper, urging that Hotspur *depart from Cadiz as soon as possible, while the tide was still high. The consul feared a one-sided encounter between* Hotspur *and hostile Spanish warships in or near Cadiz, in view of recent intelligence revealing that Spain would soon ally with France against Britain, if it had not already done so.*

As the consul was leaving, Bush nervously approached his captain to report Doughty's escape. After feigning surprised outrage and then self-condemnation for his own foolish negligence, Hornblower awkwardly changed the subject, informing Bush of their imminent danger should Hotspur *remain in port and also of the tantalizing prospect of gold on Spanish ships out at sea. Thus the episode of Doughty's escape was almost immediately forgotten by the crew of the* Hotspur *amid the frantic bustle of preparations to set sail for the safety of open waters. Forgotten, that is, by all but Hornblower, who hours later sat alone in his cabin, consumed in despair and self-loathing.*

He sat with drooping head, deep in depression. He had lost his integrity,
and that meant he had lost his self-respect. In his life he had made
mistakes, whose memory could still make him writhe, but this time he had
done far more. He had committed a breach of duty. He had connived
at—he had actually contrived—the escape of a deserter, of a criminal. He
had violated his sworn oath, and he had done so from mere personal
reasons, out of sheer self-indulgence. Not for the good of the service, not
for his country's cause, but because he was a softhearted sentimentalist.
He was ashamed of himself, and the shame was all the more acute when
his pitiless self-analysis brought up the conviction that, if he could relive
those past hours, he would do the same again. (p. 313)

In view of his final, and to him inexplicable, realization, it would be
the worst kind of injustice to accept at face value Hornblower's punish-
ing self-analysis. The Doughty affair does not disclose, as he supposed,
simply a victory of sentiment over duty and integrity. Instead, it reveals
that Hornblower instinctively knew, even though he could not understand, that the principles he so revered could not have ultimate proba-
tive power in guiding his actions, that all action is personal. The source
of Hornblower's heroism was also his tragic flaw: his inability to
comprehend that he acted better than he thought—while believing, to
his continuing sorrow and consternation, precisely the reverse. Because
of his morbid bent toward self-condemnation, Hornblower failed at
genuine self-reflexive understanding, but succeeded in spite of himself
in acting on humane instincts—instincts that in his mind he could only
equate with irresponsible sentimentalism. Hornblower may or may not
have made a responsible decision regarding Doughty, but it seems clear
that he did act responsibly, but did not know it.

NOTES

1. While, albeit in varying degrees, all three of these writers harbored democratic
sentiments, there is nothing inherently democratic about the notion of responsibility
deriving from their views. The idea that administrators should be accountable to policy-
makers may be consistent with either autocratic or democratic governments.

2. There is a second, and subtler, aspect of the pathology of goal displacement,
however, the cause of which has nothing to do with the consciously self-serving motives
of administrators and the cure of which cannot be found in institutional reforms or moral
persuasion. The label for it is "technicism," which Manfred Stanley (1978) describes as
the prevailing attitude of modern consciousness in which technological norms and values
have triumphed over those of personal authenticity and human community.

3. This idea may be grasped intuitively by reflecting on the experience of listening to someone whom we sense is posturing about his values, rather than authentically believing them. That is, we perceive a disjunction or inconsistency between the content of what the speaker is saying and the real reason it is being said. It is not that we judge the speaker to be deliberately deceptive or hypocritical; rather, we sense that the speaker is unaware that his words and the context in which they are spoken fail to match, that they stand in an awkward relation to one another. On these occasions, our feeling typically is not one of anger (which we would feel if we sensed a deliberate attempt to deceive us), but one of embarrassment owing to our sense that the speaker is not fully aware of what he is doing and saying.

4. In noting the contemporary pervasiveness of narcissism, in contrast to the principal psychopathologies of an earlier age, Lasch says that "psychoanalysis, a therapy that grew out of experience with severely repressed and morally rigid individuals who needed to come to terms with a rigorous inner 'censor,' today finds itself confronted more and more often with a 'chaotic and impulse-ridden character.' It must deal with patients who 'act out' their conflicts instead of repressing or sublimating them" (p. 37).

REFERENCES

Arendt, H. (1958). *The human condition*. Chicago: University of Chicago Press.

Arendt, H. (1963). *Eichmann in Jerusalem: A report on the banality of evil*. Harmondsworth, Middlesex, England: Penguin Books.

Berger, P.L., & Luckmann, T. (1967). *The social construction of reality*. Garden City, NY: Anchor Books.

Biller, R.P. (1979). Toward public administration rather than an administration of publics: Strategies of accountable disaggregation to achieve human scale and efficacy, and live within the natural limits of intelligence and other scarce resources. In R. Clayton & W.B. Storm (Eds.), *Agenda for public administration* (pp. 151-172). Los Angeles: University of Southern California Press.

Dean, J.W., III. (1976). *Blind ambition*. New York: Simon & Schuster.

Finer, H. (1941). Administrative responsibility in democratic government. *Public Administration Review, 1*(2) 335-350.

Follett, M.P. (1940). In H.C. Metcalf & L. Urwick (Eds.). *Dynamic administration*. New York: Harper & Brothers.

Forester, C.S. (1962). *Hornblower and the Hotspur*. Boston: Little, Brown.

Friedrich, C.J. (1940). Public policy and the nature of administrative responsibility, In C.J. Friedrich & E.S. Mason (Eds.). *Public policy* (pp. 3-24). Cambridge, MA: Harvard University Press.

Hampden-Turner, C. (1971). *Radical man*. Garden City, NJ: Anchor Books.

Harmon, M.M., & Mayer, R.T. (1986). *Organizational theory for public administration*. Boston: Little, Brown.

Harvey, J. (1974, Summer). The Abilene paradox: The management of agreement. *Organizational Dynamics, 3*, 63-80.

Herman, S.M., & Korenich, M. (1977). *Authentic management: A gestalt orientation to organizations and their development*. Reading, MA: Addison-Wesley.

Lasch, C. (1979). *The culture of narcissism*. London: W.W. Norton.

Lowi, T. (1969). *The end of liberalism.* New York: W.W. Norton.

Rohr, J.A. (1984). *To run a constitution: The legitimacy of the administrative state.* Lawrence: University of Kansas Press.

Sayre, W., & Kaufman, H. (1960). *Governing New York City.* New York: Russell Sage.

Simon, H.A. (1976). *Administrative behavior: A study of decision-making processes in administrative organizations* (3rd ed.). New York: Free Press.

Stanley, M. (1978). *The technological conscience: Survival and dignity in an age of expertise.* New York: Free Press.

Wamsley, G.L., Goodsell, C.T., Rohr, J.A., Stivers, C.M., White, O.F., & Wolfe, J.E. (1987). The public administration and the governance process: Refocusing the American dialogue. In R.C. Chandler, (Ed). *The centennial history of the American administrative state* (pp. 291-317). New York: Macmillan.

Weber, M. (1947). *The theory of social and political organization* (A. Henderson & T. Parsons, Trans.). Glencoe, IL: Free Press.

White, O.F. (1990). Reframing the authority—participation debate. In Gary L. Wamsley et al. *Refounding public administration* (pp. 182-245). Newbury Park, CA: Sage.

Whitmont, E. (1982). *Return of the goddess.* New York: Crossroad.

Wildavsky, A. (Ed.). (1979). *Speaking truth to power.* Boston: Little, Brown.

Wilson, W. (1941, December). The study of administration. *Political Science Quarterly, 66,* 481-506. (Reprinted from June, 1887.)

PART III:

Images of Public Administration: Visions of the Future

The chapters in this final section present images of what public administration may be in the future depending on how the questions of legitimacy, community, and practical wisdom and discourse raised in this volume are resolved. Robert Zinke depicts a future in which we have chosen to cope with the problems of deculturation and hyperpluralism by imposing on society a technicist metaphor often dear to public administrators' hearts: electronic data processing. Zinke projects a society in which data processing has become the basis for a unifying rhetoric that binds the ideational, cultural, and social fragments of modern society in a postmodern world.

He sees government and public administration playing a major role in this process. Governance is accomplished by a "cybernetic" state, which acts as a "servomechanism" to maintain political, economic, and social equilibrium. The cybernetic state is dominated by an "information-processing elite" who employ a thoroughly instrumentalized public service to tend the servomechanism of the government. This elite ensures that *reality* is defined in terms of technicist ideology and the dominant information-processing metaphor. They also "anticipate" the needs, thoughts, and actions of the citizens by virtue of their superior access to processed data.

If Zinke's image of the future is a pessimistic one, Ralph Hummel's work provides a counterbalancing optimism. In fact, if one is to believe his vision, the Phoenix project is well under way on a massive scale. Hummel sees the icon of the circle ". . . as an attempt to repair what has been torn apart by the pyramid." Among other things, this statement refers to the shift from hierarchical to team control in organizations; increased recognition of employee roles in planning and managing work; the restoration of evaluative language and mutual definition of the situation in the work place; recognition of the role the irrational and the unconscious play in administration; and democratization of the public policy process.

Hummel views the postmodern public administrator as key to the social and political transition from pyramid to circle. Crucial here is the role public administrators can play in mediating between the dying remains of a hierarchical system and the emerging economic, political, and linguistic community symbolized by the circle.

In what has been called the "Evergreen Manifesto," Guy Adams and his colleagues end the volume with a vision of the future that is nothing less than a challenge to make the Phoenix project the completion of a democratic revolution in the United States. The Evergreen Group argue that the costs of joining liberalism and democracy in the United States have been great. While we have been willing to espouse political (legal/procedural) democracy we have been unwilling to forge an economic counterpart. Thus we have been content to tolerate profound socioeconomic inequalities in our system and settle for a limited procedural democracy emphasizing rights and due process.

Based on this analysis, the manifesto calls for extension of popular democratic control over the way we operate and regulate our economic system and distribute our wealth. It is argued that only with these changes can we escape the self-serving individualism of our liberal heritage and form a genuine democratic community that rests on equality and fraternity as well as liberty.

Adams and his coauthors suggest public administrators can assist in this process in four ways, by: (a) decentralizing authority and responsibility where possible to lay citizens, (b) interpreting the public interest through a highly participative interaction among all relevant publics, (c) practicing public administration in a critical self-aware manner, and (d) rising above narrow professionalism to genuine service of the democratic electorate.

7

Administron:
The Image of the Administrator as
Information Processor

ROBERT C. ZINKE

INTRODUCTION

This chapter suggests that information processing theories of government reflect the technicist influence on administrative thought identified earlier by McSwain and White. It argues that as seen in administrative circles, technicism promises social unity through the management and control of information.

In public administration, information-processing theories have been used to characterize the nature of public organizations and to describe administrative activity. Some scholars argue, for example, that "[m]anagement—public or private—is largely a process of handling information" (Bernstein, 1976). Others suggest that "[a] bureaucracy is essentially an information producing, distributing, and consuming organism" (Porat, 1982). Reflecting these views, Harlan Cleveland (1987) writes:

> Government *is* information. Its employees are nearly all information workers, its raw material is information inputs, its product is those inputs transformed into policies, which are simply an authoritative form of information. So in a narrow sense, to consider government information policy is not far from considering the essence of government itself. (p. 605)

Information-processing theories of public administration are technicist because they seek to describe and account for political phenomena with computer-based languages and concepts. As Stanley asserts, "technicism" constitutes "a state of mind that rests on an act of conceptual misuse, reflected in myriad linguistic ways, of scientific and technological modes of reasoning" (1978, p. 12). This misuse occurs when scientists too quickly adopt a technological metaphor to simplify the analytical and explanatory stages of their research or when they act on the assumption that the same theoretical model can be used to explain the physical, the organic, and the human realms of nature. It also occurs when standards of "proper scientific research" are taken as the only criteria for knowledge and are applied in domains of inquiry where other criteria may be more appropriate (e.g., in ethics, politics, religion) (pp. 12-13).

Two of the most important criteria often misapplied are: the *technological test of truth*, which is based on the twin assumptions that "the *ultimate* standard of verification of a scientific theory is the ability to control the world's behavior by means of technological operations deduced from the theories," and that scientific understanding entails "the ability to deconstruct and reconstruct the object of understanding at will"; and *determinism*, which assumes that with enough knowledge about the world and its natural laws, any event can be predicted (p. 13).

Insofar as it insists that scientific and technological modes of inquiry and discourse are appropriate in all domains of human experience, technicism constitutes "a species of cognitive conquest," a form of cultural imperialism which, "through linguistic reinterpretation," leads all realms of discourse and action "as vassals into the dominion of the new [technological] metaphors and their assumptions" (p. 14).

This essay traces the paths on which public administration might be led into the domain of the information-processing metaphor. Specifically, this essay seeks to show that (a) the information-processing metaphor of human thought has had significant implications for the identity and self-understanding of administrative practitioners, (b) this metaphor has directly influenced the characterization of public organizations and administration in the contemporary literature, (c) when taken literally, the metaphor has served as a rhetorical form that promotes control of information as the basis for community, and (d) information-processing theories of public administration reflect larger currents in society that see in the Information Age a new spirituality that embraces the single-minded commitment to scientific and technological rationality and glorifies the instrumental uses of human beings.

THE COMPUTER METAPHOR: PEOPLE AS INFORMATION PROCESSORS

In many ways, the computer has begun to serve as a metaphor for describing various aspects of nature, including human beings. The computer metaphor derives its intellectual force from the view that the way human beings think is analogous with the way computers process information. When taken as a worldview, the information-processing model of nature has significant implications for how administrators conceive their role in public organizations.

The computer has become a "defining technology" in contemporary society (Bolter, 1984). A defining technology "defines or redefines man's role in relation to nature" and "develops links, metaphorical or otherwise, with a culture's science, philosophy, or literature." It "resembles a magnifying glass, which collects and focuses seemingly disparate ideas in a culture into one bright, sometimes piercing ray" (pp. 11-12). Changes in technology alone do not bring about changes in man's view of nature, "but clearly the technology of any age provides an attractive window through which thinkers can view both their physical and metaphysical worlds," and defining technologies "bring ideas into a new focus by explaining or exemplifying them in new ways to larger audiences" (pp. 10, 11-12).

The computer has become a way to metaphorically describe reality. It has facilitated a growing worldview that everything in the universe involves the receipt, processing, and transmission of information. Here, *information processing* refers to single or multiple chains of hierarchically arranged processes and subprocesses that work sequentially to take information received in one form and transform it into other forms. From this perspective, everything in nature—human and nonhuman, animate and inanimate—is involved in information processing, and this common trait provides the link between human beings and nature (Ashby, 1964; Weiner, 1961). The study of nature, according to this worldview, involves the creation of languages that can help describe and explain the continuous exchange of information between subprocessing units—people, machines, and so forth—and can set forth easily understandable rules and algorithms that govern the way these units use information inputs and transform them into usable outputs. Of this perspective, Weizenbaum notes: "Language capable of describing ongoing processes, particularly in terms of modular subprocesses, have already had an enormous effect on the way computer people think of every aspect of their worlds, not merely those directly related to their work. The information-processing view of the world so engendered qualifies as a genuine metaphor" (Weizenbaum, 1976b).

In contemporary society, many ordinary people see computers as "second-selves," attributing human qualities to computers (Turkle, 1984). In addition, as Bolter (1984) notes, "the computer is constantly serving as a metaphor for the human mind or brain: psychologists speak of the input and output, sometimes even the hardware and software of the brain; linguists treat human language as if it were a programming code; and everyone speaks of making computers 'think'" (p. 11).

The most systematic development of the information-processing perspective has occurred in the interdisciplinary cognitive sciences. Among the main features of cognitive science "is the faith that central to any understanding of the human mind is the electronic computer. . . . Not only are computers indispensable for carrying out studies of various sorts, but more crucially, the computer also serves as the most viable model of how the human mind functions" (Gardner, 1985, p. 6).

The way computers process information, for example, has served as a metaphor to describe human memory. According to this view, human memory resembles "a somewhat computer-like *set of transformations* of information from the moment of perception on; these transformations change the incoming information anywhere from slightly to greatly, and thereby cause it to be retained everywhere from momentarily to permanently. . . . In short, the new likeness of memory is not that of a structure but of a *series or system of processes*" (Hunt, 1982).

The information-processing image entails at least five parallels seen to exist between people and computers:

1. The mind in humans tells the brain how to handle information in the same way that software programs tell the central processing unit—the hardware of computers—how information should be handled.
2. Human beings, like computers, can be trained or retrained (programmed or reprogrammed) to solve problems and to behave in certain ways by changing the experiences (the information base) that inform their actions.
3. Human beings function as cybernetic systems. Just as computers send, receive, and process electrical signals, and rely on electrical feedback

loops to ensure proper functioning, human beings communicate by sending and receiving information, and they must utilize information loops to properly give and receive instructions in complex situations where continuous behavioral adjustments are necessary for correct performance and for survival.

4. Human thought is totally adaptive. Just as the degree of complexity observed in the operation of a computer program is a function of the parameters built into it by its programmers, the apparent complexity of human thought is merely a function of the complex environment in which human beings operate.

5. As with computers, human beings can be seen as artifacts, amenable to systematic comparison and study. Human behavior can be broken down into simple operational rules and algorithms, mathematically modeled, and then studied.

On the basis of these parallels, researchers in the cognitive sciences see the use of computer models as a valid way to test hypotheses about the operation of the human mind. Schank (1984) argues that "Artificial Intelligence [AI] is really just a new term for the ancient enterprise of the study of mind, which must be tested at every stage," and he explains, "The only way to know that we have developed an accurate theory of natural language processing is to create a program or build a machine that tests the theory. One can see what goes wrong with one's initial theory, and then improve it. AI thus is very close in spirit to philosophy, linguistics, psychology, and a host of other fields—except that AI tests its hypotheses on a computer" (p. 32).

Similarly, Simon (1982) has argued: "Perhaps the greatest significance of the computer lies in its impact on Man's view of himself. No longer accepting the geocentric view of the universe, he now begins to learn that mind, too, is a phenomenon of nature, explainable in terms of simple mechanisms. Thus the computer aids him to obey, for the first time, the ancient injunction, 'Know thyself'" (p. 201).

The worldview of information processing suggests that truth is relative to the processing functions and structures built into particular information-processing systems. The criterion used to determine what is true depends on the limitations for processing information that inhere in particular information processors under consideration. Thus, true knowledge as defined by human beings will be different from that defined by computers, organizations, or societies. Epistemology becomes the study and classification of the limitations for processing information that inhere in different structurally and functionally built information processors (Mouloud, 1984). Insofar as the judgment and evaluation of individual human behavior is sought, the realm and level of information processing—personal, organizational, social, technological, natural, and so forth—that is producing the information used for judging or evaluating must be specified. Put another way, human beings no longer possess the exclusive ability to define truth and evaluate their behavior on the basis of that truth. Instead, truth is the computational product of "parallel processing" carried out by multiple information processors (Thagard, 1988).

The information-processing image also suggests that human behavior largely consists in theorizing about how information should be processed to solve social problems. Simon (1982) argues that "learning how to think and learn, and learning how to design an information-processing system are not really separate and distinct topics." He continues:

> They are parts of the same topic. A human thinker is an organization of memories combined with a system of basic information processes that uses those memories, together with new information, to solve problems. But that is a definition of a business organization, too, whose components—men and computers—are, in turn, systems of the same general sort. This is the kind of system—at the level of the individual, and at the level of the organization—that we must understand if we are to continue our technical progress. (p. 120)

Ultimately, the information-processing perspective embraces the notion that knowledge represents "power to produce new outcomes, outcomes that were not previously attainable," and that the preference of knowledge over ignorance stems from the belief that "the human species is capable of progress and, on balance, has progressed over the centuries." In this regard, "[k]nowledge about the human mind can make an important contribution to that progress" (Simon, 1982, pp. 200-201). In and of itself, this view of knowledge is not new, but as Schank's (1984) and Simon's remarks suggest, the information-processing view adds an interesting twist: the ultimate test of human progress is whether human beings can consciously design, reproduce, and improve upon the human mind through the structuring of their technological and their institutional environments.

For public administration, the information-processing image provides administrators with a new identity and self-understanding. The "public executive" becomes a "social programmer" who designs "artificial systems" that adapt public institutions to "a changing social, technical, and physical environment" (Crow & Shangrow, 1989), or, to use Simon's words, "a designer and maintainer of man-machine systems that process information" (Simon, 1982, p. 120). Moreover, public administration becomes a "design science," the role of which is "to design and evaluate institutions, mechanisms, and processes that convert collective will and public resources into social profit" (Crow & Shangrow, 1989, p. 156).

The recent work of Harlan Cleveland, (1985, 1987) best exemplifies the new self-understanding of public administrators. Cleveland argues that society has become "informatized," that is, it sees "the production not of things but of symbols as its dominant activity," and that effective leadership in public administration means being able to integrate and put together the disparate sources of information so that society can be managed (1987, p. 605).

What is required, according to Cleveland, is that administrative leaders "think hard about the impact of the new information environment on their own responsibilities—using the information technologies that have made such rethinking both possible and imperative" (1987, p. 607). In addition: "[T]he critical dimension of leadership, and the centerpiece of education for leadership, is . . . organizing your mind for the analysis and projection of breadth. Breadth is a quality of mind, the capacity to relate disparate facts to a coherent theory, to fashion tactics that are part of a strategy, to act today in ways that are consistent with a studied view of the future" (1985, pp. 9-10). Computers and systems analyses represent some of the basic techniques that provide knowledge executives with a "studied view," since "[t]ools such as these empower those who learn to use them to make complex judgments in the more mindful knowledge of alternative futures" (p. 197).

PUBLIC ADMINISTRATION AS INFORMATION PROCESSING

The information-processing view has been used in the administrative literature as a way to describe office work, public organizations, and the relation of government to society at large. Together, these descriptions present a composite image of public institutions as "thinking organizations," symbiotic man-machine systems that shape society through their ability to control information.

Since the early stages of the computerization of governmental operations, in the 1950s and early '60s, the view of *office workers as information processors* has gained favor among some writers and scholars. A book review written in 1954 by an employee from the U.S. Bureau of the Budget and entitled "The Automatic Handling of Office Paper Work" states, "Although the office is engaged in handling masses of papers and cards, 'the primary function of the office is the handling of information'" (Gammon, p. 63). A 1957 article concerned with "automatic character reading for data processing systems" provides the first explicit mention of the information-processor image in the *Public Administration Review*. Referring to office workers, the article states that "[a]ny data system can be symbolized with three components: input, processor, and output." It goes on: "This symbolism is not limited to a machine system. For example, handwritten invoices (INPUT) can be summarized by a clerk (PROCESSOR) in a hand operation into a report (OUTPUT) for combination with other accounting data or for direct use by management" (Hattery, p. 159).

Since the mid-1960s and early 1970s, other scholars have conceptualized *public organizations as information-processing* systems. This version of the metaphor has received its clearest expression in the works of Galbraith (1987) and Simon (1960, 1976, 1982). Galbraith's information-processing model of organizations seeks "to explain why and through what mechanisms uncertainty and information relate to structure" (p. 294). Galbraith's model envisions organizations as collections of interdependent subunits, each responsible for carrying out subroutines and subtasks. Coordination among these subunits occurs through channels of communication and information that are governed with explicitly stated rules, programs, and procedures. Galbraith argues that differences in organizational structure are related to differences "in the capacity of the organizations to process information about events that could not be anticipated in advance" (p. 302). The greater the uncertainty, he assumes, the greater the complexity of communication and of information handling within the organization.

Galbraith's views complement the influential ideas of Herbert Simon, who has generally argued that human abilities to make rational decisions are limited and that to achieve full rationality, organizations must adopt machine-based intelligence systems to complement human decision making. Simon has argued that decisions in organizations can be classified as either structured or unstructured. He suggests that structured decisions can be handed over almost fully to computers while unstructured decisions can at least partially be handled by heuristic computer techniques (1960). In addition, he has argued that by viewing an organization "as a decision-making and information-processing system," it is possible to focus "on the decision-making process itself—that is, upon the flows and transformations of symbols." Here, "[i]nstead of watching a man or computer as information reaches him and he processes it and transmits new information in his turn," Simon can "watch information as it flows from one man or computer to another and is transformed in the course of the flow" (1976, pp. 292-293). In his work on the development of General Problem Solver in the early 1970s, Simon sought to embody in a computer program a few heuristic rules believed to guide human problem solving (Johnson, 1986, pp. 47-48). Overall, Simon's work has emphasized that administrative behavior is a function of the relationship between the information-processing behavior of human administrators and that of machines.

The information-processing metaphor has also been used to describe *the relation of government to society at large.* As Dunn (1982) has argued, "the information-processing metaphor opens up a novel and enlightening view of social structures and processes" (p. 292). The image that best characterizes the use of the metaphor is that of the *cybernetic state.*

The cybernetic approach sees public organizations as components of larger social systems, and it emphasizes the need to improve the functions that governmental systems serve in these larger systems. The notion of man-machine systems serves to separate administrators from the functions of administration, and similarly, the cybernetic approach separates governmental institutions from the functions of government; that is, public administration is seen as an information exchange process that goes beyond the boundaries of public organizations and institutions.

The cybernetic version of the information-processing metaphor rests heavily on the works of Karl Deutsch (1963) and David Easton (1965). In the combined view of these two scholars, government represents a servocontrol mechanism of information and communication that maintains equilibrium in the economic, the social, and, ultimately, the political system. In addition, it seeks to develop and regularize the inputs from society (resources conceived as information) that will allow it to adequately process those inputs (through legislative, executive, and judicial processes, conceived as information-subprocessing functions) and transform them into outputs (public policies and regulations). Government relies on feedback (program evaluations, public opinion polls) to see how well its policies are working and to determine whether additional policy changes—that is, steering corrections—are needed. From this perspective, the purpose of public administration lies in developing and refining the various input, processing, and output instruments that government uses to maintain equilibrium in society.

Ultimately, the notions above suggest a composite image of administrative institutions as "thinking organizations" (Sims, Gioia, & Associates, 1986). In the thinking organization, the goals of individuals and those of the organization coalesce into a single goal-directed entity: "Thus, the individual not only acts on behalf of the organization in the usual agency sense, but he also acts, more subtly, 'as the organization' when he embodies the values, beliefs, and goals of the collectivity" (Chatman, Bell, & Straw, p. 211). This coalescence is not accidental, however, for in the thinking organization thought is "managed" (pp. 91-214). The organization develops schemas, scripts, and social cognitive structures that present and reinforce organizational self-identities. In this context, the organization "seems to take on a life of its own." It becomes a "symbiosis of human beings and machines" where the human component—human brains and cognition—are fused with technological organs—computer-based knowledge systems—for the purpose of improving the intellectual functions of the organization (pp. 91-214).

The idea of the thinking organization involves two interpretations. On the one hand, it "is merely an expressive metaphor intended to reflect the notion that thinking organization members make the decisions that influence the actions of themselves, others, and their organizations." On the other hand, the notion of the thinking organization "is a rich metaphor chosen to recognize the view that there is no essential difference between organizations and their members. . . . According to this position, people *are* the organization; their cognitions, visions, and subsequent actions define the essence of 'being organized.' Thus, when people in organizations think, organizations think. In this interpretation the metaphorical title therefore applies more literally" (Sims, Gioia, & Associates, pp. 1-2).

It is the more literal interpretation that gives the information-processing metaphor its power in public administration.

INFORMATION PROCESSING AS
TECHNOLOGICAL RHETORIC

When taken literally, the information-processing metaphor provides powerful rhetorical justification for sustained social and political commitment to computers and information technology. A form of technological rhetoric, the information-processing metaphor in public administration proceeds from the assumption that "[m]odern government and public administration can no longer do without information technology" (Horton & Marchand, 1982, p. 3), and it portends a reality that accepts the full integration of computers in public organizations and institutions as natural and necessary. On this basis, the metaphor holds open the promise that technology can unify a fragmented, pluralist society.

As suggested earlier, a defining technology—such as the computer—unifies a culture's worldview by providing a single metaphorical image that makes the world easily describable and comprehensible to diverse audiences and intellectual communities (Bolter, 1984). The whole notion of a defining technology, however, reflects the convergence of rhetoric and technology in the Information Age. Richard McKeon, a contemporary philosopher, argues that "technology itself" has undergone a "rhetorical transformation" (1987, p. 12).

According to McKeon, *rhetoric* refers to more than just a mode of discourse, with statically conceived sets of arguments and tactics. It also represents an "instrument of cohesion," an "organizing principle," a dynamic method that changes from one historical age to the next and formulates the problems and challenges facing each new age. For McKeon, the rhetoric in any age produces "actions as well as words, and it connects disparate things—cultures, disciplines, sciences, languages, ideologies—by extrapolating commonality from the uncommon" (Backman, 1987, p. xxiv). Technology has become a rhetorical form.

As a unifying force, 20th century rhetoric justifies technologically induced social change by appeals to information technology as an ordering principle, or what McKeon refers to as the "logos of techne" (McKeon, 1987, p. 13). In this regard, contemporary rhetoric finds its "commonplaces," or accepted starting points, in a world constituted of advanced telecommunication and information technologies. As McKeon explains: "rhetoric again has assumed a dominant place in our thought and action. Whereas the rhetoric of the Romans took its commonplaces from the practical arts and jurisprudence and the rhetoric of the Humanists took its commanplaces from the fine arts and literature, our rhetoric finds its commonplaces in the technology of commercial advertising and of calculating machines" (McKeon, 1987, p. 34).

Information-processing theories of government assume that social cohesion rests with society's ability to maintain a common conceptual structure of understanding, and that such maintenance involves the control of management of information (Thompson, 1982). Thus, "it is its data gathering and communicating that ties a community together, maintains the cohesiveness and consistency of its underlying conceptual structure" (p. 80).

As a natural human activity, the assumption continues, scientific theorizing inevitably creates new views of reality, and technological innovation requires significant environmental restructuring—the "technological imperative" (Winner, 1977). Unless the results and consequences of these activities are rapidly communicated across the society and integrated within the community's common conceptual structure, they promote cultural divisions and social disintegration. These divisions can be minimized, however, if the society can maintain rapid and efficient communication channels and if the society's social institutions can create new languages and learning systems that facilitate conceptual integration. As one theorist contends: "Fractionization occurs when rates of innovation exceed the ability of the community to communicate the results of innovation. Thus if the technological means of communication can keep pace, the moment of fractionization can be postponed" (Thompson, 1982, p. 80). From this perspective, telecommunication and information-processing technologies, as well as the organizational structures and social institutions that develop, process, and control information, hold the key to social maintenance and cohesion.

The assumptions above have led information-processing theorists to contend that fragmented knowledge and information bases have made public communication inefficient and thus have hampered government's ability to maintain social equilibrium (Horton & Marchand, 1982). Potentially useful policy information, it is argued, "if forthcoming at all, is garbled and distorted, or is packaged in ways that make it incomprehensible or difficult to use" (p. 2). This occurs because no uniform and comprehensive managerial policies exist that govern the production, retrieval, and dissemination of information. If left unchecked, social "fractionization" will result. Such a situation implies an "information imperative" that requires "mechanisms whereby existing and new *sources* [of information] . . . are recognized when they emerge, identified accurately and completely as to scope and content, catalogued under professionally acceptable but yet easily used and flexibly maintainable classification systems, and with efficient but cheap search and accessing capabilities that would permit tailoring to a universal audience of users whose inquiries would inevitably range widely in form and content" (Horton, 1982, pp. 371-372).

The notion of an information imperative appeals to an older, ongoing goal in public administration: to forge a common language or organizational framework that facilitates communication among myriad communities of expertise and specialization. Indeed, public administration itself has its roots in the public desire to bring numerous communities of discourse—such as political science, economics, sociology, urban planning, and social work—together under one umbrella, labeled "the polity profession" (Stever, 1988).

The attraction of the information-processing metaphor within public administration derives from its apparent rhetorical power to provide unity amidst diverse conceptual orientations and views of reality. Through its conception of public administration as a design science that structures public institutions as "inquiring systems" (Churchman, 1971), the information-processing metaphor provides administrators with a rhetorical meta-vision of reality that sees the establishment of governmental man-machine systems as a necessary component of social and communal integration. It provides a language of natural processes and subprocesses that seeks to legitimate governmental institutions and structures in an age where the commonplaces of political discussion are seen to reside in science and technology.

INSTRUMENTAL ORIGINS OF THE INFORMATION-PROCESSING METAPHOR

To explain the appeal of the information-processing metaphor—indeed of technological rhetoric as a whole—as a basis for community is not to explain the social and cultural origins of the appeal itself. These origins are complex and cannot be fully explicated here. However, a few cursory remarks about them are relevant in the present context.

A number of theories have been advanced that could explain the rise of information processing as a rhetorical form in contemporary society. The most common explanations have centered on the political, administrative, and economic motivations to justify computer technologies in society. Noble (1984), for example, suggests that throughout the Cold War era, the military industrial complex has seen computer-guided factory automation as a way to subdue Russia, abroad, and labor unions, at home. In addition, the emerging concepts of cybernetics have provided a language useful for justifying computers as a command-and-control device in the workplace. More recently, this same argument has arisen in connection with computing in public sector organizations.

Finding that "the most important variable correlating with overall success of computing implementation proved to be the organization's commitment to advanced technology," a recent study of public organizations suggests that "computing is a complex social enterprise that involves the continuing mobilization of social forces internal and external to the user organizations for its initiation, development, and maintenance" (Kraemer & King, 1986, p. 492). As the authors explain:

> Generally, data processing leadership is the pivotal force, but it requires the support of top management and of literally hundreds of others who are managers and end-users in the operating departments of the organization. Husbanding that support involves: socializing each new wave of top management, department management, and department users; reinforcing that socialization by creating a positive culture complete with rituals, stories, and heroes; operating near capacity so that resources are adequate for current tasks and demonstrate technical efficiency, but obviously inadequate for new tasks without data processing growth; and planning for and justifying data processing growth in terms of organizational performance (e.g., "services to clients," "market share"). (pp. 493-494)

The overall level of commitment needed to implement computing has led other writers to suggest that computer innovations draw upon a contemporary "cult of information" (Roszak, 1986). Examining the implications of computers in education, Roszak contends that many classroom uses of computers serve to foster and reinforce the information-processing model of human thought and that a host of economic and political interests stand behind these uses in education.

Implicitly, all of these theories reflect the notion of an "information elite" that stands behind the creation and maintenance of a "computer state" (Burnham, 1980). In such a state, government agencies allow this elite to "anticipate the probable future thoughts and activities of groups of people" (pp. 14-15). In addition, it facilitates a "dossier society" where elite decision makers give primacy to computer-aided interpretation of social reality over all other forms of interpretation (Laudon, 1986).

A second set of theories suggests that computer-based rhetorical forms reflect the culmination of larger historical and evolutionary developments. Beniger (1986) suggests that during the past 100 years, society has undergone a "Control Revolution" and that information processing lies at the heart of that revolution. He believes that "[n]o human technology has more in common with all living things than do our various capabilities to process information, whether they be institutionalized in the formal structures and procedures of bureaucracy, input electronically to computer memory, or photolithographed into the silicon wafers of microprocessors," and that "[i]t is through the understanding of these capabilities, the essential life processes of organization, programming, and the decision to effect control, that we can best hope to answer the many challenging questions raised by the Control Revolution" (pp. 59-60).

Taking a more critical view, Weizenbaum (1976a) suggests that "the computing machine represents merely an extreme extrapolation of a much more general technological usurpation of man's capacity to act as an autonomous agent in giving meaning to his world" (p. 9). The modern reliance on computer technology represents the latest stage in a historical process moving toward increased conformity among individuals in Western society and increased reliance on processes that human beings neither comprehend nor fully understand. He states:

> It is perhaps paradoxical that just when in the deepest sense man has ceased to believe in—let alone to trust—his own autonomy, he has begun to rely on autonomous machines, that is, on machines that operate for long periods of time entirely on the basis of their own internal realities. If his reliance on such machines is to be based on something other than unmitigated despair or blind faith, he must explain to himself what these machines do and even how they do what they do. This requires him to build some conception of their internal "realities." Yet most men don't understand computers to even the slightest degree. (p. 9)

Weizenbaum's remarks point to a final set of theories that might explain the growing pervasiveness of information processing as a mode of discourse. These theories suggest that a pervasive "experience of nothingness" characterizes the sense of being for a growing number of people in modern culture (Novak, 1972). This experience has elicited a number of philosophical, religious, and cultural responses (Jonas, 1963). The faith in natural, but partially mysterious, pervasive structures that maintain order and community through the processing of information reflects one of these responses. It reflects one attempt to find meaning in a culture that no longer seems to provide spiritual stability and purpose. Because of its technological basis, however, this faith involves something else: the belief that human beings are merely instruments of larger historical and evolutionary forces that they themselves have put in motion. As Jonas comments: "Now, *techne* in the form of modern technology has turned into an infinite forward-thrust of the race, its most significant enterprise, in whose permanent, self-transcending advance to ever greater things the vocation of man tends to be seen, and whose success of maximal control over things and himself appears as the consummation of his destiny" (Jonas, 1984, p. 9).

Whether these theories, individually, adequately explain the rise of the information-processing metaphor as a rhetorical form, together they portend a society and culture that glorify the instrumental uses of human beings as a spiritual experience, manifest in a total commitment to human behavior that is scientifically and technologically validated. The information-processing view of government reflects the growing influence of these social and cultural currents in public administration.

CONCLUSION

This essay has traced a few of the paths on which public administration could be led into the technicist domain of the information processing metaphor. This metaphor conceives public leaders as "design scientists" who seek to create symbiotic man-machine systems—"thinking organizations"—that will provide a sense of artificial order and community in a world where many individuals have lost all sense of personal autonomy and significance, the world of Administron. Concomitantly, those who work and live in public organizations are conceived as technological artifacts—information processors—who can be spiritually manipulated and environmentally conditioned to instrumentally achieve the goals and visions of the communal artificers.

At the turn of the century, Max Weber (1958) spoke of the "iron cage" created when the protestant ideals underlying capitalist development eroded. He noted:

No one knows who will live in this cage in the future, or whether at the end of this tremendous development entirely new prophets will arise, or there will be a great rebirth of old ideas and ideals, or, if neither, mechanized petrification, embellished with a sort of convulsive self-importance. For of the last stage of this cultural development, it might well be truly said: "Specialists without spirit, sensualists without heart; this nullity imagines that it has attained a level of civilization never before achieved." (p. 182).

Perhaps, in the technological age, a new "cage" is now being fashioned, this one from the language of information processing and the technicist rhetoric which such language reflects. Could those who see information processing as a worldview be the new prophets of whom Weber spoke? Prophets who see in an artificially contrived civilization a world secured from personal ideals and aspirations? Let us hope that a few autonomous individuals will be left in the future to look back on this time and say: 'Programmers without foresight, information processors without ideas; that civilization allowed its designers to create minds that saw only thoughtless action as the basis for community.'

REFERENCES

Ashby, W.R. (1964). *An introduction to cybernetics*. London: Methuen. (Originally published 1956.)

Backman, M. (1987). Introduction: Richard McKeon and the renaissance of rhetoric. In R. McKeon, *Rhetoric* (M. Backman, Ed.). Woodbridge, CT: Ox Bow Press.

Beniger, J.R. (1986). *The control revolution*. Cambridge, MA: Harvard University Press.

Bernstein, S.J. (1976). *Computers in public administration*. New York: Pergamon Press.

Bolter, J.D. (1984). *Turing's man*. Chapel Hill: The University of North Carolina Press.

Burnham, D. (1980). *The rise of the computer state*. New York: Random House.

Chatman, J.A., Bell, N.E., & Straw, B.M. (1986). The managed thought: The role of self-justification and impression management on organizational settings. In H.P. Sims, Jr., and D.A. Gioia (Eds.), *The thinking organization* (pp. 191-214). San Francisco: Jossey-Bass.

Churchman, C.W. (1971). *The design of inquiring systems*. New York: Basic Books.

Cleveland, H. (1985). *The knowledge executive*. New York: E.P. Dutton.

Cleveland, H. (1987). Government is information (but not vice versa). *Public Administration Review, 46*(6), 605-607.

Crow, M., & Shangrow, R.F. (1989). Public administration as a design science. *Public Administration Review, 49*(2), 153-158.

Deutsch, K. (1963). *The nerves of government*. New York: Free Press.

Dunn, E.S., Jr. (1982). Information problem no. 2: The symbolic representation of entities. In F.W. Horton & D.A. Marchand (Eds:), *Information management in public administration*. Arlington, VA: Information Resources Press.

Easton, D. (1965). *A systems analysis of political life* (pp. 292-315). New York: John Wiley.

Galbraith, J. (1987). Information processing model. In J.M. Shafritz & J.S. Ott (Eds.), *Classics of organization theory* (2nd ed., pp. 294-303). Chicago: Dorsey Press.

Gammon, H. (1954). The automatic handling of office paper work. *Public Administration Review, 14*, 63-73.

Gardner, H. (1985). *The mind's new science*. New York: Basic Books.

Hattery, L.H. (1957). Automatic character reading for data processing systems. *Public Administration Review, 17*, 159-163.

Heim, M. (1987). *Electric language*. New Haven: Yale University Press.

Horton, F.W. (1982). The information imperative. In F.W. Horton & D.A. Marchand (Eds.), *Information management in public administration* (pp. 364-372). Arlington, VA: Information Resources Press.

Horton, F.W., & Marchand, D.A. (Eds.). (1982). *Information management in public administration*. Arlington, VA: Information Resources Press.

Hunt, M. (1982). *The universe within*. New York: Simon & Schuster.

Johnson, G. (1986). *Machinery of the mind*. Redmond, WA: Microsoft Press.

Jonas, H. (1963). *The gnostic religion*. (2nd ed.). Boston: Beacon Press. (Originally published 1958.)

Jonas, H. (1984). *The imperative of responsibility*. Chicago: University of Chicago Press.

Kraemer, K.L., & King, J.L. (1986). Computing and public organizations. In B. Bozeman & S. Bretschneider (Eds.), Public management information systems [Special issue]. *Public Administration Review, 46*, 488-496.

Laudon, K.C. (1986). *Dossier society*. New York: Columbia University Press.

McKeon, R. (1987). *Rhetoric* (M. Backman, Ed.). Woodbridge, CT: Ox Bow Press.

Mouloud, N. (1984). Machines and mind: The functional sphere and epistemological circles. In S. Torrance (Ed.), *The mind and the machine* (pp. 88-98). New York: Halsted Press.

Noble, D.F. (1984). *Forces of production*. New York: Knopf.

Novak, M. (1972). *The experience of nothingness*. New York: Harper & Row.

Porat, M.U. (1982). The public bureaucracies. In F.W. Horton & D.A. Marchand (Eds.), *Information management in public administration* (pp. 16-27). Arlington, VA: Information Resources Press.

Roszak, T. (1986). *The cult of information*. New York: Pantheon Books.

Schank, R.C. (1984). *The cognitive computer*. Reading, MA: Addison-Wesley.

Simon, H.A. (1960). *The new science of management decision*. New York: Harper & Brothers.

Simon, H.A. (1976). Applying information technology to organization design. *Administrative behavior* (3rd ed.). New York: Free Press.

Simon, H.A. (1982). *Models of bounded rationality* (Vol. 2). Cambridge, MA: MIT Press.

Sims, H.P., Jr., & Gioia, D.A., and Associates. (1986). *The thinking organization*. San Francisco: Jossey-Bass.

Stanley, M. (1978). *The technological conscience*. Chicago: University of Chicago Press.

Stever, J.A. (1988). *The end of public administration*. Dobbs Ferry, NY: Transnational.

Thagard, P. (1988). *Computational philosophy of science*. Cambridge, MA: MIT Press.

Thompson, F.B. (1982). The dynamics of information. In F.W. Horton & D.A. Marchand (Eds.), *Information management in public administration* (pp. 74-84). Arlington, VA: Information Resources Press.

Turkle, S. (1984). *The second self*. New York: Simon & Schuster.

Weber, Max (1958). *The Protestant Ethic and the Spirit of Capitalism*. New York: Charles Scribner. (Originally published 1904)

Weiner, N. (1961). *Cybernetics* (2nd ed.). Cambridge, MA: MIT Press.

Weizenbaum, J. (1976a). *Computer power and human reason*. San Francisco: W.H. Freeman.

Weizenbaum, J. (1976b). On the impact of the computer on society. In S.J. Bernstein (Ed.), *Computers in public administration* (pp. 455-470). New York: Pergamon Press.

Winner, L. (1977). *Autonomous technology*. Cambridge, MA: MIT Press.

8

Circle Managers and Pyramid Managers: Icons for the Post-Modern Public Administrator[1]

RALPH P. HUMMEL

American society is on the move from one reality to another: from modern times to the postmodern era. What will public managers find in postmodernity?

Postmodernity is not simply a new physical world; it is first a state of mind. It is certainly not computers replacing machines, service businesses replacing factories, or product firms yielding to financial mergers in the private sector. It is not tax revolts, retrenchment, cutback management, or privatization in the public sector. These are but the symptoms of late modernity. It is late modernity's terminal disease that abstraction becomes the equivalent for and replaces all that is solid and concrete. Postmodernity is a response that rises up against the absolute equalization of any and all things with any and all values. It is a spirit, not a place. In that spirit, human beings again find themselves as human beings. There is a reassertion of human values, social relations are again between people and not between roles, work again becomes meaningful and not alienating, ethics is again given content and integrated into organizations and society, and politics is restored to its supreme place in the progress of human populations. Yet this is no return to premodernity; the ways of the postmodern spirit are new. To the extent that its promises are not as yet fulfilled, postmodernity is not yet here; but its pathways are emerging. The human being that emerges with it is more synthesizing than analytic. There is a reflective and complex, yet integrative, being such as modernity never knew. Postmodernity is a new state of mind—full of strange meaning, undreamed possibilities, and ominous portent. In traveling there everyone is a Columbus of the mind. One must grasp that world, mentally seize hold of it, before it can be mapped.

For this task there is available the most powerful tool that humankind has invented to encompass the meaning of an entire world: the icon. Icons already contain within themselves all the possibilities of pathways of worlds of meaning. The icon of the waning modern world is a familiar one. It is the pyramid. In the shape of pyramids, we draw the most important and most widely recognized map for modern organizations: the organizational chart. The pyramid has represented the idea of top-down control that has governed not only the modern world but its predecessors back to the ancient Egyptians. But if the pyramid is the icon for the modern world, what is the icon through which we can map out the postmodern world? Both in language use and as visual symbol, the emerging icon for the postmodern world appears to be the circle.

THE COMING OF THE CIRCLE

For the way we relate to each other, we have the circle of the encounter group in social life and the T-group, the work team, and program management in working life.

For the way we work, we have quality circles, in which the knowledge of the worker is recognized for the first time as a source of knowledge all of its own. It must be added to managerial or engineering knowledge before work can be done.

For the way we think, we have the circle of knowing pursued by the reflective practitioner—the individual who derives his knowledge from what he does while he does it and is at the same time able to correct that knowing by reflecting on it.

For the way we feel, we live in an age that values reestablishing the broken connection between rationality and feelings. Reason meets emotion when conscious again meets unconscious. To psychologists such connections signify the recovery of the unified psyche. Its symbol since ancient days has been the circle.

For the way we speak, we have a new approach that limits the modern idea that every act of speaking can freely define the words we use. This approach recognizes the costs of arbitrary definition. Meanings given to terms will not be fully understood, the world will not become fully powerful, unless terms are used in a context understood by all speakers and listeners as it was by those who have spoken before. Referring to ancient religious days, when the god Hermes was messenger between gods and men, linguists refer to this definition of language by language itself as the hermeneutic circle.

For the way we politick, especially in organizations, the most adaptive organizations involve all their members in a circle of discourse to say what it is that the organization might do. The select inner circle— exclusive, secluded, and cut off atop the pyramid—has given way to the larger circle of an organization-wide network for evoking new ideas and convoking the commitment to enact them. There emerges a new and enlarged circle of widely legitimated political discourse.

THE CIRCLE VERSUS THE PYRAMID

Each of these circles is an attempt to repair what has been torn apart by the pyramid. In modern organizations, the prevalent symbol in the shape of the pyramid was the organization chart. There is nothing so apparent to anyone working in organizations today than the fact that the organization chart no longer does its job; it does not show us important realities of how we relate to each other, how we think, how we feel, how we work, how we communicate, and how we politick. But before we can understand why and how the organization chart is no longer a good map for today's postmodern realities, we need to take one last look at the reality that the chart not only described but imposed in the pyramidal organization.

Socially, the pyramidal organization divides people from one another. This is the dark side of the secret of its success. The division of labor makes possible specialization in a new kind of working: working according to standards developed scientifically with efficiency in mind and set at the top and transmitted downward. Mass production and mass service are the result. But separating people who work on the same project from each other makes sense only to the extent that both the object of the work and the work itself lend themselves to being perfectly grasped from the top down and therefore to being rationally divisible into work roles. As early as Elton Mayo (1949) and Frederick Roethlisberger (1941), corporations had to admit that informal organizations existed in the most rationally designed formal organization. This was the first concession that the pyramid needed to be repaired by the circle.

Technically, in terms of how we work, the builders of the pyramid assumed, beginning with Frederick W. Taylor, that an individual worker's hands-on knowledge of a craft could be totally translated through scientific measurement into technical knowledge. This could then be standardized and, after being extracted from the crafts worker, handed in bits and pieces back down to the new worker of modernity, the factory worker. That there were limits to this assumption did not dawn on American industry until the late 1970s when the total quantification of work processes was pushed so far in the automotive industry that, as one engineer was forced to exclaim, "we're shipping junk!" (Moritz & Seaman, 1984, p. 92). Confronted with the Japanese competition and its inroads into traditionally American markets, the industry began studying Japanese work processes and discovered—wonder of wonders—that total translation of hands-on crafts work into units of measurement left out one crucial element: the numbers had to be translated back again. Numbers have no hands to lay on the work. Today, quality circles in over 40% of all American companies with over 500 employees recognize that the worker, no matter how specifically managed, always retains a kind of knowledge that comes only from hands-on work. Here the icon of the circle is called on not simply to repair a knowledge relationship that the pyramid and its reliance on hierarchy's knowledge monopoly ripped apart but to establish for the first time in a hundred years a kind of knowledge—workers' hands-on knowledge—whose very existence had been denied.

Cognitively, the pyramid separated the worker from a sense of mastery. How work was to be done was decided by managers up in the hierarchy or by production engineers. The worker lost the cognitive ability to make judgments about how to master the work—at least officially. In an American attempt to put the worker back in touch with the cognitive ability to make judgments about how to master a piece of work, American scholars (among them Vaill, 1971, 1984; Schoen, 1983, 1987; Hummel, 1985, 1987a, 1987b) recovered from workers' own experience and from European philosophy a basis for recognizing how hands-on knowledge worked, something that Japanese management could not explain. Concepts like knowledge-in-action showed that the origins of any knowledge about work lie in the working itself. How does a tightrope walker know how to walk the tightrope? By walking the tightrope. At the same time, concepts like reflection-in-action showed it is possible to correct one's knowledge-in-action even while one is using it at work (Schoen, 1983, 1987; Hummel, 1985, 1987a, 1987b.).

Emotionally, the pyramid pushed all feelings out of the modern organization. *Sine ira ac studio*—in this Latin phrase the greatest theorist of modern organizations summarized the attitude of the public or private bureaucrat: without hatred or passion, without any feeling— thus would he treat all clients and customers alike. By the 1970s in business administration (e.g., Zaleznick & Kets de Vries, 1975) and the 1980s in public administration (Diamond, 1984, 1986a, 1986b; Diamond & Allcorn, 1985, 1986), the lid had been pried off a snake pit of feelings hidden behind the clockwork image of the rational pyramid (Schwartz, 1986). With mastery and moral judgments officially assigned to management in modern organizations (Hummel, 1977), the hierarchy attracted into management positions individuals who were psychologically deficient (though contextually functional) to begin with or were made so by their position. Arrogant-vindictive or perfectionist narcissists used their positions as managers to force those formally subordinated to make up for managers' personal deficiencies (Diamond, 1987, pp. 168-178). One psychoanalyst treating both public and private managers found that "different roles call for more or fewer irrational attitudes," admitting that irrational and pathological individuals had deeply penetrated the "rational" modern organization (LaBier, cited in Hummel, 1987b, p. 162). With the recognition that emotional exploitation of employees by managers was not unusual but typical, psychoanalytic organization theory and a therapeutic movement developed on the principle of developing healthy emotional relationships by recognizing rather than denying feelings (Zaleznick & Kets de Vries, 1975; Diamond, 1984, 1986, 1987; Diamond & Allcorn, 1985, 1986; Schwartz, 1986).

Linguistically, the pyramid reached an extreme of top-down determination of what could be said and what it could mean in the programming and processing of information through computers. Terms in programs were given merely functional definitions corresponding to electronic operations triggered by the engineering language but arbitrary in a social context. Encapsuled in a program, a word or term was protected against any redefinition by any outsider while it was being processed.

The problem of defining an order and passing it on from top to bottom without distortion seemed solved perfectly and forever. Those who controlled the top, it seemed, now could perfectly control the parts. This would have held true if the entire system had been an information machine. But information machines like computers or rationalized bureaucracies take their life from and feed back into an environment in which human beings deal with their programs through the constant creation, passing away, and recreation of the terms of ordinary language that fit their situation. As Hans-Georg Gadamer (1976b, p. 86) says of the interface between technical language and ordinary language: ". . . precisely defined, unambiguous terms live and communicate only in so far as they are embedded in the life of the [ordinary] language. . . ." Also, machine-processed information cannot answer fundamental questions that human beings need to have answered before knowing what to do on the receipt of an order. Did the speaker mean it—was he or she sincere? Did the speaker have the authority to send the messenger—was the order legitimate? What was the context in which the order was given? Does it make sense in the context of the recipient? Questions like these are involved in all human communications; when human communications are translated into machine information, a great deal of what goes into human communication does not go into the translation. To repair what damage the pyramid has done to human speech, communications theorists and interventionists try to get people to speak to each other as if they meant it (Habermas, 1979; Forester, 1980; Fish, 1987).[2] What is most important here is that people are put back into the communications model with the recognition that even as people define the terms of the system it is also true that the system defines what they say: the hermeneutic circle (White, 1987a, 1987b). As Gadamer and Searle, among others, have observed, to use language does not mean one can simply use a word as a sign to represent an object in a way that is adequate only to him- or herself. In language use, a word is uttered to place the represented object before the eyes of the person being spoken to (Gadamer, 1976a, p. 65) and unless the other person "recognizes that I am trying to tell him something and what I am trying to tell him, I do not fully succeed in telling it to him" (Searle, 1969, p. 47). To succeed in doing this each word must find its place in the tradition of the shared language, which already defines the word. Words are not simply logically defined, they take their meaning from their use and the tradition within which they stand. Just like Hermes, the messenger of the gods, the manager can only say what people, in some sense, are ready to know. The postmodern manager communicates within the hermeneutic circle.

Politically, the democratic tradition in public politics has long defined the idea, implicit in the pyramid, that decisions as to what a society should do are made at the top. However, in both private and public organizations the tradition of elite decision lingers on, although less so in private than in public. Privately owned organizations received their first major blow to the premise of elite decision making in 1889 when a financier named Wharton sent Frederick W. Taylor to Bethlehem Iron Company in Pennsylvania to make the firm more efficient. Taylor promptly asserted that scientists, engineers, and managers schooled in what was later to become known as scientific management were more qualified than owners to design work processes—and promptly got fired by the owner (Copley, 1923). By the 1930s, managers started taking over the actual control of businesses from owners in massive numbers (Berle & Means, 1968). But it took until the 1980s for American corporations to hear from Japan inklings that it might be advisable to involve all levels of the organization in, for example, setting new goals for the company. Similarly, the practice of legislators consulting administrators in the public service as to what policies might be doable, while it had been held politically wise for decades, still had not been considered quite legitimate in the 1980s. Nevertheless, at least at the program level within public organizations, the recognition dawned as early as the 1970s that it was advisable to engage all members of a unit in a communications process Rivlin (1973) calls "forensic discourse" before setting goals for the unit or making other major decisions. Other forces helped flatten out the pyramid: the democratic theory of public participation impacting on a variety of levels from community school boards to coproduction methods; the conceptual framework imposed by systems analysis on all government planning through, for example, environmental impact statements; and the explicit recognition of the autonomy of politics and of the utility of qualitative research into political values choices espoused by policy analysis. In putting all levels in touch with each other, traditional political thought and contemporary methods of analysis create expanded political circles (Cf. Waldo, 1952, 1984; Marini, 1971; Schoen, 1971; Jun, 1986, pp. 88-91).

THE PUBLIC ADMINISTRATOR:
BETWEEN CIRCLE AND PYRAMID

Despite the growth of T-group circles, quality circles, and circles of knowing and reflecting at work; circles of reason and emotion; hermeneutic circles; and circles of political discourse, the pyramid with its division of labor and hierarchy still looms over all organizing and managing, even where its shadow is pushed into the background.

The administrator, the manager, the supervisor—all are caught between circle and pyramid. Only the circle can produce effective work. This is especially clear in public service where social outcomes define success. Only circles can produce quality work, even and especially in private organizations on the cutting edge where success is measured by demanding customers insisting on quality products and quality service. Managerial success depends on closing the circle with workers who are in touch with each other, with their hands-on knowledge, with their own integrated psyche, and ultimately with the social goals of the private and public enterprises they work in. Yet the pyramidal organization continues to promise and deliver—up to a point—massive and standardized production of goods and services quantitatively defined.[3]

What kind of individual would the public administrator have to become to take full advantage of the circle? What kind of individual does he or she still have to be to fulfill the functions imposed by the traditional pyramid?

THE CIRCLE-ORIENTED PUBLIC ADMINISTRATOR

Because he or she is a public administrator, the organizer and manager in public service has always had—in contrast to generations of private executives—an orientation toward the larger circle of the public. Where the private executive could take a limited view, the American public administrator was and is ultimately responsible to the realm of all things public, what the Romans called the *res publica*, what we call the republic. Republicanism, unlike aristocratic rule or pure democracy, unites the levels of the society although they may be divided by economic or social position in the pyramid. When the founders decided on a republic they guaranteed in this country's political institutions a flow of discourse that ran from upper class to middle class to lower class and back again. While its institutional channels and its mechanical sluices and gates that could block power were a far cry from the openness of the pure circle of discourse, the American political system from its beginning also was not a pure pyramid. This we owe not only to the democratic idea but to the republican idea.

Within such a system, the American public administrator, unlike the ideal-typical German bureaucrat, would commit a serious error if he or she saw authority or power or orders as flowing simply and merely from above—or if he or she expected clients simply and merely to adapt themselves to institutionally given rules and orders.

Politically, in fact, the American public administrator has always been both responsible up the ladder and responsive down the ladder. Policies are implemented, as they must be, but the changing needs of clients must be considered as they emanate from below in the power pyramid. At the same time, powerful groups at each side of the pyramid must be consulted and admitted to power even after legitimate policy is promulgated. The politically successful public administrator, indeed, often treats the pyramid of authority as a pyramid but sometimes, perhaps even frequently, as if it were a circle.[4] Yet the new circles at work—social, technical or work-oriented, reflective, emotional, and linguistic—make demands on the administrator entering postmodernity that no modern administrator has had to face before.

Socially, there are the leveling demands of the encounter group or the T-group. There is the requirement to reveal oneself to one's sub-ordinates by quantifying and stating one's goals in management-by-objectives. There are the numerous face-to-face interactions, the by-passing of a strict chain of command both upward and downward to form task groups that will interact well and get things done: work or program teams. The pyramid still leaves the manager responsible and in charge, yet the circle forces her or him to share intentions, open up relationships, and be responsive. Formal status may be attacked, even successfully challenged, by functional position within the group. In a sense the pyramid protected the administrator or the manager more. Everyone knew who the manager was: a title on the door and Bigelow on the floor. Now what you are is open to negotiation—and constant renegotiation. Status nourishment is taken away to feed the health of the informal work circle. Role autonomy now yields to role flexibility. Dominance over the group yields to membership in the group, with all its possibilities of dissolution in the group as it inexorably forces members to change to achieve group poise in the encounter with the work to be done. What the social group demands is eternal readiness for change and adaptation on the part of its members; those in charge cannot escape this demand any more than those formally subordinated.

Technically, or in the working, also, the administrator must leave him- or herself open—wide open, he or she may fear—to what a hands-on employee may try to communicate about the knowledge he or she has obtained from the experience of hands-on work. The administrator who runs a taut ship top-down and by the numbers may find him- or herself in the position of the managers who ignored the hands-on advice of the O-ring engineers and let the space shuttle fly because the numbers were not yet there or not yet clear. If any one event symbolized the demise of the purely pyramidal administrator, it may have been the crash of the space shuttle Challenger in 1986. Here again formal position or authority based on book knowledge has to yield or find its proper realm in autonomy when confronted by bottom-up knowledge. The growth of management information systems, like the proliferation of technical knowledge in general, demands judgment more than ever.

Cognitively, just like the postmodern worker, the postmodern professional or manager will have to develop a special felt sense. Through such felt sense, he or she will be able to acquire the hands-on knowledge of knowledge-in-action. Managers and their helpers must develop reflective judgment on when to respect such bottom-up knowledge. They must learn how to integrate it into the general overview across the larger picture of an organization to which the supervisors, professionals, and managers will continue to be oriented. The member of the most modern organization will have to have a mind sensible to things as they present themselves during work while at the same time being reflective so as to be able to appreciate and correct what he or she does even while he or she is doing it.

Emotionally, the postmodern administrator will be in touch with his or her feelings. He or she will admit to those feelings while needing at the same time to control them when they are inappropriate to hierarchical or other contractual relationships with subordinates or coworkers. Wherever there are power relationships, there are emotions that are projected—both ways. The new administrator will be aware of love and hate, need for autonomy or need for dependence, both as his or her own feelings and as such feelings are transferred by a subordinate. This new awareness will give rise to new possibilities for manipulation. What will keep such manipulation in check? Only its cost. Manipulation can destroy the willingness of subordinates to communicate their hands-on knowledge. They can refuse to admit the manager into their social circle, and even more so into their selves, when teamwork needs to be done.[5]

Linguistically, the postmodern manager, like the modern manager, will have an unquenchable thirst for knowledge. The modern manager kept knowledge to him- or herself: out of secrecy grew power. The new manager, while not naive about the power of knowledge, appreciates a second face of knowledge: to the extent that he or she keeps information, interpretations, or standards to him- or herself, he or she will be excluded from the hermeneutic meaning-giving circle that defines the reality of the organization. Employees can be kept from participating in discussions as to the meaning or intent of a program. But this will result in the construction of two half-circles, one above the other. The outcome would be the reconstruction of a pyramid of knowledge in which as Max Weber said, even the second rank after the lawgivers no longer knows the intent of a law (Weber, 1968, pp. 472-473).[6] Professionals aiding managers in the design of management information systems will have to become more conscious that the arbitrary choice of terms, for example in computer programming, denies both the program designer and the user the power of both the tradition from which these terms are taken and the social situation in which they must be used. The manager will become more conscious of this political role of crystallizing new problems, but, in addition, he or she will now be aware that to do so means to evoke new meaning in old words.

This presentation does not exhaust the discussion of the orientations or the problems of the circle-oriented public administrator by any means; in fact, it hardly begins them. Yet a set of conflicts can be outlined from this initial analysis (see Table 8.1).[7] The postmodern manager lives in the tension between these points of conflict.

CLOSING THE CIRCLE

The analytic categories dividing this discussion—social, technical, cognitive, emotional, linguistic, political—are still analytic. They are not only artificial and inappropriate to real life in the postmodern world, they are directly derivative from the time of the pyramid. Such a style of communicating is unavoidable at a time in which termination of an era and the resulting turbulence begin to crystallize into transition and emergence. Emerging from within the pyramid is not only a whole

TABLE 8.1: The Administrator between Circle and Pyramid

	Circle-oriented Administrator	Pyramidal Administrator
Socially	Open to group, changeable, functional part of work teams	Closed to group, rigid and autonomous, above group
Technically (work orientation)	Reflective practitioner, integrates sensibility to hands-on work and judgment	Top-down administrator; separates management and work(ers), planning and doing
Cognitively	Both reflective and intuitive: knows how to integrate rational knowledge of system and hands-on knowledge of employees	Rationalist, scientific; knows rational plan, receptive to scientific correction; ignorant of any other type of knowledge
Emotionally	Aware of own emotions and others' transferences; in touch with self, others, and rationalism of system	Denies emotions of self and others; perpetrator of emotional "crimes" illegitimate in rationalist system
Linguistically	Part of hermeneutic circle; speaks the new, but in the context of what others already know; treats language innovation in a dialectic with tradition	Cut off; under illusion others divine meaning; under illusion of understanding others without talking things out
Politically	Responsible but responsive; engages in forensic discourse when goals for entire unit are at stake; legitimates	Rules top down; relies on legal authority

variety of small circles, each of which connects or integrates a form of life that the pyramid has rent asunder, but a larger, all-encompassing circle. The larger circle emerging asserts that all the smaller circles— that is, the individual life forms (social, etc.)—do not exist in separation from each other. This means the postmodern public administrator must adopt the circle as the icon of postmodernity in full.

It is not possible to be open to a T-group during a weekend's retreat from the hustle and bustle of management and at the same time to expect to return to work on Monday with one's psyche rigidly intact. It is not possible to enter the circle of a training group without at the same moment talking with other group members in a hermeneutic circle—just as it is not possible to relate to others fully without speaking with them in mutually agreed upon terms. It is not possible to learn the new way of thinking, to be at the same time both sensible to things and reflective, without having both worked and managed. It is not possible to do the new politics without doing the new social relations, the new thinking, the new working, the new communicating, and without being in touch with one's emotions or at least working on developing an integrated psyche.

A new image of a human being is emerging here; much is expected of him or her. It might almost seem too much. But when the total image is broken down into its components, we see already in place the approaches, the methods, the techniques or ways of working that this world of synthesis requires.

This synthesis, after all, is the key distinction between modernity and postmodernity. Modernity is an analytic world; postmodernity is a synthesizing world. In modernity, things, including human beings, are taken apart. The whole modern world takes itself apart—by the hypothesizing approach of science, which can test and recognize in reality only that which is already preconceived, as much as by the top-down approach of management. In the heyday of modernity, it was assumed that once the pieces of a problem or a person were known, they could then be put together again, and the totality of the problem or person would be understood. Science and rational-quantitative analysis, however, failed in this promise. Postmodernity, not only in its initial stages but in its essence, tries to deal with people and the problems within which they exist not by cutting them apart but by understanding: reading one's self into the whole situation of others. With the advance of the circle over the pyramid, the analysis of scientific/rational explanation is not so much replaced as put in its place; analysis is bounded by the synthesis of reading one's self into the relationships between the human being and the world.

Just as the manager has always been immersed in his or her world of work, the researcher in the postmodern world no longer can separate him- or herself totally, as did the modern researcher, from the problems with which the research deals. He or she is aware that, no matter how detached the analysis, at some point the ultimate question must be faced—not so much what should be done, but what is possible and appropriate that might work.

Within the work of understanding and for the understanding of work, the postmodern manager finds a place for both empirical experiment and rational analysis. Science and reason are not dead; they are given their proper place in a process of reasonableness whose inhabitants recognize that the ultimate question in managing life is not answered by defining the pieces of life but by judging how the pieces fit together.[8]

The first step on the way to becoming the circle manager of postmodernity is to recognize the ways of understanding where they already exist. In action research, in qualitative methods, in policy studies, in the work teams of quality management, and elsewhere, such ways of understanding what is going on are already elaborated into highly sophisticated and workable methods. These are ultimately methods of good judgment, something with which the successful manager has long been acquainted but to which those running management schools gave no legitimacy. These synthesizing methods are not only competitive with scientific/rationalist methods, but ultimately superior because they connect science and reason to practicality.[9]

Two friends and I developed a simple self-test for the prospective circle manager: Assume your assistant comes running into your office and shouts, "Quick, they're killing each other on the second floor!" You rush down and find your employees are tearing each others' hair out. What is the first thing you say? Organization theorist Jay White suggested you would say, "What is going on here?!" Public management theorist Charles Levine suggested you would say, "Who's in charge here?!" Without making too much of this, the person who seeks understanding is a circle manager, the person who seeks control is a pyramid manager.[10]

We must take the next step in the development of public sector circle managers. This step will entail a strategy that uses training as well as public production and service institutions as permanent apprenticeships in the postmodern world of synthesis.[11]

NOTES

1. I dedicate the thoughts in this chapter to the memory of Charles H. Levine, who died while leading the fight for the dignity of the American public servant. This is the fifth draft of a paper originally delivered at the First National Conference of Public Administration Theory, American Society for Public Administration. The definition of *postmodernity* at the beginning of the chapter is the result of a dialogue with Jay White.

2. Also see the following: Gadamer (1976a, 1976b) and Searle (1969).

3. See the discussion in Hummel (1987a).

4. The pyramid demands circle solutions even in times of cutback management, as Charles Levine pointed out: "Growth slowdowns, zero growth, and absolute declines—at least in some sectors, communities, regions, and organizations—will increase the probability of rancorous conflict, decrease the prospects for innovation by consensus, and complicate the processes for building and maintaining support for administrative systems and democratic processes. In this potentially turbulent environment the dominant imperatives will likely involve a search for new ways of maintaining *credibility, civility,* and *consensus*; that is, in an era of scarcity, we will need new solutions to problems of how to manage public organizations and maintain the viability of democratic processes (Levine, 1980, p. 305).

5. This is not too early to point out that the changes necessary for the postmodern public administrator in any one area—for example, the psychological emotional area—cannot be taken successfully without reference to all other areas, in this case the social, cognitive, technological or working, linguistic, and political areas. This problem—which I call the problem of closing the circle—is discussed below.

6. There is perhaps no better recent example of this than the finding that a large portion of American generals in Vietnam said they did not understand the goals of the war; see Kinnard (1985).

7. I have developed the details of how the circle affects the administrator socially, technically, cognitively, psychologically, linguistically, and politically in two related and as yet unpublished documents: a two-part paper entitled "An Iconography for the Post-Modern World" and a proposal for a book to be entitled *The Circle and the Pyramid*. These are available from the author.

8. Among the people who have reflected on this are a number of college graduates talking about what their education gave them (analysis, or how to take life apart) and what it did not (synthesis, or how life fits together); see Schuman (1982).

9. Contemporary standards of knowledge demand that any method of acquiring knowledge must have as its foundation a sound theory of knowledge. The epistemology of qualitative or synthesizing methods has been developed in a number of places. The source that informs the reading of such methods in this chapter is Immanuel Kant's aesthetic in the *Critique of Pure Reason* as interpreted in Heidegger (1967).

10. Personal communications with Jay White and Charles Levine, 1986.

11. For the academic scholar of public administration the problem arises as to what conceptual framework can be developed for explaining and understanding the total reality of the postmodern administrator. This problem has been attacked already by Habermas (1979); see especially the translator's discussion on pp. xi-xii. It might seem, as Robert Denhardt (1981) has suggested, that some sort of critical theory would have to be used to integrate at least some of the social, technical, cognitive, emotional, linguistic, and political elements of postmodernity. I have serious misgivings, however, about the possibility of adapting German critical theory to the American context, primarily because a central theme of German critical theory—the descent of the world spirit upon a series of nations—is fundamentally alien to American culture. In fact, it has been argued by political theorist H. Mark Roelofs (1976) that America lacks the critical tool for understanding itself exactly because it was isolated from world history for so much of its life. Without some fulcrum in history, however, it is ultimately impossible to judge whether contemporary developments are merely fads or part of a historical direction. Compare Denhardt (1981), Schmidt (1980), and Roelofs (1976). On the more practical level, the

problem of practitioners acquiring entry into the postmodern world has been approached by Donald Schoen (1987); see especially Chapter 11, How a Reflective Practicum Can Bridge the Worlds of University and Practice.

REFERENCES

Berle, A.A., & Means, G.C. (1968). *The modern corporation and private property.* New York: Harcourt, Brace, & World.

Copley, F.B. (1923). *Frederick W. Taylor: Father of scientific management* (Vol. 2). New York: Harper & Brothers.

Denhardt, R.B. (1981). Toward a critical theory of public organization. *Public Administration Review, 46*(6), 628-635.

Diamond, M.A. (1984). Bureaucracy as an externalized self system: A view from the psychological interior. *Administration and Society, 16*(2), 195-214.

Diamond, M.A. (1986). Resistance to change: A psychoanalytic critique of Argyris and Schoen's contributions to organization theory and intervention. *Journal of Management Studies, 23*(5).

Diamond, M.A. (1987). The psychological dilemma of bureaucratic self integrity. In R. Hummel, *The bureaucratic experience* (3rd ed., pp. 168-178). New York: St. Martin's Press.

Diamond, M.A., & Allcorn, S. (1985). Psychological responses to stress in complex organizations. *Administration and Society, 17*(2), 217-239.

Diamond, M.A., & Allcorn, S. (1986). Role formation as defensive activity in bureaucratic organizations. *Political Psychology, 7.*

Fish, S. (1987). Nurturing straight talk in organizations. In R. Hummel, *The bureaucratic experience* (3rd ed., pp. 207-210). New York: St. Martin's Press.

Forester, J. (1980). Critical theory and planning practice. In P. Clavel, J. Forester, & W.W. Goldsmith (Eds.), *Urban and regional planning in an age of austerity* (pp. 326-342). New York: Pergamon Press.

Gadamer, H.G. (1976a). Man and language. In D.E. Linge (Ed. and Trans.), *Philosophical hermeneutics* (pp. 59-68). Berkeley: University of California Press. (Original work published 1966.)

Gadamer, H.G. (1976b). Semantics and hermeneutics. In D.E. Linge (Ed. and Trans.), *Philosophical hermeneutics* (pp. 82-94). Berkeley: University of California Press. (Original work published 1972.)

Habermas, J. (1979). *Communication and the evolution of society* (T. McCarthy, Trans.). Boston: Beacon Press.

Heidegger, M. (1967). *What is a thing?* (W.B. Barton & V. Deutsch, Trans., E. Gendlin, Analysis.). South Bend, IN: Regnery/Gateway Press.

Hummel, R.P. (1977). *The bureaucratic experience* (1st ed.). New York: St. Martin's Press.

Hummel, R.P. (1985, September). *Bottom up knowledge in organizations.* Paper delivered at the conference on Critical Perspectives in Organizational Theory, New York City.

Hummel, R.P. (1987a, Summer). Behind quality management: What workers and a few philosophers have always known and how it adds up to excellence in production. *Organizational Dynamics.*

Hummel, R.P. (1987b). *The bureaucratic experience* (3rd ed.). New York: St. Martin's Press.

Jun, J.S. (1986). Public administration: Design and problem solving. New York: Macmillan.

Kinnard, D. (1985). *The war managers.* Garden City, NY: Avery.

Levine, C. (1980). More on cutback management: Hard questions for hard times. In C. Levine (Ed.), *Managing fiscal stress: The crisis in the public sector* (pp. 305-312). Chatham, NJ: Chatham House.

Mayo, E. (1949). *The social problems of an industrial civilization.* London: Routledge.

Marini, F. (Ed.). (1971). *Toward a new public administration: The Minnowbrook perspective.* Scranton, PA: Chandler.

Moritz, M., & Seaman, B. (1984). *Going for broke—Lee Iacocca's battle to save Chrysler.* Garden City, NY: Doubleday (Anchor Press).

Rivlin, A. (1973). Forensic social science. In *Perspectives on inequality* (Harvard Education Review Reprint Series No. 8). Cambridge, MA: Harvard University Press.

Roelofs, H.M. (1976). *Ideology and myth in American politics: A critique of a national political mind.* Boston: Little, Brown.

Roethlisberger, F.J. (1941). *Management and morale.* Cambridge, MA: Harvard University Press.

Schmidt, A. (1980). Die "Zeitschrift fuer sozialforschung": Geschichte und gegenwaertige bedeutung. In M. Horkheimer (Ed.), *Zeitschrift fuer sozialforschung* (Vol. 1, pp. 51-63). Munich: Deutscher Taschenbuch Verlag.

Schoen, D. (1971). *Beyond the stable state.* New York: Norton.

Schoen, D.A. (1983). *The reflective practitioner: How professionals think in action.* New York: Basic Books.

Schoen, D.A. (1987). *Teaching the reflective practitioner.* New York: Basic Books.

Schuman, D. (1982). *Policy analysis, education and everyday life: Empirical reevaluation of higher education in America.* Lexington, MA: D.C. Heath.

Schwartz, H.S. (1986, April). *The clockwork and the snake pit: An essay on the meaning of teaching organizational behavior.* Paper delivered at the annual meeting of the American Society for Public Administration, Anaheim, CA.

Searle, J.R. (1969). *Speech acts: An essay on the philosophy of language.* London: Cambridge University Press.

Vaill, P.B. (1971). *The practice of development.* Madison, WI: American Society for Training and Development.

Vaill, P.B. (1984). Process wisdom for a new age. In J. Adams (Ed.), *Transforming work.* Alexandria, VA: Miles River.

Waldo, D. (1952). Development theory in democratic administration. *American Political Science Review, 46*(1), 81-103.

Waldo, D. (1984). *The administrative state: A study of the political theory of American public administration* (2nd ed.). New York: Holmes and Meier.

Weber, M. (1968). *Gesammelte aufsaetze zur wissenschaftslehre* (3rd ed.). Tuebingen: J.C.B. Mohr.

White, J.D. (1987a, September). *The interpretive framework: Prospects for theory development in public administration.* Paper delivered at the annual meeting of the American Political Science Association, Chicago, IL.

White, J.D. (1987b, November). Action theory and literacy interpretation. *Administration and Society.*

Zaleznick, A., & Kets de Vries, M. (1975). *Power and the corporate mind.* Boston: Houghton Mifflin.

9

Joining Purpose to Practice: A Democratic Identity for the Public Service

GUY B. ADAMS
PRISCILLA V. BOWERMAN
KENNETH M. DOLBEARE
CAMILLA STIVERS

Public administration in the United States has always lacked genuinely democratic purpose, identity, and image. Generations of well-intentioned apologists have simply missed the point: they have sought to rationalize and justify an expert role for administrators amidst a very partial understanding of democracy. To be consistent with a full understanding of democracy, administrators will need to change their identities and their practice in fundamental ways—as we describe later in this chapter. Similarly, education for the public service will need to be profoundly different. We shall also describe an ongoing effort to develop a curriculum and pedagogical practice appropriate to a society in the process of realizing full democracy.

But first, the many meanings of democracy must be unpacked and a definition of *full democracy* defended as both historically grounded and socially imperative. Democracy is, of course, one of the key "contested concepts" of our culture. As the dominant meaning of the concept evolved to a rhetorical symbol of everything good about the American political system, it has been drained of content. Today, the meaning of *democracy* is at best exclusively procedural—civil liberties, voting, fair procedures in decision making, and the like.

The present authors argue that this definition is only partial. It lacks the concern for outcomes, conditions of people's lives, and realization of all people's political potential that made democracy a politically explosive concept in the past. We briefly trace the loss of this crucial dimension of democracy's content in American history and, as briefly, identify moments when the full version surfaced again—usually in popular movements.

The main thrust of the analysis is to the effect that seeing the world as an integrated political-economic entity moving through time leads inexorably to a full version of democracy. Only those who split the social world into separate compartments—economics here, politics over there—can accommodate great inequality in one sphere with supposed equality in the other. But that is the great achievement of American liberal-capitalist ideology and the reason for widespread acceptance of the partial definition of democracy today.

We offer a definition of what full democracy might entail as a benchmark and grounding for a new understanding of the role of the public service. We posit a society in the process of reaching for full democracy and ask what part administrators might play in the process of realization of that goal. We suggest that administrative action is legitimate to the extent that it decentralizes authority, achieves determinative interaction with the citizenry, and is critically aware of the political-economic context. Finally, we show how public administration education might reflect democratic purpose so as to contribute to that end.

THE ROAD TO PARTIAL DEMOCRACY

A contested concept is a basic way of organizing reality whose connotation is highly valued but whose operational meaning is the focus of struggle among contending forces. In current American usage, *democracy* is a central and highly valued goal *and* a term often used to describe the American political system. But it does not mean the same thing to all Americans today, and there has been a continuing struggle throughout our history to affix an authoritative meaning on the term. Clearly, whoever can control the meaning of this valued symbol can legitimate or challenge conditions and policies under its banner.

Democracy was not always so highly valued. Most of the leading thinkers of the founding era feared and rejected democracy, which they understood as a leveling mob rule (Shoemaker, 1966). Only a few propertyless social revolutionaries, followers of Sam Adams or Tom Paine, actually embraced the notion. It was not until after the French Revolution and Jefferson's use of the term to describe his new political party that democracy began to have broad general appeal. By the 1830s, however, its appeal was so strong and widespread that all manner of policies and practices could be legitimated in its name, and none rose in opposition to its claims.

While this history is often noted, a vital parallel change—one that may go far to explain this rapid shift in *democracy* from bad to good symbol—is much less often recognized. We refer to the way in which statesmen and citizens alike conceptualized their social worlds. Historically, and certainly in the founding era, people thought of their social worlds as holistic political-economic entities. *Democracy* thus meant a whole set of roughly equal social and economic conditions, as well as the right of common people to participate in politics and control the circumstances in which they lived. As such, democracy was clearly a threat to the established social order, which simply could not accommodate the demand for equality.

In time, however, politics became understood as a sphere of activity separate from economics, which was taken to be private in character. The popular demand for expansion of the right to vote—political equality—could eventually be granted, because the (separate) economic world was insulated by the principles of *laissez faire*. With industrialization, economic inequality became a shaping fact just as political equality (among white men) was established in principle. And democracy, applicable only to the political side of life, could be celebrated as an American fact *and* symbol.

The contested character of the concept of democracy is thus bound up with the way in which we understand the social world of which we are a part. When it is understood as an integrated political-economic whole, democracy can be a call to class conflict and drastic social change, or what is called here *full democracy*. When the social world is understood in two separate compartments, one politics and another economics, gross (economic) inequality can be accommodated with supposed (political) equality and the achievements of American democracy celebrated. This is what we call *partial democracy*.

Democracy During the American Founding

Clearly, there were genuinely democratic impulses during the American Revolution. While political beliefs were widely divergent, there was widespread popular support for the revolution; there had to be for the armies to be manned, and for the struggle to be successfully pressed against the British. What lingers decisively, however, is not the revolutionary rhetoric, but the state that was built following the war, during a time that has been appropriately called counterrevolutionary. The constitutional framework that was laid down during the founding period was decidedly antidemocratic.

Although many men made thoughtful and active contributions to our constitutional framework, James Madison and Alexander Hamilton stand above all the others. Major contributors to *The Federalist Papers*, they vie with each other for who trusts the people less; their question is always how far removed from the people an institution must be in order to be "prudent," that is, safe from democratic rule. To be sure, these papers were written to secure ratification of the Constitution from arguably the single most conservative and antidemocratic audience in the United States at that time, the landed and commercial elites in the state of New York. Yet it is one of the great ironies, and, for our purposes, perhaps the most significant irony, of American history that *The Federalist Papers* came to be accepted as the authoritative interpretation of the framers' intent.

From the modern perspective wherein we so readily fragment the social world and its artifacts into discrete compartments—the political here, the economic there; the public there, the private here—we comfortably label Madison the Father of the Constitution. Certainly it was the methodical, careful, puzzle-solving Madison who deserves the credit for the intricate constitutional devices, such as the separation of powers and checks and balances, that so many applaud as hallmarks of American democracy. He was the prime craftsman of a governmental structure secured from concentration of power within and insulated from the electorate without.

But it is a fundamental error of our social understanding and a measure of the limits of our social imagination to view the Constitution as just a political document, just a blueprint for government. For the Constitution confirmed an entire social order embracing specific political/economic relations, private/public divisions, power configurations, and developmental directions—and simultaneously disallowed others. From this perspective, Hamilton, not Madison, was the chief architect of the American state. Hamilton foresaw the special greatness the United States could achieve with a national government reconstructed by the Constitution. His vision was stunningly prescient: The United States would be a great commercial republic ready and able to trade as an equal among the nations of the world, with an energetic and potent national government ready to ensure that the wheels of commerce turned smoothly. He sought a government that could make business its business, a government insulated from participation by the common people. In Federalist 78 he claimed for that government a capacity to interpret its own powers through the innovation of judicial review, constitutional choices made by courts of experts thoroughly barricaded from the common people.

Madison, like Hamilton and many people of the 18th century, recognized that constitution making set a design on a total social order, but at the time of writing the Constitution, he did not realize the full import of Hamilton's vision. As early as the first Washington administration, however, Hamilton's vision began to emerge in the Reports on Credit and Manufacturing, and Madison, as Speaker of the House, was forced into explicit opposition.

Americans of the 19th century lived, as we 20th century Americans do, in an order fraught with the tension between the liberal and the democratic traditions of our founding. Imbued through and through with individualism, the notion of rights (particularly to property), the sanctity of contracts, and the rule of law, American democracy can only with the greatest difficulty be anything but *liberal* democracy. The story of the marriage of convenience between liberalism and democracy is ably told in C.B. Macpherson's *The Life and Times of Liberal Democracy* (1977). The tension in this marriage increasingly permeated every aspect of the social order as Hamilton's vision became a reality and then was supplanted by a great industrial republic.

Yet, living in the midst of ever-increasing evidence of this tension, Americans became less able to recognize it. We learned to see some matters as political and others as economic, some as proper concerns for government and others as concerns for private action. Government and the political were democratic; economics and business, run on liberal principles of contract law and the rules of the free market, could exist right alongside this democratic government in a category we thought of as totally separate and discrete. Because we thought this way, we were better able to acclaim democracy. The term, indeed, lost its pejorative sense in the 19th century as it became identified solely with representative government (Williams, 1985). But the price we have paid is very high, indeed exorbitant: we cannot comprehend, without tremendous effort, that the political and the economic are thoroughly integrated in our social reality, and we can hardly admit, much less entertain, a vision of full democracy.

The Second Hamiltonian System

The dominant image of the period 1896-1916 is perhaps still the age of reform. It was a time of popular outrage against the depredations of big business, against social ills, against exploitation of all kinds. It resulted in a wave of progressive reform: child labor legislation, minimum wage legislation, woman's suffrage, direct election of senators, and trust busting, as well as eliminating patronage, instituting clean government, and regulating industry. But this image obscures as much as it reveals. Some individual reforms were enacted. Overall, however, the reforms of the period inaugurated a new Hamiltonian system, still wedded monogamously to business interests but adjusted to the realities of an industrial nation for whom the promises of great profit and growth depended on the organization of large-scale, capital-using industries; on stable financial markets and prices; and on keeping a growing unpropertied industrial working class quiescent.

The Progressive Era was a time of debate over the substance and language of American democracy. Conservative businessmen, especially small-business men, used Jeffersonian language to emphasize a laissez-faire, limited government, counter to the interests of big business. Reformers, interestingly, adopted Hamiltonian language to extend the proper sphere of action of an active, assertive government to social principles as well as economic goals. Essentially, the reformers' aim was a Hamiltonian national government in the service of Jeffersonian ideals (Croly, 1909).

But Gabriel Kolko (1963) was right in calling this age of "reform" the "triumph of conservatism," for the legacy of this era to us was a Hamiltonian national government with Jeffersonian rhetoric in the service of corperate and financial interests. Far-sighted corporate leaders secured government regulation in order to eliminate competition and to rationalize the economy significantly. Clientele agencies, such as the Department of Commerce, formed in 1913, straightforwardly served their clients' interests. Regulatory agencies created in response to public outcry often became client agencies of the regulated (Nelson, 1982). Proposals for substantive reform were translated regularly into enactments of procedural reform (and these often reforms in name only). The history of the Federal Reserve Act of 1913 (Kolko, 1963, Chap. 9) is the most revealing illustration.

During this era, the American sense of democracy was bled of substance. Proceduralism reigned triumphant and continues to do so today. The broad superstructure and ideational base of the modern welfare/corporate liberal state came together in this era, rather than much later, as the conventional wisdom has it (Weinstein, 1968). And the era set parameters and a trajectory as well for the field of public administration, from which it has not since deviated significantly (Skowronek, 1982).

The scientific mindset and technological progress that combined during the Progressive Era unleashed a current of rationalism and professionalism that can only be termed a juggernaut. Impressed by the tremendous achievements of science and technology in the physical world, the Progressives naturally wanted to apply them in the social and political world, to achieve science-like precision and objectivity in these spheres as well.

Rationalism led irresistibly to specialized, expert knowledge, the very lifeblood of the professional, and also to the explosion of professional associations in the latter half of the 19th and early part of the 20th centuries. Without the legitimacy derived from specialized knowledge, the professional could not have gained the social status nor the autonomy and control over the practice of the profession that are the ultimate goals (even if sometimes unstated) of every profession. But the compartmentalization of knowledge demanded by rationalism also inevitably led to a contextless, or placeless, practice: Witness the lack of historical consciousness across the professions and disciplines. The practice of a profession with little or no sense of context has precluded meaningful engagement with the larger ethical and political concerns of a society. That is to say, professionalism, fed and nurtured by rationalism, led inexorably to a naked public square.

The professional's incessant drive for legitimacy, status, and autonomy is fundamentally antidemocratic. The nature of experts and expertise has changed since Hamilton's time, but the experts are, if anything, more removed from the people. Moreover, lacking a meaningful public discourse around the central ethical and political dilemmas of the time, citizen and expert alike have no opportunity to see themselves practicing (full) democracy. Procedures are left alone to degenerate into meaningless ritual, bled as they are of all substance.

Moments of Full Democracy

While the American founding and our constitutional framework constrain democracy, they have clearly admitted fully democratic impulses from time to time in American history. Shay's rebellion in the early years of the Republic and the antiwar and other activism of the 1960s can be counted among such democratic impulses. The populism of the late 19th century was also a moment of full democracy. For a long time, historical scholarship considered populism to be many things—primarily unthinking or strange (Hofstadter, 1955)—but seldom democratic. But, as historical scholarship has begun to look for democratic impulses in American history, democratic moments have been "rediscovered" (Goodwyn, 1978).

Devastated by the post-Civil War contraction of money and the dead hand of the crop lien system, Southern and Western farmers, over a period of less than 20 years (roughly 1877-1896), allied themselves into first a mass movement and then a mass political movement. Alliance-men learned from experience that economic problems are political matters too and that economic struggles must be pressed in the political arena. The People's Party was born. So-called mid-road populists, those who stood by the Omaha platform of 1892, sought nothing less than to democratize control over the nation's supply of money and credit. Their campaign foundered on the problems of forging a premature alliance with urban labor and on the quagmire of fusion politics in the election of 1896. So passed this democratic moment. But its lessons are being recovered by historians: that mass organization can be effected around common struggles, and that political economic problems, ostensibly economic in nature, are, in truth, capable of resolution only in the political arena.

The state of Washington, for example, has also had democratic moments. Reform efforts there during the Progressive Era had outcomes sufficiently different from the national reform movement that in 1936 Postmaster General (and Democratic Party Chairman) James Farley captured the state's national image by referring to it as "the Soviet of Washington." Thirty-six years as a territory ending with statehood in 1889, with major local decisions made in the "other" Washington and a long history of a colonial, resource-based economy owned and controlled by out-of-state interests, created the kind of dependencies and disparities between classes that fostered a powerful surge for local (sub-state level) control over government institutions and practices. The state was known for its enactment of initiative, referendum, and recall practices; for the nation's first workmen's compensation law; and other such legislation. But it was the Port District Act of 1911 that was the significant local control legislation and the sign of a democratic moment. Control of the waterfront was wrested from the railroads and vested in public districts. Henceforth, citizens had power to make the important decisions. Not only were port commissioners elected, but all decisions about acquiring land and about significant changes in operations had to be put to the voters in the district. For three decades, the port district served as a model for numerous attempts at other forms of participatory (i.e., politically democratic) economic development, but only the public utility districts were successful (in the 1930s).

Since the Second World War, the state of Washington has been delivered into the hands of modern managerialism. Nonetheless, the Washington example demonstrates that democratic impulses are not necessarily stillborn. Outcomes that put control closer to the people and that threaten, even overturn, the sanctity of private enterprise are possible.

RECOVERING FULL DEMOCRACY

We have no wish to add to the many carefully crafted definitions of *democracy* that are available in the scholarly literature. Our goal here is to restore and develop the socially revealing, integrated political-economic perspective; to recapture the full version of democracy that is consistent with such a view of the social world; and to seek its realization in practice. Nevertheless, specification of the nature of the democracy involved is incumbent upon us, if only to provide a grounding for the argument about changes in administrative practice that is to follow.

Presuppositions

The definition of *full democracy* offered here is a prescriptive one. To be adequate, a definition of democracy or democratic rule must answer four questions: (a) who rules, (b) to what end, (c) what is meant by *rule*, and (d) what enabling conditions are necessary to realize such rule? In our answers to these questions, some familiar political and/or democratic notions were rejected and some significant substitutions were made.

We reject a purely procedural conception of democracy that ignores outcomes. We reject the necessity and/or desirability of significantly concentrating decision-making authority in a group of experts or professions. We deny that there is an achievable or even desirable separation of politics and administration. We eschew (a) the liberal substitution of the concept of preference or desire for need, (b) the liberal notion of atomistic individualism, (c) the positivist notion of objective knowledge, and (d) the liberal definition of *liberty* that entitles individuals to amass property with no limit other than not interfering with the exercise of the same right by other individuals.

We define a full conception of democracy in which procedural and substantive prescriptions are not only congruent but mutually reinforcing. Because administration is political and often politically powerful, we maintain that administration must not be relegated for long periods of time to one part of the citizenry. We limit narrowly the decision-making authority of experts qua experts.[1]

We hold that people have some common needs that are distinguishable from individual preferences and that people are able to identify these commonalities. We also maintain that people are defined in essential ways by and through their relations with others, and, further, that each person's individuality can be recognized and realized only through social relations. These positions explain our rejection of the liberal and positivist notions named above. They also open us to affirming the possibilities of consensus politics and of a definition of the good, but our definition of *democracy* does not depend on the full prior achievement of either.

As advocates for a particular conception of democracy, we have the obligation not only to define our conception adequately but also to show how, under current conditions, we can begin to realize it in our society. We shall do this in the remaining sections of this chapter.

The Definition

Full democratic rule (a) ensures that all adults have a genuine opportunity to participate in public discussions of issues that affect the conditions of their lives and to exercise decisive judgment about public actions that may affect those conditions, and (b) achieves outcomes that are consistent with choices the people collectively make about the public conditions of their lives.

Clearly, we ascribe rule to all adults. Some adults may have particular incapacities that make them incapable of discussion and/or judgment. However, a first cut need not struggle with such niceties, significant as they may be; rather we want to affirm the posture of including everyone as rulers.

By our definition, to rule means to have "a genuine opportunity to participate in public discussions of issues that affect the conditions of people's lives in the society and to exercise decisive judgment about public actions that may affect those conditions." Genuine opportunity requires that the democratic society guarantees a legal right to participate and ensures that each adult has the means to exercise it. In order to exercise democratic rights, people need time free from the responsibilities of earning a living and free from social responsibilities, like child care, that are borne by them as individuals. They also need free access to information requisite to informed discussion and judgment. To satisfy these needs, government may have to engage in income subsidy programs, child-care programs, and the like.

Public discussion is an essential prelude to any decision about public action. The purpose of a discussion open to all adults is to inform public decisions with the multiplicity of perspectives in the citizenry. Such discussion does not aim at, nor need it be characterized by, an egalitarian airing of any and all viewpoints that might be brought to an issue. Rather it aims to find a perspective persuasive to all and, thereby, a decision for action (or inaction) deemed judicious by all.[2]

The public agenda—that is, what issues shall be discussed publicly—should be decided democratically too. That is, all adults should have a genuine opportunity to participate in public discussion of, and exercise decisive judgment about, what issues shall be placed on or struck from the public agenda. The determination of what is a public issue and what is a private matter, unsuitable for public deliberation and the exercise of public authority, should be made through a democratic judgment predicated upon public discussion. What issues to discuss, how they should be framed, what alternative public actions should be considered, and what specific votes should be taken—all these should be *outcomes* of discussion. Certainly, an issue must have some definition at the start of any discussion, but that definition should not set bounds on the perspectives admitted to discussion. So, in the course of discussion the issue may be newly understood and the array of public actions considered and voted on greatly reconfigured.

The aim of democratic rule is to achieve outcomes that are consistent with promoting or sustaining a state of affairs in which all people determine the procedure (who rules and how) and the substance (to what end) in our conception of full democracy. Basically, outcomes that undermine democratic procedure are unacceptable. Each public decision need not aim directly at maintaining democratic procedure, but each must be considered in terms of its impact on procedure, on whether it excludes or increases the number of adult participants in public decision making, enhances or detracts from the quality of their participation, and improves or hinders their access to information relevant to public matters.

Just as the array of acceptable actions is limited by effects on democratic procedure, so acceptable procedural behavior is limited by the end of democracy. Someone should call foul when a speaker advocates a public action that, however conducive to some social good (e.g., economic growth), undermines the right of some adults to rule. Agreeing with George Will (1983) that statecraft is necessarily soulcraft, we expect that the practice of full democracy will reshape our people's character and hope that it may engender habits of thinking and speaking out of a sense of a common good.

The enabling conditions for realizing this conception of democracy are both procedural and substantive. We assume a constitutional framework, civil and political rights, and a structuring of governmental units so that they are as small and as localized as is compatible with effectively addressing present and anticipated public issues. Substantively, the following are required: economic security sufficient for ruling; the provision of social goods, such as health care, education, and child care, sufficient for ruling; and the willingness to start to realize democracy.

THE DEMOCRATIC ADMINISTRATOR

What does this conception of full democracy imply for governance and for the practice of public administration? An active share in governance for ordinary people—supported by basic economic security and other enabling social policies—requires a considerable but not impossible shift in current thinking about the role of the public administrator. The norm we offer is an ideal; nevertheless, it offers workable guidance for real-world public administrators under current circumstances. If public administrators will take some initiative in the direction we suggest, they can move public affairs in a democratic direction. Public administrators need not wait for the advent of full democracy to begin democratic practice.

The Current Image of the Public Administrator

Current ethical arguments about public administration (e.g., Chandler, 1987) are perceptive and compelling in many ways. But all are problematic because they assume that current practice, though flawed, is in some sense fundamentally just. From the mainstream perspective, democracy need not be substantive, and public administration can be confined to facilitating minor adjustments in established arrangements: for example, correcting for market failures, promoting growth and stability, and extending civil liberties.

The reigning moral image of the public administrator is in line with this view and is exemplified in varying ways by the chapters in Part II of this volume. The virtuous public administrator is guided in governance (in the exercise of discretion) by regime values—individual liberty, private property, and procedural equality. These values, established at the founding and supported by our constitutional system of separated powers, are reflected in current administrative practice and lend it legitimacy.

But constitutional values account for only a part of the ethical identity of the modern public administrator. In the mainstream view, the Constitution did not anticipate the large and complex dimensions of the modern state nor the role public administration would be called on to fulfill therein. Responsiveness and accountability have become profoundly problematic, and tendencies of stasis and drift, engendered by the dynamics of interest group politics, have brought into question the very governability of the modern state. In the prevailing view, these trends suggest the need for public administration to play a decisive, if not determinative, role as a "fourth branch of government" and the public administrator to assume leadership in "steering the ship of state."

As Morgan suggests in Chapter 2, public administration is assigned a key part in governance as a fulcrum on which to balance competing or conflicting forces engendered by separated powers and checks and balances. The role of the virtuous public administrator is not merely to manage the public's business but to interpret the public interest in particular situations acting for and responsible to the people. Qualified by a commitment to public service and by expertise in governance, which has become too specialized a task on too great a scale for any but a restricted few, the public administrator serves, as Kass suggests in Chapter 4, as faithful steward for those less able or less willing to bear the burdens of public service.

Dissonance with Democracy

Some call this image of public administration democratic because of its commitment to regime values and the public interest, but there is considerable dissonance between it and full democracy. Genuine participation by ordinary people in governance is at odds with the image of the public administrator as an expert specially qualified by knowledge and commitment not only to "manage the public's business" but also to interpret the public interest on behalf of others. Despite its lineage, the idea that elected officials and professional administrators are the only citizens who are wise, virtuous, and energetic enough to have a say in decision making is too convenient a justification of administrative authority to be taken at face value, as it usually is. Even the framers were suspicious of arrangements that depended too much on the virtue of individual statesmen.

The emphasis on virtuous expertise skews priorities and choices toward values, such as comprehensiveness and order, that make democracy a cost of doing business rather than the nature and end of governance. Reliance on consistency with regime values and the civil liberties that flow from them introduces another bias. Because these values emphasize individual liberty and neglect social justice and community, citizens can be seen as bearers merely of rights rather than of obligations and positive capacities. The view of administrators as specially qualified to determine the public interest promotes a "weak" view of citizenship. Finally, restricted to making marginal adjustments in the status quo, current public administrative practice helps maintain economic and social conditions favored by vested interests that bar people from being able to share in governance, much less economic abundance.

A critical analysis such as ours presents a fundamental challenge to individual public administrators. We recognize that their ability and willingness to respond will depend on the conditions of their own lives and how much risk they can afford. We do submit, however, that defending an elite role for public administration as *democratic* rests comfortably in the well-intentioned apologetic tradition, and represents a *Phoenix* hardly in need of revival.

Democratic Practice

Our critique implies that there is another way of viewing the role of the public administrator, one that fosters full democracy, as we have defined that term. In our conception, administrative governance is legitimate to the extent that it (a) decentralizes authority and responsibility to lay citizens; (b) interprets the public interest in particular situations through determinative interaction with affected stakeholders, including neglected groups and the public at large; and (c) is practiced by self-conscious administrators who are critically aware of the political-economic context. Let us consider each of these briefly.

Decentralization of authority

Democratic public administration can be fostered by laws, regulations, policies, procedures, and ongoing actions that share authority and responsibility with citizens in conducting agency affairs. Within given legislated mandates, democratic administrators can use their discretionary authority to approach rule making and the design of agency processes so that not just clients and interest groups but members of the public at large participate as fully as possible in policy-making and in implementation.

We do not imply divestiture of responsibilities from government to the private sector, as in the current privatization trend. Instead, democratic public administration entails substantive forms of cooperation between citizens and administrators in which citizens are seen as co-governors and co-decision makers, not simply as consumers or providers of services.

One example of this kind of relationship is the federal Community Health Center program in the Department of Health and Human Services. Groups of grass-roots citizens hold authority for expending federal grant funds to organize and deliver a complex array of health services in deprived areas. While public administrators are responsible for monitoring what citizens do, the latter have considerable authority within their sphere for making discretionary judgments about how to translate legislative intent and agency policy into specifics that are responsive to the needs and priorities of particular communities as well as to the public interest in the largest sense. In addition, through substantive interaction with agency officials, citizens participate in shaping what amounts to a shared interpretation of relevant rules. Public administrators do not simply tell citizens "how things are"; instead, together, citizens and officials work out agreements of meaning and action that bind them both. A similar kind of arrangement is reflected in the transfer to tenants of authority for managing public housing developments.

Determinative interaction

Democratic public administrators view their agencies as open communities of knowledge that admit citizens to membership in the process of interpreting the public interest in particular situations. By this we mean that administrators interact with citizens in order to determine the possible range of policy choice and the type and content of knowledge relevant to decision making. They provide information to citizens, call attention to neglected perspectives, raise consciousness, educate, and even organize. They also receive information from citizens, have their attention drawn to neglected perspectives, have their consciousness raised, and are educated and organized by citizens. Together, citizens and administrators develop an agenda of possibilities—a substantive vision of democratic alternatives specific to the perspective and mandate of particular agencies.

An example of democratic interaction is the process followed by the Berger Inquiry in Canada, which evaluated the proposed natural gas pipeline from Prudhoe Bay through the Mackenzie Valley. All parties to the Inquiry were required to submit a list of all pertinent documents in their possession and to share this information on request. Funding was provided to native groups, environmental groups, municipalities, and small businesses to improve their ability to participate on an equal footing with the pipeline companies. Community hearings were held throughout the affected area, in which all participants could speak their own languages.

As a result of the process, a range of views was heard that broadened the usual definition of costs and benefits beyond the contexts of industrialization, modernization, business, and employment expansion to take in renewable resources, the cultural identity of native peoples, and cooperative endeavor. The Inquiry was one factor in the decision of the Canadian Cabinet to reject the Mackenzie Valley proposal, though vigorously promoted by petroleum corporations, in favor of another pipeline project (Torgerson, 1986).

Self-consciousness in context

Democratic public administrators reflect upon their own world views and values as well as those of the agency within which they work. They develop critical awareness of existing economic and power arrangements and the extent to which their agencies help to maintain them, so that, although they may not have the power to change particular structures or practices, they watch for and, indeed, foster opportunities to advance democratic practices such as those outlined above.

IMPLICATIONS FOR PUBLIC ADMINISTRATION EDUCATION

For those who would presume to "produce" the new generation of public administrators, the implications of this emphasis on full democracy are profound. *Everything public administration educators do* is at risk—fundamentally challenged. But the task before us seems much more difficult than it is. Two preliminary steps will get us more than halfway. First, we must learn to see the social world as a truly integrated political-economic context in which unequally distributed wealth, status, and power are constantly shaping understanding and action. Second, we must genuinely accept the imperative of realizing full democracy in our lives. When we take these two steps, as the saying goes, all that remains is implementation.

The Problem of Professionalism

To be sure, our notions of professionalism will be an initial obstacle. We shall need to separate intellectual and moral integrity from mere elitism, status-assertion, and personal convenience. How much of what we associate with professionalism is truly essential to carrying out public policy in the citizen-developing world of full democracy? Tomorrow's public administrators will be facilitators, educators, and co-participants, rather than deference-demanding experts or independently responsible decision makers. They will need to learn humility and respect for the developmental potential of others and to enjoy apparently self-limiting transfers of authority and responsibility to citizens. Without such self-discipline on the part of full-time public servants, citizens will not be able to grow in their capacities and become the practicing democrats that they can be.

In all probability, some substantial share of administrative offices and positions will be filled by citizens on a rotating basis. Full-time administrators of the future will have to be enthusiastic practitioners of an enabling, empowering kind of education. The measures of success on the part of such administrators will be as much the extent of citizens' democratic development as the quality of the work actually accomplished.

Tomorrow's public employee unions in particular will take on new roles. Instead of primarily promoting higher wages and better working conditions or defending members' rights and privileges, they will exercise leadership in engaging citizens in understanding and managing their public affairs. The unions can become the forum for collective choices about how tasks are to be organized, and sources of new ideas for better serving the common good. Gone—or at least greatly reduced—will be the adversary nature of the unions' role; instead, they will facilitate democratic practice by citizens.

Educating the Future Administrator: Substance and Process

Clearly, the new generation of public administrators will require a different kind of educational experience to prepare for this different set of public functions. Their education will be different in both what is taught, and in how it is taught. Both kinds of difference have been mentioned in the discussion so far; neither can be fully described as if in a blueprint, because they can only fully mature as faculty and students become clearer about their goals and capabilities. The authors' initial experience in exploring new approaches to teaching public administration has shaped the tentative suggestions about substance and design that follow.

The substance of the curriculum will be informed throughout by the two initial commitments to integrated political-economic analysis and full democracy as a goal-in-realization. For example, a first course will develop these two conceptual and methodological concerns and help students begin to become aware of (and eventually "unlearn") their

American liberal-capitalist ideology and identities. They will make a start on appreciating what is involved in a multicultural learning-living experience through the systematic use of race, gender, and class as analytic concepts. They will also systematically apply their developing understanding of integrated political-economic analysis and full democracy to their own immediate state and local government setting as well as to the national government.

Other standard courses will have to be adapted in similar ways. In the organizational theory and behavior course, for example, the emphasis will be on developing an awareness of authority relations in organizations and learning what democratic authority relations might look like. The intended prominence of citizen-administrators will present a special opportunity (and challenge) in this regard. In the budgeting course, emphasis will have to be placed not only on the skills of constructing and understanding a budget but on ways of unpacking the choices and opening them to citizen scrutiny and decision.

The methods course must emphasize the limits of positivism, the extent to which various qualitative techniques can make up for those deficiencies, and the alternative ways of knowing that are extant in the multicultural world. The critique must reach to the level of epistemological coherence with cultural values, social structures, and personal identities. This experience will make it much easier for the public policy course to focus on the need for multiple value perspectives, and to raise the essential questions about the real premises and purposes of public policy and its analysis.

Much of the learning process should be cooperative, with regular opportunities for group projects. Regular small group seminar discussions provide a major opportunity for sustained interaction and collective analysis. Crucial to the success of the seminar method, of course, is mutuality and social support. Intellectual rigor does not depend upon authoritarian didacticism or law school-style Socratic bullying. Personal intellectual development, not to mention self-confidence, proceeds faster and more genuinely when it occurs in the context of group efforts at building collaborative analyses and interpretations.

The classroom process should emphasize self-development—that is, development of self-consciousness about the nature and sources of values and ways of thinking—and development of self-confidence about the ways in which purposeful practice can change oneself and the world. It is important that students be in the same classes together for the duration of the program. As noted in an earlier section of this chapter a person is shaped in and through social relations, and stability in the classroom membership promotes self-definition and helps foster the trust and confidence necessary to finding one's voice and hearing the voices of others.

The teacher-student relationship will be fundamentally altered—in a way modeling the manner in which the administrator-citizen relationship will develop. The teacher-administrator becomes a citizen-participant who learns with and through the same process in which students are learning. Lines break down, and authority is contextual and earned, rather than positional and ascribed.

Teachers of public administration need not await a full democratic transformation of American political, economic, and social structure to initiate democratic practices where they live, work, and teach. Through these practices, we can prepare ourselves and others for future fully democratic moments. If we start now, wherever we can in whatever small and large ways we can, the possibility of full democracy—a *Phoenix* truly worth evoking—is kept alive and the hope that democratic moments can be more than passing is made more realistic.

As we have considered our own practice of teaching, and the practice of public administration more broadly, we have been increasingly moved by the need for a purpose larger than mere professionalism, one grounded in the social and political values of the American tradition that offers hope of a better future to Americans. We believe such a purpose is unlikely to be found in the bled-of-substance proceduralism of partial democracy—that way lies the Administron of Chapter 7. Rather, genuine purpose, identity, and image depend on a political and economic world seen whole; we argue here for a fully democratic identity and image. The practice of public administration in the 21st century badly needs such a democratic purpose. Surely we are not alone in that conviction.

NOTES

1. In a more detailed development of our conception of democracy, we would anticipate (a) limiting the numbers of experts exercising decision-making authority at any given time and the policy areas in which their expertise legitimated their authority to make decisions; (b) advocating substantial decentralization and localization of decision making; and (c) arguing for citizen rotation into offices with decision-making authority as an effective means of spreading some forms of expertise through the citizenry.

2. Ideally, consensus on specific public actions is the outcome, but it is not an aim. Consensus, which appears utopian to us all, may be more realizable in a polity like the one we envision where decision making is greatly decentralized and localized. But consensus is not the aim or means of our notion of rule, it is merely a livelier possibility. Practically, voting is an acceptable means of determining the public's judgment about public actions when, again, the vote has been preceded by public discussion.

REFERENCES

Arendt, H. (1958). *The human condition*. Chicago: University of Chicago Press.

Barrett, W. (1979). *The illusion of technique*. Garden City, NY: Anchor Press/Doubleday.

Bellah, R., (1985). *Habits of the heart*. New York: Harper & Row.

Bendix, R. (1956). *Work and authority in industry*. New York: Harper & Row.

Caldwell, L.K. (1976, September/October). Novus ordo seclorum: The heritage of American public administration. *Public Administration Review, 36*, 489-504.

Chandler, R.C. (Ed.). (1987). *A centennial history of the American administrative state*. New York: Free Press.

Croly, H. (1909). *The promise of American life*. New York: Macmillan.

de Tocqueville, A. (1956). *Democracy in America* (R.D. Heffner, Ed.). New York: New American Library.

Dolbeare, K.M. (1986). *Democracy at risk*. Chatham, NJ: Chatham House Publishers.

Fay, B. (1975). *Social theory and political practice*. London: Allen and Unwin.

Follett, M.P. (1918). *The new state*. Gloucester, MA: Peter G. Smith.

Goodwyn, L. (1978). *The populist moment*. New York: Oxford University Press.

Goodwyn, L. (1981, January). Organizing democracy: The limits of theory and practice. *Democracy, 1*, 41-60.

Greenberg, E.S. (1985). *Capitalism and the American political ideal*. Armonk, NY: M.E. Sharpe.

Hamilton, A. (1904). *The works of Alexander Hamilton* (H.C. Lodge, Ed.). New York: Putnam's.

Hamilton, A., Madison, J., & Jay, J. (1961). *The federalist papers* (C. Rossiter, Ed.). New York: New American Library.

Hanson, R.L. (1985). *The democratic imagination in America*. Princeton, NJ: Princeton University Press.

Hofstadter, R. (1955). *The age of reform*. New York: Vintage Books.

Karl, B.D. (1976, September/October). Public administration and American history: A century of professionalism. *Public Administration Review, 36*, 489-504.

Kolko, G. (1963). *The triumph of conservatism: A reinterpretation of American history, 1900-1916*. New York: Free Press.

Larson, M.L. (1977). *The rise of professionalism*. Berkeley, CA: University of California Press.

Macpherson, C.B. (1962). *The political theory of possessive individualism*. New York: Oxford University Press.

Macpherson, C.B. (1977). *The life and times of liberal democracy*. New York: Oxford University Press.

Mosher, F. (1982). *Democracy and the public service*. New York: Oxford University Press.

Nelson, M. (1982, Winter). A short ironic history of American national bureaucracy. *Journal of Politics, 44*, 747-778.

O'Toole, L.J., Jr. (1984, Winter). American public administration and the idea of reform. *Administration and Society, 16*, 141-166.

Shoemaker, R.W. (1966, May). "Democracy" and "republic" as understood in late eighteenth-century America. *American Speech, 41*, 83-95.

Skowronek, S. (1982). *Building a new American state: The expansion of national administrative capacities*. Cambridge: Cambridge University Press.

Stever, J.A. (1986, August). Mary Parker Follett and the quest for pragmatic administration. *Administration and Society, 18*, 159-177.

Torgerson, D. (1986). Between knowledge and politics: Three faces of policy analysis. *Policy Sciences, 19*, 33-59.

Waldo, D. (1948). *The administrative state*. New York: Ronald Press.

Weinstein, J. (1968). *The corporate ideal in the liberal state, 1900-1918*. Boston: Beacon Press.

Wiebe, R.H. (1967). *The search for order, 1877-1920*. New York: Hill and Wang.

Will, G.F. (1983). *Statecraft as soulcraft*. New York: Simon & Schuster.

Williams, R. (1985). *Keywords: A vocabulary of culture and society*. New York: Oxford University Press.

Wilson, W. (1887, December). The study of administration. *Political Science Quarterly, 56*, 481-507.

Epilogue: Reflections on Practical Wisdom—Enacting Images and Developing Identity

BAYARD L. CATRON
BARRY R. HAMMOND

INTRODUCTION

The chapters in this volume were written in response to a call to reflect on the image and identity of public administration. These chapters and 8 or 10 other papers provided the basis for discussion at the first annual meeting of the Public Administration Theory Network, which was held in Portland, Oregon, in conjunction with the 1988 National Conference of the American Society for Public Administration.

The authors were asked to use the process Gareth Morgan (1986) calls *imaginizing*—that is, generating images or metaphors in order to stretch customary ways of thinking and play with new ideas. Almost without exception, the authors rose to the challenge, and the multilogue at Portland generated even more images.

At the opening of the conference, Gareth Morgan described an exercise he uses in his work with organizations, in which he asks individuals to name an animal that best characterizes their organization now and one that best fits their ideal image. Without exception, the ideal private sector organizations were expressed as sleek, fast, beautiful wild animals—lynx, cheetah, eagle, and so forth. In contrast, one person characterized the ideal public organization as a lizard—because it survives with little food and water, lives patiently under a rock, and can change colors to avoid danger.

If public administration were described as an animal, it would surely be one quite domesticated, albeit with wild ancestors and cousins. Given the range and diversity of images generated at the conference, perhaps no one animal would suffice. Perhaps some mythological creature would emerge, one which for all its strangeness would be as familiar as a barnyard animal—an animal, say, with the head of a pig, the body of a horse, and the feet of a chicken.

This epilogue provides an occasion to reflect, now at some remove, on what can be learned from the imaginizing. What can be inferred from the spate of images about the identity of public administration? As the chapters selected for this volume reveal, a common concern for the identity of public administration also entailed a search for its nature and its legitimacy.

The next section introduces and discusses seven images that provide at least partial identities for public administration. Next, these images are discussed in relation to each other as a developmental framework within which administrators may enact their own images. Then, the final section assesses the state of the dialogue—of practical discourse.

MULTIPLE IMAGES, COMPOUND IDENTITY

Seven images of the public administrator are discussed below: functionary, opportunist/pragmatist, interest broker/market manager, professional/expert technician, agent/trustee, communitarian facilitator, and transformational social critic. While these are conceptually distinct, they are not mutually exclusive. The intent is not to choose among and between them, nor to pigeonhole administrators as all one or another of them. As will be discussed in the next section, these images should be seen as comprising a developmental frame of reference, rather than read as a simple typology.

Functionary

Historically, the classic and perhaps the most prevalent image of the public administrator, dating back to the very early forms of social organization, is that of functionary. In this view, administration is entirely subordinate and instrumental to politically defined ends. As

Woodrow Wilson expressed it, administration ". . . is part of political life only as the methods of the countinghouse are a part of the life of society; only as machinery is part of the manufactured product" (1887). If administration is only instrumental, the image of the administrator is that of cog in the machine. Public administrators who believe that their role can be adequately characterized as such will make it true by their (in)action.

Most of the chapters in this volume can be seen as attempts to discover or invent a viable basis for a more active portrait of—and identity for—public administration. This is perhaps most evident in the chapters in Part II, but none of the authors could be content with this passive view of public administration, even though no one spends time discussing it. It seems peculiar that the authors think it unnecessary to identify this image, if only to discredit it, particularly when this is the identity most often attributed to "bureaucrats" by the American public.

Opportunist/Pragmatist

At the most rudimentary level, the administrator as actor is seen as self-interested, goal-seeking, and "utility-maximizing," just as other actors seem when viewed through the lens of neoclassical economics. The sinister image is that of the wily survivalist who constantly broods upon the next move in an intricate ego-gratifying game of power seeking and organization aggrandizement. To confirm this image, all behavior that suggests that administrators are primarily concerned with organization growth, stability, and defense of the status quo is interpreted as selfish. The public administrator is thus seen as seeking private, personal goals in the context of the public organization and therefore as little better than a parasite on the body politic.

A more sympathetic image of the public administrator as pragmatist is that of the policy entrepreneur who uses the same skills effectively in the competition for scarce resources not for narrow selfish reasons, but to advance the programs for which they are responsible. "Iron triangles" and other coalitions are forged by the conscientious efforts of pragmatic agency actors in order to defend and advance their agency perspective against the competing interests of both other agencies and private interests.

Even though the administrator's action is not reduced to pure selfishness in this image, it is not elevated to any concern with the public interest either. Public administration is simply another special interest in a political system of interest groups, each seeking its own advantage in the political marketplace.

Particularly during periods of administrative activism, the public administrator has emerged in the public mind and/or the literature as a significant (albeit subordinate) political actor. The issue of an appropriate political role for the administrator was debated during and following the Progressive Era, when the pragmatists argued for a more activist role. Those who White and McSwain dub the traditionalists in this volume—that is, the leaders of the field during and after World War II—fit into this category in many ways, but with at least one crucial exception: They all assumed and acted as if the public interest was a sensible concept and one which was indispensable in guiding public action.

Interest Broker/Market Manager

Also drawing on the basic concepts of the market-centered society is the image of the public administrator as market manager. This is the image drawn from public choice theory, in which public administrators correct market deficiencies where necessary and design programs consistent with consumer preferences, resulting ideally in "delivery systems" that match the supply of "goods" provided to the demand for them.

In this view, public administrators have a special role to play. They are not just another special interest group as above, but are asked to be honest brokers for the wishes and desires of all the other interest groups. As such, they bring together and translate among various points of view, some of which may be program or clientele based, some politically based, and some managerially based (or organization specific). This image sees the public administrator as skillful at the design of incentive systems, at devising a system of carrots and sticks that will maximize or optimize the values sought by the contesting parties. The model assumes that the exercise of choice is the fundamental value to be preserved and enhanced through the actions of the public agency.

Despite the similar basis in market concepts with the image above, there is a fundamental difference. Here the public administrator is somewhat paradoxically not part of an interest group, but a disinterested arbiter. This is the image of the neutral civil servant taken to its logical extreme: Administrators may claim no rightful say in the allocations of the market, nor may they insert into the process their professional and technical expertise beyond that of negotiator/mediator for the political actors.

While this image has gained currency in some quarters over the past 15 years, none of the chapters in this volume has utilized it. In fact, the public choice perspective was not represented in any of the papers written for the conference.

Professional/Expert Technician

In Weber's "ideal type," bureaucracy is staffed by experts. Administrators occupy positions defined by functional specialization, and the authority of the position was established by written rules. The expert offered the mastery of a body of knowledge produced and expanded by the application of an epistemology to the information available. The information available to the expert is determined by the hierarchical arrangement of positions. This image is consistent with the icon of the pyramid, as described by Hummel, rather than that of the circle.

The image enacted by the occupant of such a position is that of the competent analyst. The body of knowledge mastered by the expert is usually not explicitly related to the public nature of the information analyzed. We do not, for example, have public economists or public chemists or public foresters. We employ experts to apply their expertise to the information made available to them. Their actions conform to the image of expertise as enacted in the community of experts of which they are a part.

The tension between professionalized expertise and managers is a well researched and understood process. As a result of graduate training in the unique concepts and language of the specialty, by the time a person is granted a terminal professional degree he or she may define his or her very personhood by the body of expertise commanded. After joining a complex organization, professional experts may have more frequent contact with other professionals outside the organization at conferences or other professional meetings. By mid-career many professionals find it difficult to adopt the more generalist point of view of managers, who are responsible for organization-wide performance.

If a person bases his or her sense of self-worth (and sense of appropriate organizational role) on mastery of a body of knowledge or the holding of a degree, and uses as a reference group others who have mastered the same or similar bodies of knowledge, then the self-image enacted is that of "expert." In this image, the autonomy, credibility, and legitimacy of the administrator is bought at the price of isolation. This is the technicist image so vividly portrayed by Zinke. According to White and McSwain, this is the dominant "modern" image.

Agent/Trustee

If public service is a public trust, the public administrator can be seen as a trustee. While the analogy is not perfect, it is sufficiently rich to command significant attention. Moreover, when it is put in the context of a constitutional tradition, as it is in Morgan's chapter in this volume, public administrators bear the responsibility to protect the public interest. They can be seen as "guardians," to use the Platonic language used by Fox and Cochran. This role may seem to put the agent beyond criticism as in the case of the professional above. But the agent is not the repository of special knowledge so much as a person with a special obligation to act on behalf of, and for the protection of, the interests of the public.

Kass takes the notion a step further in this volume by characterizing the administrator's role as that of "steward." This is a subtle, but significant, shift that moves away from the language of social contract to the quasi-religious notion of "covenant," and thus fits better the communitarian facilitator image discussed below.

Communitarian Facilitator

This image is one of facilitator for the reemphasis of the communitarian themes in American life. If hyperpluralism is our problem, as White and McSwain argue, enacting a more cooperative and collaborative environment within which to carry out the common project of human life, and the more complex project of collective life, seems to be the answer.

The image of communitarian facilitator requires that public administrators devote more attention to reforming themselves than to reforming others. It requires that public administrators "reinvent themselves" and shift their attention from the "distal" environment of the clientele to the "proximate" environment of the face-to-face work group. This is consistent with the image and language of the circle that Hummel describes. It requires that those preparing others for service do the same. Perhaps the era of the "educated human being" is still to come: we may yet

understand that training is obtained "on-site," while education is preparation to create a reality in which to live.

Adams and The Evergreen Group exemplify this attitude most thoroughly in this volume. They try to identify the directions that are
necessary to complete the democratic revolution, and they gear their
ideas to administrators as persons, rather than by class or role. And they
do not hesitate to apply the same standards and expectations to themselves, in their role as teachers. Community building in a more modest
sense is also the mission of the enclaves that White and McSwain
identify as our best hope to survive the technicist assault.

Transformational Social Critic

In this image, the public administrator serves as the critical thinker
who, because of the strategic location and the public nature of his/her
vocation, serves as the monitor of social and political processes on
behalf of the citizens. (The presumption is that the citizen is either too
distant to effectively influence the outcome of policy processes or
that the citizen is too occupied with other, more private, concerns to
be capable of obtaining the information needed to analyze policies.)
In a sense this image would convert public administrators from the
blind instruments of others into the whistle-blowers for the common
conscience.

The administrator does not act for citizens so much as acting on social
conditions that tend to oppress and dominate them. Under this image,
the public administrator tries to provide "protection of the individual from domination by rational, impersonal, and hierarchical authority . . ." (Harmon & Mayer, 1986, p. 333). This image suggests that
public administrators have a role to play in developing the capacities
of citizens for critical thinking and sensitive analysis of the potential
and actual results of the policies and practices undertaken by government. This image offers public administrators a role in shaping and
molding public policy based solely on their positions in government
service.

The transformational social critic image has been advocated by academic writers out of the traditions of critical social theory and interpretive theory based on phenomenology. They are represented most clearly
in this volume by Jay White, who cites Habermas, Gadamer, and others
at some length. As White argues, interpretive and critical reasoning are

essential if one is to engage in meaningful practical discourse, which is at least implied by many of the essays in this volume.

The public administrator is to be more than typically aware of the rationalizations of current social relationships and become proactive in his/her intentions toward others. The goal of the public administrator is first to transform his/her own awareness of language, thought, and action from the acceptance of the given social context into an ability to actively participate in the enactment of social reality. This transformation also entails the responsibility to take action to enable others to transform themselves. The ultimate value of this image is the possibility of an ethical and moral basis for public administrators based on both a general recognition of the human condition and an awareness of the particularly crucial nature of those who interact in public authority relationships.

This image seems to give a very expansive role to public administrators, and one for which they are not necessarily well-suited by training or inclination. Yet it is quite consistent with the position advocated in the "Evergreen Manifesto" in this volume, and the move from the pyramid to the circle that Hummel sees as necessary to a postmodern society.

In this image, responsibility necessarily exceeds authority, and administrative action is not clearly demarcated by rule or role. Administrators faced with multiple and conflicting responsibilities might well be "tortured souls," as Harmon has so clearly presented it in his contribution to this volume.

ENACTED IMAGES AND THE DEVELOPMENT
OF IDENTITY

The seven images described in the preceding section should not be viewed as a simple typology, but as a developmental frame of reference to illustrate how administrators enact their own identities. The developmental framework is not intended primarily in a historical or psychological sense, although either of these might well be explored. In a sense, the developmental framework is similar to Kohlberg's scheme for describing moral development (Kohlberg, 1963). For example, the first two stages (functionary and opportunist) are rudimentary as are the two stages in the "pre-conventional" phrase of Kohlberg's scheme. The next three (interest broker, professional/technician, agent/trustee) are altogether conventional in the straightforward sense that they are designed as social roles. The final two (communitarian, social change agent) are clearly postconventional in that they are not merely instrumental, nor entirely definable by role. It is only at the level of these last two (and perhaps the agent/trustee) that practical discourse is fully possible.

Each succeeding image is more complex than the one before it, but each is layered onto instead of simply replacing the preceding one. For example, those who are employed to fill conventional roles may nonetheless act opportunistically from a motive of self-interest, or work within that role to build community or free citizens from domination.

The increasing complexity can be seen in the broadening of the concept of context from the rudimentary state of competition of all against all to the face-to-face personal work-group [agency perspective], to the broader concept of context as the "project of human life" (as it is called by White and McSwain and other emergent theorists) at the postconventional level. At this level, the enterprise of public administration is seen not as a specialized technical function, but as one of many ways to contribute to the development of the human community. While this may seem to deemphasize the importance of public administration, it reemphasizes the crucial nature of those who contribute to the enrichment of the symbols of community.

None of this means, of course, that public administration ceases to function in its traditional role of delivering goods and services and implementing public policy. Rather, what has changed is the meaning of the role and the context to the public administrators themselves. The more complex images create a wider repertoire of responses, a new awareness of a range within which discretionary actions are legitimate, and a sense of power to enact one's own identity.

We all have considerable influence in enacting our own images as a response to beliefs about our appropriate social role. As indicated earlier, public administrators who view themselves as "mere functionaries" tend to make that true by their inaction. In contrast, as changes are recognized and the capacity for affecting those changes is appreciated and utilized, public administrators enact images selected from a wider range of choices. Public administrators enact their images within an emotionally charged set of concepts that define a social and political community. Contributions to that set of concepts/symbols have effects on the entire society's sense of self. This explains, for instance, why ethics are important for all public actors. Unethical actions by public administrators undermine trust and damage the very symbols by which political and social communities are experienced and seen as meaningful by their members.

THE STATE OF PRACTICAL WISDOM

The Phoenix project would investigate how public administrators can change their images from those arising from the patterns of the past to those that may meet the challenges of the present and future, and how they might address the limitations of the social context within which they act and of which they are a part. Changing images for public administrators may facilitate the emergence of public authority structures that enhance the possibilities of a higher quality of intellectual and emotional life for the society. If public administrators are expected to serve this expanded purpose for society, they will need to adopt the more complex images that have been examined in this volume.

The adoption of additional images is not an activity engaged in by solitary individuals. Discussion with others (and reflection on that discussion) is the process by which public administrators will deepen their own appreciation of their roles and enhance the image of public service. We are calling this process practical discourse. It is the interaction of ideas and concepts, leavened with the experiences of active service, that will expand the rigid stereotypes of public administrators.

These richer and more complex images argue that public administrators are, and cannot help but be, change agents by acting to create certainty in the face of uncertainty. This is where the circle closes on the discussion of the proper role of public administrators. This image would argue that political actors are no more nor any less legitimate sources of certainty. All actors in the public authority structures are capable of creating certainty in the face of ambiguity. All enactments are value choices of individuals in the face of ambiguity and uncertainty. The social roles of the enactors are less important than the vision carried forward by the enactments of individuals. The visions mentioned above, say emergent theorists, emerge as part of a process whereby unconscious energy is transformed into actions under the conscious control of responsible human beings. According to White and McSwain this is the project of human life (White & McSwain, 1983, p. 294). No selection by social, political, economic, or academic process is needed to be engaged in this project. We are all engaged, and we all share a vision of personhood.

The success of this project—imaginizing—and its limitations seem to point the direction for the next. While there is no end to the images that might be generated, the search for identity requires a constructive or convergent phase. Perhaps the many images discussed in works such as this will begin to define a core of identity upon which public administrators can build. Despite the differences in style, concern, literatures used, and so forth, there are numerous points of agreement among the various authors. If identity is necessarily compound (or layered), perhaps we are ready for convergence.

Imagination can be seen as the opposite of reification. Discourse is intended to expand rather than restrict the possibilities in our future. Practical discourse is only possible, however, with a common language and undistorted communication. The current volume has tried to present a vision of the richness of public administration, rather than an argument about what is its "proper role." Now what is needed is attention to the possibilities of public service. Neither the resources nor the perseverance to do so are lacking—but above all else imagination will be needed.

REFERENCES

Harmon, M.M., & Mayer, R.T. (1986). *Organization theory for public administration.* Boston: Little, Brown.

Kohlberg, L.K. (1963). The development of children's orientation toward a moral order: 1: Sequence in the development of moral thought. *Vita Humana, 6.*

Morgan, G. (1986). *Images of organization.* Beverly Hills, CA: Sage.

Ostrum, V. (1975). *The intellectual crisis in public administration.* University: University of Alabama Press.

Wamsley, G., & Zald, M. (1973). *The political economy of public organization.* Bloomington: University of Indiana Press.

White, O.F., Jr., & McSwain, C.J. (1983). Transformational theory and organization analysis. In G. Morgan (Ed.), *Beyond method: Strategies for social research.* Beverly Hills, CA: Sage.

Wilson, W. (1887). The study of administration. *Political Science Quarterly, II*(20), 197.

Index

253

About the Editors

BAYARD L. CATRON received his doctorate from the University of California, Berkeley. He is currently a professor of public administration, editor of *Ethnet*, chairman of the American Society for Public Administration Standards and Ethics Committee, and the program director for "Ethics and Government: An Intricate Web," the first ASPA ethics conference. Catron is also the author of a wide variety of articles dealing with ethics in administration.

HENRY D. KASS received his doctorate from American University. He has taught at Eastern Washington University and is currently professor of public administration in the School of Professional Studies, Lewis & Clark College, Portland, Oregon. He coedited a recent issue of the *International Journal of Public Administration* dealing with ethics in public administration. Kass is a past chairman of the American Society for Public Administration Standards and Ethics Committee. His current research deals with the application of the normative theory of agency to public administration. He is also senior associate with JMA Associates, Boston, a management consulting firm.

About the Contributors

GUY B. ADAMS has his doctorate in public administration from George Washington University and has taught at California State University, Hayward and The Evergreen State College, where he is currently a member of the faculty. His recent publications have been in the area of organizational symbolism and culture.

PRISCILLA V. BOWERMAN received an M.Phil. in economics from Yale University Graduate School in 1971. She has taught at The Evergreen State College for 16 years, serving as director of the Graduate Program in Public Administration since 1986.

CLARK E. COCHRAN is professor and chairman of the Department of Political Science at Texas Tech University. He has published articles on the public interest, political theory, and religion and politics in the *American Political Science Review*, the *Journal of Politics*, and the *Journal of Church and State*. He is coauthor of a public policy text and is currently working on a book about religion and politics.

KENNETH M. DOLBEARE's Ph.D. in political science is from Columbia University. He has taught at the Universities of Wisconsin, Washington, and Massachusetts and is presently a member of the faculty of The Evergreen State College. He is the author of a number of books on American politics, political thought, and public policy.

CHARLES J. FOX is assistant professor of political science and director of the MPA program at Texas Tech University. He has published on public administration theory and ethics, epistemological issues in social science research, and public policy and its implementation in *Administration and Society*, the *Western Political Quarterly*, *Public Personnel Management*, the *International Journal of Public Administration*, and *Policy Studies Review*, and has contributed chapters on these topics to several books. He is currently researching new union strategies in public sector labor relations and writing a manuscript on professionalism in public administration.

BARRY HAMMOND completed his graduate work at the University of Pittsburgh. He is currently chairperson of the Department of Public Administration, Slippery Rock University. Hammond is editor of *Dialogue*, the journal of the Public Administration Theory Network. He has served on the American Society for Public Administration National Program Committee since 1984.

MICHAEL M. HARMON is professor of public administration and associate dean of the School of Government and Business Administration at George Washington University, where he has taught since 1970. Before and during his tenure at GWU he has also taught at the School of Public Administration of the University of Southern California; the Federal Executive Institute, Charlottesville, Virginia; Carleton University, Ottawa, Canada; the University of International Business and Economics, Beijing, China; and Kuring-gai College, Sydney, Australia.
   Professor Harmon has written two books: *Action Theory for Public Administration* (1981) and, with Richard T. Mayer, *Organization Theory for Public Administration* (1986). His chief research interests include organization theory, especially as it bears upon issues in political theory, moral philosophy, psychology, ethics, and public sector organizations. His heroes are Mary Parker Follett, Edward R. Murrow, Adlai Stevenson, and, as one might expect, Horatio Hornblower.

RALPH P. HUMMEL completed his doctorate at New York University. He is currently professor of public administration in the Department of Political Science at the University of Oklahoma. Hummel is the author of *The Bureaucratic Experience*, now in its third edition. He is the author of numerous papers and articles and is currently working on a book entitled *How Managers Think*.

CYNTHIA McSWAIN is an associate professor in the Department of Public Administration at George Washington University. Her research interests include organizational psychology and theory and social/political philosophy. She has authored and coauthored numerous articles and book chapters on transformational theory and its implications for organizational behavior, ethics, leadership, and the reemergence of the feminine. Professor McSwain has worked as an organizational consultant internationally and throughout the United States in the areas of organization change, executive development, and action research.

DOUGLAS MORGAN, professor of public administration and director of the Masters Program in Public Administration at Lewis & Clark College in Portland, Oregon, received his B.A. from Claremont McKenna College and his M.A. and Ph.D. in Political Science from the University of Chicago. He has held several academic administrative positions at both Lewis & Clark College and Sangamon State University, including the directorship of both disciplinary and interdisciplinary programs in the social sciences.

Dr. Morgan's teaching and research focus on his interest in public law and political theory. His articles on administrative ethics have appeared in various journals and books, including *Administration and Society*, *Problemi di Administrazione pubblica*, and Shumavon and Hibbeln, Eds., *Administrative Discretion and Public Policy Implementation*.

CAMILLA STIVERS earned her Ph.D. in public administration from Virginia Polytechnic Institute and State University. She is presently a member of the faculty at The Evergreen State College. Her recent publications are in public health and public administration theory.

JAY D. WHITE is currently associate professor of public administration at the University of Nebraska at Omaha. He teaches Organization Theory and Behavior, Quantitative Methods, and Management Information Systems. He also conducts interpretive and critical research in organization.

ORION F. WHITE, JR., is currently a professor at the Center for Public Administration and Policy, Virginia Polytechnic Institute and State University. He has done research and consulted for government agencies at all levels, in the United States and internationally. His areas of research interest are organizational psychology and change and social theory, and he has authored and coauthored numerous writings on these and related topics.

ROBERT ZINKE received his doctorate from New York University. He has taught at William Paterson College in New Jersey and Eastern Washington State University, where he is currently director of the graduate program in Public Administration. He has published in the fields of cost/benefit analysis, administrative rule making, and administrative ethics. Zinke is coeditor of a special issue of the *International Journal of Public Administration* and is working on a book that deals with computers and their impact on American constitutional government.

NOTES

NOTES

NOTES

NOTES

NOTES

NOTES